CHURCH
PLANTING
from the ground up

edited by
TOM JONES

forewords by
Thom Rainer and Ed Stetzer

College Press Publishing Company • Joplin, Missouri

Cover design and artwork by Michael Lotenero/BarkingPhish.com

Library of Congress Cataloging-in-Publication Data

Church planting from the ground up/ edited by Tom Jones
        p.   cm.
Includes bibliographical references (p.   ).
  ISBN 0-89900-490-3 (hardcover)
  1. Church development, New.   I. Jones, Tom, 1955–
  BV652.24.C493 2004
  254'.1—dc22

                                        2004003389

What Leaders Are Saying about *Church Planting from the Ground Up*

"This book is an encyclopedia of church planting. I am strongly encouraging our staff to require this book of every church planting student."

Thom Rainer, from the Foreword
Author of *Surprising Insights from the Unchurched and Proven Ways to Reach Them* and *The Unchurched Next Door*.

"The church planting movement within the independent tradition of Christian Churches is strategically significant. In ratio to their number of prior churches, they seem to plant more churches that become large regional churches than any other tradition or denomination. They have been teaching each other 'how to do it' for years. While any collection is uneven, this one permits a wider audience to access much of their practical wisdom."

George G. Hunter, Distinguished Professor of Evangelization
School of World Mission and Evangelism
Asbury Theological Seminary (Wilmore, Kentucky)
Author of *Church for the Unchurched* and *Leading and Managing a Growing Church*

"Here is a valuable contribution to the literature on church planting. The authors are biblically grounded. They bring credibility in that their insights are birthed and nurtured in personal experience. The range of topics covered is comprehensive. It is one thing to birth a church (as painful and challenging as that might be), but it is another to see those new churches grow to maturity, become a breeding ground for new church planters, and demonstrate that they are reproducible."

Eddie Gibbs, Donald A. McGavran Professor of Church Growth
Fuller Theological Seminary (Pasadena, California)
Author of *ChurchNext* and *I Believe in Church Growth*

"The pace of population growth continues to race faster than the growth of the church. Visionary, focused, healthy, and strategic new churches are our best and maybe only hope for bridging the gap. Yet church planting is fraught with numerous land mines that can derail even the best of prayerful intentions. Here's a tool designed to keep you on course and out of the ditch from leading practicioners who've been in the trenches and a few ditches themselves. Every team considering the adventure of church planting will serve their vision well by reading this book before taking another step."

Gene Appel, Associate Pastor
Willow Creek Community Church (S. Barrington, Illinois)
Coauthor of *How to Change Your Church*

"Every church planter, denominational supervisor and pastor needs to read and benefit from the practical wisdom, raw urgency, and passion in *Church Planting from the Ground Up*. Not the product of theoreticians, *Church Planting from the Ground Up* . . . was forged in the heat of experience. Developed by a team of church planters, this wonderful resource reads, at times, like dispatches from the front lines of a war and at other times feels like that much needed cup of coffee with an experienced friend. This welcome addition to the much needed field of church planter resources will empower, encourage, and equip you the reader to a more effective and fruitful ministry."

Tom Clegg, Vice President
Church Resource Ministries (Anaheim, California)
Coauthor of *Lost in America: How You and Your Church Can Impact the World*

"This resource is for everyone—denomination executives, college and seminary administrators, professors, pastors of established churches, scholars and researchers, students, members of the laity as well as church planters. Found in the pages of this handbook are engaging chapters that integrate sound foundational principles on specific topics with practical ministry application."

Charles Ridley, Professor & Associate Dean, The University Graduate School
Indiana University
Author of *The Leadership Files—Real Solutions for Real Problems*

"Here is a most useful book on church planting that combines practical wisdom with theological substance. It is written by practitioners who have learned not only by doing but also from Scripture and from significant literature on the church and church planting. The range of topics covered is impressive. Anyone engaged in church planting, or wanting to know more about it, will benefit from this book."

Howard A. Snyder, Professor of the History and Theology of Mission,
Asbury Theological Seminary (Wilmore, KY)
Author of *The Problem of Wineskins* and coauthor of *Decoding the Church*

"Hearing experts on church planting who have never planted a church seems strange. I prefer to learn about carpentry from carpenters. *Church Planting from the Ground Up* is just that—a wealth of wisdom from a diversity of practitioners. Tom Jones has provided a great service to the church—practical insights from people who have been there and speak from experience. They help the church planter to start a biblically faithful and contextually relevant church. This book is a gift to the church that will help its planters think biblically, missiologically, and experientially about church planting."

Ed Stetzer, from the Foreword
Author of *Planting New Churches in a Postmodern Age*

"Dr. Tom Jones practices what he teaches in this book. I know because I met regularly with him as he built Princeton Community Church in Princeton, New Jersey. This is not just a basic church planting book. The writers of this book cover everything from contextualizing the message to developing a leadership culture, and they do it out of their front lines experience. Church planters and church leaders of existing churches will all benefit from reading this book."

Robert Cushman, Senior Pastor,
Princeton Alliance Church, http://www.paccma.org/

Don't put this book down if you are thinking about planting a church. Historically, nearly 80 per cent of new church plantings fail. But Tom Jones knows solid advice when he sees it. He is both a seasoned theologian and a veteran church planter—plus an effective coach of church planters. In this volume, Tom handpicks a cadre of crack troops from the church planting trenches to address crucial issues of church planting with him. The result is profound yet immensely practical, and it reads like a primer.

Dr. Lynn Anderson, President Hope Network Ministries.
Author of *They Smell Like Sheep*

Acknowledgments

I regularly tell my seminary students and anyone else who will listen, "It's all about relationships!" The church, ministry, family, work, and life itself is all about relationships. This book is about a lifetime of relationships.

I have had the pleasure to know and relate to some of the writers of this book for over twenty-five years. I am indebted to their friendship and the commitment they have to church planting. These men and women are on the front lines getting the job done with incredible creativity and excellence. Their passion to fulfill the mission of the church is manifested in this labor of love we are calling, *Church Planting from the Ground Up*.

I am also grateful to my faculty colleagues, students, administration and staff at Emmanuel School of Religion. They provide a rich learning community that not only encourages, but also expects contributions to the Body of Christ at large. My church planting passion is fueled by Stadia, a national church planting movement, who allows me to recruit, assess, teach, and coach an incredible group of church planting types. I particularly cherish our Southeast Stadia team. Thanks Greg, Peggy, and Bobby!

A word of thanks needs to be extended to Dru Ashwell and the good folks at College Press Publishing. In addition, special acknowledgment is given to my assistant for this project, Erin McDade. Her writing, editing, insight, and servant's heart make me look better than I am.

The Lord has blessed me with the wonderful experience of being directly involved in the birth of four babies: Melanie, Tom, SouthBrook Christian Church, and Princeton Community Church. My partner in all of these births has been my wife of twenty-seven years, Debbie. She is the love of my life and my partner in the gospel. We have been blessed with two great kids who have been there with us every step of the way. They always understood the mission of the

Acknowledgments

church beyond their years and allowed our family to share the gospel through new church work.

The good folks of SouthBrook Christian Church and Princeton Community Church will always have a special place in my heart. The launch and leadership teams in each of these churches were made up of wonderful people. They get what it means to be the Bride of Christ. I am honored to have played a small part in the birth of these two communities of faith.

Grace and Peace,
Tom Jones
January 2004

Table of Contents

Forewords

Irecently returned from a speaking engagement in Montana where I met a few minutes with a young pastor. He shared with me that the attendance of his church was 400 a couple of years ago, 200 last year, and almost back to 400 this year. "What is happening?" I inquired of the roller coaster growth and decline and growth. "We grew to 400, planted a church of 200, and have almost replaced all of our 'losses,' all in just three years."

His story amazed me. This pastor and church planter grew a church, planted a church, and grew a church again in one of the most sparsely-populated states in America. "What are your future plans?" I asked. He smiled and responded, "We plan to do it again and again and again. God blesses when you 'give away' people and resources. We are just going to keep giving it all away."

This young man has not had the opportunity to lead research teams as I have the past decade. But his on-the-field experience is just as credible as the national research we have conducted. God blesses church planting.

One of my first research projects was on effective evangelistic churches in America. We discovered that churches that have a DNA of reproduction are among the most effective churches at reaching the lost and unchurched across America.

Starting new churches is always important. The biblical narratives of the early Church certainly attest to that reality. But starting churches today is critical. There are roughly 400,000 churches in the United States. We estimate that approximately 60,000 of those churches will close in the next 10 to 15 years. We will need at least 60,000 churches just to stay even!

> ## Starting new churches is always important. But starting churches today is critical.

But even if churches were not closing, we would need new congregations. These new churches tend to be more effective at reaching people for Christ, and for penetrating areas not reached by existing churches. One cannot have a true passion for reaching our world for Christ without also having a passion for planting churches.

In your hands is a book that surprised me for at least two reasons. First, I thought I was fairly knowledgable about church planting. But, as I devoured the pages of this tome, I was surprised to find out how much I did not know!

But I was also surprised by the incredible quality of each chapter I read. In most multiauthor books, the material ranges from bad to good to very good. In this book, each contribution was good, or very good, or very, very good. There is no weak link in this work.

My original plans were to write the foreword to *Church Planting from the Ground Up* and to thank Tom Jones for the opportunity to provide my input. I now have different plans. As soon as I finish these words, I am giving the manuscript to the church planting department of the seminary where I serve as dean. I am strongly encouraging our staff to require this book of every church planting student. It will also become required reading for a course I teach on growing evangelistic churches.

This book is an encyclopedia of church planting. Every chapter is written by someone who knows his or her stuff. These are no pie-in-the-sky theories that just might work. Every contributor writes from an incredible background of real-world experience. They have been there and done that. And now you have the opportunity to hear their insights on a wealth of church planting topics.

> ## Be prepared to enjoy some great stories.

Be prepared to enjoy some great stories. Be prepared to hear from some great men and women. But, above all, be prepared to hear the work of a great God who honors the work of His servants who take church multiplication to heart.

Thom Rainer
Dean of the Billy Graham School of Evangelism & Church Growth
Southern Baptist Theological Seminary
Louisville, Kentucky

I remember the first time Donna, my wife, asked, "So what do we do now?" It is easy to remember because I had no answer. It was 1988 and we were planting our first church in Buffalo, New York. We were 21 years of age and right out of college. We had arrived full of enthusiasm and passion, but with little knowledge and no experience. So, we started knocking on doors. Fifteen years, several new churches, and much more training later, I still knock on those doors—but I do a lot more when I plant a church now.

Over the years, Donna and I learned that church planting is hard work, but incredibly rewarding. I remember the day we baptized 50 people, the Sunday we had a great outreach service with hundreds of new people, and the day our new church pulled off a great story in the local paper. But, I also remember the many things we tried that did not work. I recall vividly the failure of an incredibly expensive mailer that generated no guests, building a building that sat unfinished for months, and core members leaving because they "needed" something more established.

I remember the times when I did not want to go on.

I remember the times when I did not want to go on. I remember quitting many times but never telling anyone but God. I wish I could have had someone tell me what they did right and wrong, so that I could have learned from their experience. I wish I could have learned from someone else's hindsight.

3

Outside of the text of Scripture, the greatest tool I could find along the way was experienced church planters. I found a coach to help me, I read everything out there, and I asked questions of every church planter I could find. It made a difference. Our second church plant was four times larger at its first service than our first church plant five years earlier.

What would have been different if I had had some experienced church planters to guide me—like the church planters in this book? Could I have avoided some of the obvious and painful mistakes? Probably. We are always more effective when we discern lessons from those who have gone before us.

The Tools for the Task

Ultimately, we combine several things when we plant a church. First, we bring the Word of God and the gospel message. Ultimately, we are planting the gospel and the kingdom, and the content of our message must be "the faith once delivered to the saints" (Jude 4). If we plant something else, it is not a church, but a religious club. There is always the stumbling block of the cross (1 Cor 1:23); that, no matter how contextual we want to be, we must never discard. We learn from history that those who go too far end up with a shipwrecked faith.

But, we must bring the tools of missions to the task. North America needs to be treated as a mission field. Biblically faithful churches are churches on a mission in their communities. They are missional by the commands of Jesus (though some do not live that mission). As such, we need to think like missionaries think and discover how the unchurched think, how we are most likely to reach them, how we can lead them to an encounter with God, and how we can create a biblically faithful church that is indigenous in its context.

> We need to think like missionaries think and discover how the unchurched think.

Mission principles teach us that the church needs to be indigenous (to some degree it looks like the community it is called to reach), contextualized (its worship and outreach are meaningful to those in the context), and faithful (it cannot become so much like its community that the gospel is compromised). Needless to say, that is a difficult task—and over the years, many more have failed than have succeeded.

Lastly, we bring the tools of experience to the task. When we plant a new church, we are not the first ones to discover the adventure. People have been planting churches for two thousand years, and we have learned some things along the way.

Entrepreneurs Learning by Experience

Church planters are, by their nature, entrepreneurs. Entrepreneurs tend to start things from "scratch." Effective entrepreneurs learn from those who went before them. Today that might mean reading everything we can find on the topic of church planting. It might involve delving into the deeper principles of missions that undergird the church planting task.

Effective entrepreneurs learn from those who went before them.

We can learn power encounters from Boniface who cut down the sacred Oak of Thor leading to the conversion of Germany (700s), contextualization from Raymond Lull who taught us to learn the culture of Muslims to reach them (1300s), the need for each church planter to have a deep devotional life from Philip Jacob Spener (1600s), the importance of culturally relevant worship from Rufus Anderson (1800s), and even strategies from the Church Growth Movement (late 1900s). Finally, we can learn from experienced pastors and leaders who are just a few years further along the journey than we are.

Learning Practice from Practitioners

I have always found learning practical skills from theorists to be an odd thing. Hearing experts on church planting and growth who have never planted and grown a church always seemed strange. I prefer to learn about carpentry from carpenters. *Church Planting from the Ground Up* is just that—a wealth of wisdom from a diversity of practitioners.

Tom Jones has provided a great service to the church—practical insights from people who have been there and speak from experience. They help the church planter to start a biblically faithful and contextually relevant church. This book is a gift to the church that will help its planters to think biblically, missiologically, and experientially about church planting.

Ed Stetzer, Ph.D.
Author, *Planting New Churches in a Postmodern Age*
www.newchurches.com

A veteran church planter and pastor for over twenty years, **Dr. Tom Jones** is a widely sought after new church development coach, consultant, assessor, seminar leader and teacher, and mentor. He has a Doctor of Ministry Degree from United Theological Seminary in Dayton, Ohio, with an emphasis in church planting. Tom received his Master of Divinity Degree from Emmanuel School of Religion and his Bachelor of Arts Degree from Milligan College. Among other things, he now directs the Supervised Ministerial Experience (SME) Program, teaches in the Christian Ministries area at Emmanuel School of Religion in Johnson City, Tennessee, and is Director of Recruitment and Assessment for Southeast Stadia, a national church planting movement. Tom and his wife Debbie led the church planting teams at SouthBrook Christian Church in Dayton, Ohio, and Princeton Community Church in Princeton, New Jersey. They have two children, Melanie and Tom. Tom can be reached at **jonest@esr.edu**.

Why Plant Churches?

Recently, I've been thinking quite a bit about my home church. I have a special place in my heart for that little church, located on the corner of Penn and Neville Streets, in Follansbee, West Virginia. Do you know what a sure sign of a home church is? It's when you are 49 years old and the good folks still call you "Tommy Jones."

I have so many fond memories of my home church, like when I was eleven years old and stole communion grape juice from the church refrigerator with my best friend Randy Weaver. We drank right out of the bottle. Randy's an elder there now. I also attended Vacation Bible School there every summer. In that church, I met Jesus and was baptized on Easter Sunday in 1967. My third grade school teacher, Mrs. Stemple, sang in the choir. My Boy Scout troop met there. Al Cooper, an elder in our church, was our scout leader. I received the Boy Scout's "God and Country" award in that church. I remember going to Elkorn Valley Christian Service Camp and holding hands with a girl for the first time around a campfire. My home church sponsored me during that camp.

When my father struggled with alcoholism, the church was there for my family. I remember my dad going forward one Sunday morning and rededicating his life to Christ. He wasn't judged or condemned. Instead, he was loved and accepted.

I developed a heart for ministry at my home church. There, I

preached my first sermon when I was fifteen years old and a soph-
omore in high school. Two years later, I shared my faith at a high
school assembly of 2200 students. My youth group days under the
leadership of one of our elders, Bill Cooper, prepared me for this
public testament of faith.

I developed a heart for ministry at my home church.

Throughout the years, my home church always encouraged
my move toward vocational ministry. Our preacher, John Barto, and
his family took me to Milligan College's School of Ministry. I fell in
love with Milligan and attended college there. My home church
helped pay my way through both Milligan College and Emmanuel
School of Religion. I can still remember going to my post office box
at Milligan and receiving mail that included a ten-dollar bill from
George and Adda Mae Heckman. George worked for the city as a
trash collector. He didn't have much, but what he had, he shared
with me.

My home church financially supported both churches I started. With their mission-oriented hearts, they helped the down and
out, ministered to alcoholics, loved and accepted unwed mothers,
and invested in their youth. All of this was just part of their DNA.

My sister was married in my home church. I was ordained
there in 1977. My father's funeral was held there in 1982, and now
that same group of believers are caring for my ill mother. Words cannot express the depth of gratitude I have for that church. They
understand what it means to be a community of faith. Are they perfect? No. But they "get it!" That seemingly insignificant group of
people, who meet every Lord's Day around the Lord's Table on the
corner of Penn and Neville Streets in that small river town of three
thousand people, made a huge difference in my life.

They understand what it means to be a community of faith. Are they perfect? No. But they "get it!"

Why am I sharing this with you? As we think about the world
events of recent years, does any intelligent, thinking man or woman
doubt that this planet is in trouble? Do you question the fact that a

global spiritual famine is responsible for the human disaster we daily see on the news?

How do we fix this desperate situation? Better laws? Better political leaders? Better government? Military force? These solutions have been tried before and, historically, are always lacking. That's not to say better government and laws are not needed, but spiritual and moral change cannot be legislated. Lasting change can only occur through the transformation of hearts as people and communities meet Jesus Christ.

Transformation happens through the faithful witness of "home churches," communities of faith like my home church in Follansbee, West Virginia. The Bride of Christ has more to offer than a better set of laws. What the people of God have to offer is a new and better heart that Christ gives to people when they experience Him through His church. The church does not offer the transformation of political systems; it offers personal transformation. As people are brought into God's family and involve themselves in God-honoring relationships with others, they are encouraged in the strong name of Jesus. Where else are people going to find Jesus Christ and the kind of sacramental community Christians have? No one else can offer what the church has to offer. Home churches are the best things going. We just need more of them, lots and lots that do what they do best—nothing more, nothing less.

The church does not offer the transformation of political systems; it offers personal transformation.

In August of 1985, our family was living in Springfield, Ohio, but had recently been called by the Miami Valley Evangelizers Association (MVEA)[1] to start a new church in Centerville, Ohio. As we prepared to move, I wondered if my three-year-old daughter, Melanie, really understood why our family was being sent out by MVEA. On a warm August day, I thought I would try to help her understand. I asked her, "Melanie, why do you think we are moving to Centerville?" She looked up at me with an expression on her face that said, "Why are you asking such a stupid question?" Then she answered very simply by saying, "Well, Daddy, to tell those people about Jesus." That little walk, which was intended to be a father-daughter teaching time, instead was a personal learning experience. Melanie already knew something about mission that was simple, but profound.

Six years later that learning event was repeated. Although we planned to spend the rest of our lives in Centerville, Ohio, God had other plans in mind. In the fall of 1991, the Go Ye Chapel Mission and the Mid-Atlantic Christian Church Evangelism—both church planting associations in the Northeast—called us to lead a church planting team in Princeton, New Jersey.

The decision was a difficult one. We loved Centerville, but felt a strong sense of call to New Jersey. Finally, one late afternoon after our kids were home from school, we sat down as a family and discussed the decision. After explaining the opportunity in Princeton, I asked our children, Melanie and Tom, "What do you think?" They thought for a few moments and then Melanie said, "Well, I would be sad to leave my friends, but if those people don't have a church to tell them about Jesus, then I think we should go." My son Tom chimed in, "Yeah, we can teach them how to worship."

If we are clearly to understand the *why* of church planting, we must begin by taking a close look at the mission of the church.

> **God's nature is at the root of mission. The living God portrayed in the Bible is a sending God.**

Mission

God's nature is at the root of mission. The living God portrayed in the Bible is a sending God. He sends because of His love for the world (John 3:16). He sent Abraham from his home into the unknown, promising to bless the world through him if he obeyed (Gen 12:1-3). God sent Joseph into Egypt to help preserve God's people during a famine (Gen 45:4-8).[2] When the time had fully come, God sent His Son. Later, the Father and Son sent the Spirit at Pentecost (Gal 4:4-6; John 14:26; 15:26; 16:7; Acts 2:33). Finally, Christ sent His church (Matt 28:19-20). John Stott writes:

> And now the son sends as he himself was sent. Already during his public ministry he sent out first the apostles and then the seventy as a kind

of extension of his own preaching, teaching, and healing ministry. Then after his death and resurrection he widened the scope of the mission to include all who call him Lord and themselves as his disciples.[3]

Lesslie Newbigin affirms Stott when he writes, "The Church is sent into the world to continue that which he came to do, in the power of the same Spirit, reconciling people to God (John 20:19-23)."[4] Emil Bruner states, "The Church exists by mission, just as fire exists by burning."[5] Wilbert Shenk expounds on Bruner's statement, "The fire of mission is God's passion for the world's salvation. When the people of God live in covenantal relationship with God, they will find this fire burning within them, too."[6] David Bosch explains further,

> . . . it is impossible to talk about church without at the same time talking about mission. Because God is a missionary God, God's people are missionary people. The church's mission is not secondary to its being; the church exists in being sent and in building up itself for its mission.[7]

"The Church exists by mission, just as fire exists by burning."

If God is a sending God, and this action culminated in the sending of His Son, and the Son sends the church, then what was Christ sent to do? What has He sent the church to do?

In Luke 19:10 Jesus emphasized the priority of evangelism in His mission when He said, "For the Son of Man came to seek and to save what was lost."[8] He later passes this same mission on to the church in the Great Commission. The Commission is given in the New Testament in five different places.

> As the Father has sent me, I am sending you (John 20:21).

> Go into all the world and preach the good news to all creation (Mark 16:15).

> Therefore go and make disciples of all nations, baptizing them in the name of the Father and of the Son and of the Holy Spirit (Matt 28:19).

> He told them, "This is what is written: The Christ will suffer and rise from the dead on the third day, and repentance and forgiveness of sins will be preached in his name to all nations, beginning at Jerusalem" (Luke 24:46-47).

> But you will receive power when the Holy Spirit comes on you; and

you will be my witnesses in Jerusalem, and in all Judea and Samaria, and to the ends of the earth (Acts 1:8).

The Great Commission teaches that disciple-making evangelism gets priority in the mission of the church. The early church took this Commission seriously, and effectively fulfilled it.

Disciple-making evangelism gets priority in the mission of the church.

As important as evangelism is to the mission of the church, it does not stand alone. God's mission, reign, and evangelistic efforts are concerned with all areas of life. Wilbert Shenk correctly asserts,

> Because the church should know its own culture best, it has a special missionary vocation to that culture. Significantly, the Great Commission includes all arenas of human life and activity in the mandate of the church. . . . At no point is the church given license to stop thinking in missionary terms.[9]

If the evangelistic mandate is best summed up in the Great Commission, the cultural mandate is expressed best in the Great Commandment. In Mark 12:31 Jesus says, "Love your neighbor as yourself" (see also Lev 19:18). Christ's concern for hurting people is an extension of Old Testament thinking. Amos's prophetic words are characteristic of a total biblical concern for social issues.

> You trample on the poor and force him to give you grain. Therefore, though you have built stone mansions, you will not live in them. . . . You oppress the righteous and take bribes and you deprive the poor of justice in the courts (Amos 5:11,12).

Certainly Christ came to reconcile lost people to God, but He also fulfilled other needs in His mission. In reference to Himself, Jesus said:

> The blind receive sight, the lame walk, those who have leprosy are cured, the deaf hear, the dead are raised, and the good news is preached to the poor (Luke 7:22).

Jesus "gave himself in selfless service to others, and his service took a wide variety of forms according to men's needs."

Jesus "gave himself in selfless service to others, and his service took a wide variety of forms according to men's needs."[10] As His church, we are to follow Christ's example of service. Ministry to the poor was an integral part of the early church's ministry and mission. Scripture adequately records the first-century church responding to the needs of the poor and marginalized of society. In the medieval church, monks ministered to the needs of the destitute. Later, hospitals, schools, orphanages, homes for the needy, and other helpful institutions were initiated by the church, not the state. As a modern example, the Hunger Site attests to a major need of the world in the twenty-first century.

> It is estimated that one billion people in the world suffer from hunger and malnutrition. . . . About 24,000 people die every day from hunger or hunger-related causes. . . . Three-fourths of the deaths are children under the age of five.[11]

Christ came into the world as one of us. He saw and felt the heartaches of people, and out of compassion, He acted to ease their suffering. Howard Snyder and Daniel Runyon write concerning the church's response to Christ's model:

> Preaching the gospel to the poor, however, does not mean preaching *at* the poor, but incarnating the Good News among the poor as Jesus Christ did, through healing, teaching, touching, preaching, and forming kingdom communities.[12]

"The Word became flesh" (John 1:14). Somehow the church must become incarnational if it truly wants to fulfill the Great Commandment and the Great Commission. John Stott writes concerning an evangelistic problem:

> It comes more natural to us to shout the gospel at people from a distance than to involve ourselves deeply in their lives, to think ourselves into their culture and problems, and to feel with them in their pains.[13]

Eddie Gibbs concludes:

> Churches cannot stand apart from society and invite people to come to them on their terms. Rather, churches must go to people where they are and communicate in terms that will make sense to them, addressing the issues that shape their lives and speaking their language.[14]

In short, the mission of the church includes fulfilling the evangelistic and the cultural mandates. Shenk and Stutzman assert,

"God's intention is that every congregation of believers in Jesus be a surprising revelation of the presence of the kingdom of God on earth. These surprising colonies of heaven are audiovisual expressions of the continuing life and ministry of Jesus. . . ."[15] Jesus says that we are to be salt and light (Matt 5:13-16). The Body of Christ is light because we point men and women who are lost in darkness to the illuminating Good News of Jesus Christ. We are also salt because the presence of God's people makes a difference in the world. The model of Jesus sends the church into the world to serve. That service includes "both words and works, a concern for the hunger and for the sickness of both body and soul, in other words, both evangelistic and social activity."[16] Snyder and Runyon state:

> It does not mean only saving the earth from oppression or ecological collapse, nor does it mean exclusively eternal life in heaven, with the total destruction of the material universe. Rather, it means the reconciliation of heaven and earth, the reign of God that is in some way the reconstitution of the whole creation through God's work in Jesus Christ.[17]

The most efficient way to fulfill the total mission of a sent church is the multiplication of local churches. God sends His church expecting a harvest.

Church Planting and Mission

The most efficient way to fulfill the total mission of a sent church is the multiplication of local churches. The world needs more home churches like mine back in Follansbee, West Virginia. It needs lots of them. Why? Because God sends His church expecting a harvest. He will not be satisfied until lost people are found and all of creation is reconciled to Him.[18] One of my former students and a contributor to this book, Laura Buffington, says the language used in the seeker philosophy is reversed. We in the sent church are *seekers*, and those we pursue on God's behalf are the *sought-afters*. Therefore, the Great Commission and Great Commandment are most effectively implemented through God-honoring, *seeking* local churches. Lesslie Newbigin states:

> It will only be by movements that begin with the local congregation in which the reality of the new creation is present, known, and experi-

enced, and from which men and women will go into every sector of public life to claim it for Christ, to unmask the illusions which have remained hidden and to expose all areas of public life to the illumination of the gospel.[19]

The church at Antioch represents a New Testament example of a sending church. When the Jerusalem church was scattered (sent out by God) because of persecution, some of the Christians relocated to Antioch. The gospel was preached, and the church was born. Barnabas was involved with this church, and he brought Paul back to disciple him at Antioch. During this time, the Antioch Christians, led by the Spirit, received an offering to help fellow Christians in Judea (Acts 11). The church at Antioch was definitely interested in fulfilling the Great Commandment. Later this same church set apart and sent out Paul and Barnabas for the purpose of fulfilling the Great Commission by starting a new church multiplication movement (Acts 13:1-4). The Antioch church was serious about mission. David W. Shenk and Ervin R. Stutzman write:

> No matter how young or small a new church may be, God wants it to be a center for world mission. One does not measure the significance of that center by the quantity of financial or personnel resources which a congregation generates. Rather, one looks at the clear vision, prayer, and sacrificial commitment of that congregation to the world mission of the church.[20]

Paul was primarily a church planter.

When the Antioch church sent Paul out, it was the beginning of his church planting ministry. He was primarily a church planter. The apostle understood that God had called him to preach the gospel (Ephesians 3) and start new churches wherever he went. Paul established churches in Thessalonica, Ephesus, Corinth, Galatia, and other places. He was especially interested in fulfilling the Great Commission's direction to make disciples of all nations.

Paul succeeded because he had singleness of mind and clarity about mission. His persistence and perseverance overcame many obstacles, including personal animosity and physical suffering. To fulfill mission, he preached the Good News and gathered believers into churches. Paul's ministry truly reflected salt and light in this world. New Testament scholar Michael Gorman writes regarding the apostle's mission, "Paul sees his mission as one means of extending the reign of Jesus the universal Lord into the enemy-occupied and enemy-governed world."[21] Groups of God's people, with different backgrounds, cultures, and needs, emerged everywhere because of Paul's church planting ministry.

The fulfillment of the church's mission must continue today. Just as in the first century, the answer to the problems humanity faces in a sin-filled twenty-first century is the multiplication of churches.[22] The world needs more churches! Great numbers of new churches that take God's mission seriously can positively influence creation for Him. Shenk and Stutzman write,

> Church planting is thus the most urgent business of humankind. It is through the creation (or planting) of churches that God's kingdom is extended into communities which have not yet been touched by the precious surprise of the presence of the kingdom of God in their midst.[23]

The whole world needs to feel the presence of God through groups of His people. Every city, community, language, people group, and town on earth has the right to have a church in its midst. Every person on the planet deserves a home church.

The whole world needs to feel the presence of God through groups of His people.

How can more churches be started? I believe every local congregation, denomination, and church tradition must restore the New Testament priority of congregational reproduction. Every local church should consider itself a center for world mission. Each church should ask, "What are we doing to fulfill the mission of the church in our community and in the world? What are we doing to fulfill the Great Commission and the Great Commandment? What are we doing to start new congregations among people that are not being reached?" Donald McGavran sums it up best.

> Being a real New Testament church means believing and doing what the New Testament church did. It means planting churches as the New Testament church did. The New Testament church was tremendously concerned with, engaged in, and successful at establishing new congregations. Churches were planted in Jerusalem, Judea, and Samaria. Christian churches were formed in many villages on the Samarian

hills. Churches sprang up in Galilee, in Antioch, in city after city, and all around the Mediterranean. Toward the end of his life, Paul was heading toward Spain to begin planting a church there. Church multiplication was an essential part of New Testament life.[24]

Conclusion

The best way to fulfill the mission of the church is the multiplication of God-honoring new churches. The evangelistic and cultural mandates can be effectively implemented when groups of God's people are sent throughout the entire world. That's God's plan, and it cannot be improved upon. Mission is at the heart of God's plan. As Lianne Roembke so appropriately concludes,

> Without the sending aspect of God's character, He remains aloof and distant. Without the Sent One, Jesus Christ, Christology becomes merely anthropocentric. Without the gifts of the Spirit of God, sending and teaching, the continuing work of Christ through the Church in the parenthesis between His ascension and return would be without concrete meaning. And without the outward orientation of missions, the Church becomes ingrown, complacent and ethnocentric. The history of the expanding Church is the history of missions.[25]

Why expand the church? Why start new churches? As my daughter Melanie said, "To tell those people about Jesus."

---

[1] The Miami Valley Evangelizers are a group of Church of Christ/Christian Churches who are a volunteer association for the purpose of starting new churches in the Dayton, Ohio, area.

[2] John R.W. Stott, *Christian Mission in the Modern World* (Downers Grove, IL: InterVarsity, 1975) 21-22.

[3] Ibid., 22.

[4] Lesslie Newbigin, *The Gospel in a Pluralistic Society* (Grand Rapids: Eerdmans, 1989) 230.

[5] Wilbert R. Shenk, *Write the Vision* (Harrisburg, PA: Trinity Press, 1995) 87.

[6] Ibid.

[7] David J. Bosch, *Believing in the Future* (Harrisburg, PA: Trinity Press, 1995) 32.

[8] All Scripture quotations are taken from the *New International Version*.

[9] Shenk, *Write*, 47.

[10] Stott, *Christian Mission*, 24.

[11] Quoted from the Hunger Site at **www.thehungersite.com**.

[12] Howard A. Snyder and Daniel V. Runyon, *Decoding the Church* (Grand Rapids: Baker, 2002) 51.

[13] Stott, *Christian Mission*, 25.

[14] Eddie Gibbs, *ChurchNext* (Downers Grove, IL: InterVarsity, 2000) 39.

[15] David W. Shenk and Ervin R. Stutzman, *Creating Communities of the Kingdom* (Scottdale, PA: Herald Press, 1988) 23.

[16] Stott, *Christian Mission*, 29.

[17] Snyder and Runyon, *Decoding*, 130.

[18] For a complete discussion on "A God Who Finds" see Donald McGavran, *Understanding Church Growth* (Grand Rapids: Eerdmans, 1970) 31–48.

[19] Newbigin, *Gospel*, 233.

[20] Shenk and Stutzman, *Creating*, 211.

[21] Michael J. Gorman, *Cruciformity* (Grand Rapids: Eerdmans, 2001) 364.

[22] See Marcus Bigelow's chapter in this book entitled *It Takes a Movement*.

[23] Shenk and Stutzman, *Creating*, 23.

[24] Winfield C. Arn and Donald A. McGavran, *Ten Steps for Church Growth* (San Francisco, CA: Harper and Row, 1977) 96.

[25] Lianne Roembke, *Building Credible Multicultural Teams* (Pasadena, CA: William Carey Library, 2000) 1.

Marcus Bigelow is the president of Stadia: New Church Strategies. Prior to that, he led the Northern California Evangelistic Association and also planted and pastored a church in northern California. Since 1996, Stadia has proudly assisted in the planting of 45 churches. The development of assessment, coaching, mentoring processes, and a business model that provides strong financial stability have all been keys in Stadia's successful church planting movement. Currently, Marcus and his coworkers at Stadia are working toward 30 new church plants in 2004. Marcus lives with his wife, Jan, in Vacaville, California. He is the father of three Christian daughters and four grandchildren.

A Church Planter . . . Who Me?
The Call to Plant

If you are thinking that God may be calling you to plant a church, then I encourage you to read on. Church planters come in all shapes and sizes. Some are tall, dark, and handsome. Others, well let's just say that Sean Connery isn't worried. Some are very young, and some are older; some are studious, and some use their theology books as coasters; some are introverts, and some wear ecclesiastical lampshades on their heads at every party. Some have been in large churches, and for some this is their first ministry; some are polished, and others are diamonds in the rough (the argument could be made that some planters are still lumps of coal that haven't been turned into diamonds yet by the heat and pressure of the refiner's fire). Some come from very successful ministries, and others come after crushing defeats in previous congregations; some give up lucrative salaries in business, and some leave "cushy" ministry positions in large churches with ample budgets and support staff. Still others leave ministries that feel like dead ends.

The seed of faith is the most important ingredient in all of church planting.

The one common denominator for these church planters is a belief that God is calling them to plant a church. Without a doubt, the seed of faith is the most important ingredient in all of church planting. If you are reading this book and there is dissatisfaction with the way things have always been done, a conviction that God has called you to better things, or a deep burning vision for what could be, then keep reading. God may be calling you to plant a church.

The Need for a Sense of Call

A sense of call provides assurance and security in the face of adversity. It contributes to staying power, confidence in ministry, and a sense of empowerment. Second Corinthians 4:1-10 is perhaps as instructive as any Scripture when it comes to the importance of a call.

Staying power
Therefore, since through God's mercy we have this ministry, we do not lose heart. . . . We are hard pressed on every side, but not crushed; perplexed, but not in despair; persecuted, but not abandoned; struck down, but not destroyed. We always carry around in our body the death of Jesus, so that the life of Jesus may also be revealed in our body.[1]

Satan is called the accuser of the brethren. If he can make us doubt ourselves, he certainly can defeat us. Spiritual warfare will be a reality of life during a church plant. When we come to those battles, it is important to know that we are indeed called to the King's business. Church planting is the fulfillment of the promise in Matthew 16:18 that the gates of Hell will not be able to overcome the church.

In a study conducted by Todd Hunter of Vineyard church plants that failed, an interesting statistic emerged: *half of those leading the failed plant were actually unsure of their call to church planting in the first place!*[2] The fact of the matter is, church planting can be incredibly difficult, and the decision to plant will often be deeply and sometimes painfully tested.

A survey of 493 mission agencies in 14 countries concluded, "A clear call was seen as the most important reason for preventing loss from the field, followed by a very supportive family or spouse, and a healthy spirituality."[3] This same sense of call is no less important for church planting missionaries in North America than it is for church planters around the world.

When a person is called to plant a church, offers and other opportunities will distract from that call at the very outset of the plant. Jeff moved to a community to plant a church, and before the boxes had been unpacked, another church contacted him, offered him a greater salary, more prestige, and the security of a larger church. Only the sense of call gave him the stability to stay with the church plant. His staying power resulted in a new church with an attendance over 1,600 after 8 years.

Dean Pense, former director of the Northern California Evangelistic Association[4] often told potential planters, "If you can do anything else, you ought to do it." It was not about talent or interests or abilities. Mr. Pense realized and taught the fact that competing interests and a double-minded focus on church planting are fatal in the long-term.

Confidence in ministry
Such confidence as this is ours through Christ before God. Not that we are competent in ourselves to claim anything for ourselves, but our competence comes from God (2 Cor 3:4-5).

Sureness in the face of adversity
We are hard pressed on every side, but not crushed; perplexed, but not in despair; persecuted, but not abandoned; struck down, but not destroyed. We always carry around in our body the death of Jesus, so that the life of Jesus may also be revealed in our body (2 Cor 4:8-10).

A sense of empowerment:
Not that we are competent in ourselves to claim anything for ourselves, but our competence comes from God (2 Cor 3:5).

"Our competence comes from God."

Understanding the Call

Phil Stevenson, a consultant with New Church Specialties,[5] identifies two distinct types of calls. The **Damascus Road** call of Paul involves a dramatic, unforgettable, watershed type event. On the other hand, the **Emmaus Call** is more developmental in nature.

Which is yours—the Damascus Road call or the Emmaus Call?

Typical of the Damascus call is the experience of Chris and Rita, both of whom had a vision of a school gymnasium filled with hundreds of unchurched people. It was a vision that came to them ten years before they actually planted a church.

Then there was Dan who knew within ten minutes of becoming a Christian that God had called him to be a missionary. During his training in seminary, he decided the best way to accomplish mission work was through planting churches. For Dan, church planting became a natural follow-through of his earlier sense of call. Dan read John Eldredge's words, "What the world needs are men who are alive,"[6] and then asked himself, "What makes me come alive?" The answer was easy—"Saving the lost and planting new churches." Following this event, Dan was led to plant a church for *Stadia: New Church Strategies*.

Other planters I have worked with experienced the Emmaus call, which took them through a developmental process to a sense of certainty. Galen said, "I think there was a long buildup for me. There were at least two things that confirmed to me the call: a fire in my belly to preach the Word, and how God took me from being scared to death of planting a church to the point that my greatest fear was not having the privilege to plant one."

Dean Pense echoed the growing desire to plant a church in saying, "My call to plant a church started with a passion for evangelism. When I discovered that studies revealed that church planting was the most effective means of evangelism in the world today, I could do no other."

Another church planter wrote, "Matthew 9:36-38 captured my heart." In a time of prayer on a clear southern California night, a picture of Christ struggling in Gethsemane and His concern for the lost brought him to the conclusion, "If He were to open the doors to plant a church, I would walk through every one tirelessly to His glory."

A third type of call commonly expressed by planters is what one calls "an anticall." Barry says, "The last thing I wanted to do was start a church with six people in my living room." As God brought educational experiences and a sense of vision that could not be accomplished anywhere else, however, he yielded to the call to plant a church.

Two other planters wrote of finishing second in several pastoral searches until God guided them toward church planting. The sense that circumstances were moving around them to lead them to plant a church is a common theme.

For many, the experience of the call also includes trusted advisors who directed them toward or encouraged them to plant.[7] In every case, seasons of prayer contributed to the sense of call, either at the beginning of the process or during confirmation of that call.

The desire to begin a new thing (spiritual entrepreneurship) is another sign of God's call. Personally, I found myself drawn to lost people, then to the need to escape the status quo mentality of many existing churches, and finally to church planting. The agenda of the lost had to take priority over the needs of the existing believers. Dissatisfaction with the status quo is a common thread in the sense of a call to plant. Time and again, Scripture illustrates God's love of doing things in new and fresh ways.

The heart of compassion may also be an indicator of a call to church planting. When listening to pastors such as Gene Appel or Bill Hybels,[8] we immediately are touched by their powerful emotions and concern for the lost. It is no coincidence that both of these men have been involved in church planting.

How Do You Discern a Call?

In the days before church planters' assessment became a routine part of understanding the call to plant, my wife, Jan, developed a rating system affectionately known as the "Mad Dog" rating. The system stemmed from her observation that every planter we hired was so passionate about it that they were like a dog on a choke chain straining to get loose and get on with the task. If a person did not rate at least a 7 on the "Mad Dog" scale, we questioned their sense of call.

The first confirmation of a call to plant a church is the presence of passion for it.

The first confirmation of a call to plant a church is the presence of passion for it. While it may be totally subjective, if you are not passionate about planting a church, I would encourage you to question your call. Enthusiasm is contagious and will draw people and resources to the plant. That passion will also see you through the lean, hard times that inevitably accompany a plant. (Be careful not to equate enthusiasm with being an extrovert. Some of the most enthusiastic and passionate planters are introverts by nature.)

Here are some examples of that deep-seated enthusiasm.

◉ When I first met Barry, he could see every detail of the church that he wanted to plant. God has since tempered that vision. We met in the library of a seminary, and Barry was so animated and passionate that everyone was looking at us by the time we were done.

◉ Randy, a "10" on the "Mad Dog" scale, couldn't wait to put legs on his vision. He told his story to everyone who would listen and often to others who didn't want to listen. The ministerial association gave him the opinion that his church plant would never top fifty. Today a congregation of over 500 exists.

◉ By the time Dan received a letter of call from the Northern California Evangelistic Association, he had already raised $650 of monthly support, made a trip to the area, and checked out options for meeting places.

◉ When Matt came to his first interview, he brought a fifteen-page outline showing the need, plan, and personnel—and we didn't even know who he was!

If you are married, God will confirm your call through your spouse.

A second determinant for the call is that, if you are married, God will confirm it through your spouse. If God makes two become one in marriage, surely He is able to confirm a call to both spouses. While a church plant may employ only one spouse, if both do not have a sense of call, the results are disastrous. One planter's spouse wrote,

> This has been a difficult year for us. The cost is high, and we knew that going in. I just didn't understand the ramifications of what it means to die every day. . . . I can tell you this: it was absolutely liberating when I realized that church planting was *my* call as well. I realized it was not about my spouse getting to do what he wanted, and then me being resentful of the time he spent away. The fight became moot when I understood God *called me* too. I think it was the intense desire filling me, which made me realize I was called. Church planting was the vehicle God decided to use to grow me up in Him as well as love His people. For me it is an act of worship.

Thirdly, wise counselors will confirm a call. Although it is not the topic of this chapter, in this era of church planting one should never consider planting a church without going through assessment and receiving the confirmation of those who already have planted. Most church planting agencies have a policy that demands all potential planters to undergo assessment before being offered employment. Because failure in a church plant always hurts both the church plant and the church planting team, assessment is essential. Conversations with leaders from several denominations and our own experience would indicate that good assessment can raise the success of church plants by as much as 50%.

> Numerous individuals have felt a call to plant churches. Many of these "called" pastors have planted churches without any objective confirmation. The usual logic is that the felt call is the obvious will of God. Tragically, many of these founding pastors have failed. It is not unusual to have more failures than successes. Throughout the history of the church, responsible leaders in the church have confirmed an authentic call to ministry. God often reveals Himself in decision making through shared wisdom and counsel. Today church leaders have the process of assessment to enhance the decision-making process. The personal call is considered necessary, but it is not the only consideration used for choosing church planters.[9]

This chapter is not intended to be a theological treatise on knowing and doing the will of God. It does not address theologically the issue of an internal call versus an external call. Rather, this has been intended to help planting couples on a practical level discern whether or not God is calling them to plant a church.

---

[1] All Scripture quotations are taken from the *New International Version*.

[2] Steve Nicholson and Jeff Bailey, "What Does a Church Planter Look Like?" *The Cutting Edge* 2, no. 1 (Winter 1998).

[3] William D. Taylor, Summary of ReMAP Survey from the WEF/MC international study on attrition of long-term missionaries by WEF Missions Commission, P.O. Box WEF, Wheaton, IL 60189, USA.

[4] The Northern California Evangelistic Association planted churches for 48 years in California until it became one of the founders of Stadia: New Church Strategies. Since 1986, they have planted over 60 churches. For more information about NCEA and Stadia, please visit **www.stadia.cc**.

[5] "New Church Specialties is a 501[c][3] non-profit organization specializing in

coaching pastors and church planters, consulting districts, and providing NewStart, ReStart, and ReFocusing education and training. They exist to serve the mission and ministry of the church." Their web site is www.NewChurchSpecialties.org.

[6] John Eldredge, *Wild at Heart* (Nashville: Thomas Nelson, 2001) 200.

[7] See Acts 13:1-5 for a New Testament precedent.

[8] Both Gene Appel and Bill Hybels are teaching pastors at Willow Creek Community Church in Southern Barrington, Illinois.

[9] Quoted from North American Mission Board Church Planting Web site http://www.namb.net/cp/About_CPG/qualified_cp.asp.

Gene Appel began serving as the Associate Pastor of Willow Creek Community Church in S. Barrington, Illinois in June of 2003. Prior to that, he spent 17 years as the Senior Pastor of Central Christian Church in Las Vegas, Nevada. In addition to being instrumental in church planting in the Las Vegas valley, Central grew during that era from 400 attendees to over 7,000. Gene and his wife, Barbara, have three children and reside in the northwest suburbs of Chicago.

"Do It Again, God! Do It Again!"
Planned Pregnancies: Churches Planting Churches

Sometimes I wear contact lenses. One spring several years ago, I'd put my contact lenses in my eyes before preaching, and everything would be fuzzy and blurry. I'd get up to speak and then have trouble focusing on my message notes. It was really bothersome. This trend of seeing the world blurred and unfocused continued until one weekend before a Saturday night service. I don't know what prompted me to think of it (in fact, I'm embarrassed to admit it), but the thought hit me: maybe somehow along the way I've gotten my lenses switched. Maybe I'm putting the lens that goes in my left eye into my right eye, and the lens that goes into my right eye into my left eye. Out of curiosity, I switched lenses, and it was just amazing how much better I could see. I saw things with new clarity and precision.

What I just described unfortunately happens to many Christ-followers, churches, and even many church leaders. We get our lenses switched, and we become fuzzy about our purpose. We focus inward instead of outward. We become exclusive instead of inclusive. We serve ourselves rather than serving others. Why the confusion? Unfortunately, the gravitational pull in me, the gravitational pull in you, the gravitational pull of the 99 sheep already in the pen is always toward *selfishness*. If you don't believe that, ask a pastor of a large and prosperous church what his or her knee-jerk reaction is to the thought of releasing a portion of the Christ-followers in his or her church to start a daughter church. Ask this pastor to be completely transparent about his or her anxiety in releasing these people—people who have been won to Christ and discipled in that church, who worship in that church, who serve and tithe in that church, who pray in that church, who sacrifice for that church, and who lead ministries in that church. I'll tell you what his or her honest answer most likely is, because as embarrassed as I am to admit it, I've had to wrestle with this sin myself over the years. It's selfishness.

Pastors of churches that are considering starting daughter churches are left asking, "How is this going to affect me? What will this do to our attendance and giving that's been increasing every year? How will this new daughter church affect our building project?" We get our lenses switched, and we lose sight of the fact that we are called to be in the Kingdom-expansion business. We have been empowered by the Holy Spirit to be witnesses in Jerusalem *and* Judea *and* Samaria *and* to the ends of the earth.

One of the best ways to expand the Kingdom involves existing churches mothering baby churches. That's what our church in Las Vegas, Nevada, did several years ago.[1] We made the decision to become indefinitely pregnant. In the process of learning about planned pregnancies and mother-daughter church planting we found four phases: conception, pregnancy, birth, and long-term family planning.

> To expand the Kingdom
> we made the decision to
> become indefinitely pregnant.

Conception: Moving beyond the Comfort of the Way Things Are

From an outward glance, it didn't make any sense; the timing seemed wrong. The church was thriving, growing, and healthy. There was spontaneity and dynamism that was magnetic. They were full to running over each week during worship. Everything was so comfortable.

You may think the church I'm describing is Central Christian Church, but the one I have in mind is the church in Antioch mentioned in Acts 13. Although Jesus told the disciples they would be witnesses in Jerusalem, Judea, Samaria, and to the ends of the earth, I'm convinced they easily forgot. They were first witnesses in Jerusalem, and after the Holy Spirit came, the church was born and grew. People began putting down spiritual roots. As you know, once you do that, it's hard to move. I truly believe that if the decision to stay or leave had been left to these Christ-followers, they would have stayed in Jerusalem forever. God, however, allowed persecution to come to the church. It served as a catalyst to push these Christ-followers out into the areas of Judea and Samaria, areas to which they never would have gone because they were so comfortable with life in Jerusalem. In this way, the church came to Antioch.

Listen to how Acts 13 describes the leadership team in Antioch,

> Among the prophets and teachers of the church at Antioch of Syria were Barnabas, Simeon (called "the black man"), Lucius (from Cyrene), Manaen (the childhood companion of King Herod Antipas), and Saul (Acts 13:1).[2]

Just think about these five guys. Barnabas was a great encourager, a man who took Saul of Tarsus under his wing and believed in him when nobody else would. Simeon (according to Scripture) was a black man, and Lucius of Cyrene, a Gentile. Both represented unique segments of the population. There's Manaen, the childhood friend of King Herod, a man with aristocratic and government connections. He was apparently from a wealthy background and had been raised among the power brokers of his day. Finally, Saul was a lawyer with brilliant, razor-sharp intellect.

Amazingly, these men were the staff of the church in Antioch. Talk about a dream team of leaders! You've got a world-class encourager, a black man, a Gentile, a man with powerful connections, and another with a razor-sharp mind. This was an exciting church. Who in the world would want to leave a church like this and go do something new?

The Question of Timing

I believe that the greatest challenge of conception when it comes to mothering a new church is the challenge of moving beyond the comfort of the way things are. This was certainly a challenge for our church as we began seriously contemplating giving birth to a new church back in the early '90s. We were first-time parents, and in many ways, the timing didn't make sense. It seemed wrong.

At the time, we were taking our first steps toward a multimillion-dollar relocation project. The church was thriving and reaching people. Why would we consider giving away hundreds of people and thousands of dollars to give birth to a new church when we needed people and dollars for our own dream?

Sometimes God's timing doesn't make sense. For example, my mom and dad decided early in their marriage to keep their family small in order to give their kids extensive opportunities in life. . . . So, they stopped at six! I was number six. After my brother Gregg was born, the folks were all finished having children, so they got rid of the crib, high chair, and baby clothes. Five years later, when my dad was 38 and my mom was 37, little Geno Brian came bouncing into their lives—the bonus baby, or as I like to think of it, the unexpected blessing. Friends kidded dad that he was going to have to ride to PTA in a wheelchair. Mom told me later that she cried and cried when she found out she was pregnant again. Dad put his arm around her and said, "Honey, don't you worry. I'll get you some help around the house." Mom anticipated someone to help with the housekeeping responsibilities; dad bought her an electric dishwasher instead.

Sometimes the timing of a birth seems all wrong. Everything is moving along smoothly and comfortably, but then God interrupts life with a different plan. Acts 13:2 says, "One day as these believers were worshiping the Lord and fasting, the Holy Spirit said . . ." *While* they were worshiping, *while* they were fasting, *while* everything was comfortable, *while* the church was thriving, the Holy Spirit interrupted.

While the Antioch church was thriving, the Holy Spirit interrupted.

That's the best illustration I can give you for what happened to us in 1991. After years of considering planting a new church on the west side of Las Vegas and after being challenged by the fact that we lived in the fastest growing metropolitan area in the country, the Holy Spirit interrupted our plans. In 1992 we moved beyond the comfort of the way things were by planting a daughter church.

Putting Legs on a Dream

The first question we faced was, "How are we going to conceive? How will we do this?" We had never given birth to a church before. We didn't know what we were doing. Instead of first developing a comprehensive church planting strategy, we set out to find a gifted, Holy-Spirit-called leader for the daughter church.[3] Had we gone the other way, we feared developing a comprehensive strategy that didn't reflect the personality and gifts of the eventual leader. Also, we feared that if the called leader wasn't a dynamic communicator and teacher, people would leave the new church plant before it even had a chance to develop.

Prior to the time we called Mike Breaux[4] to be the initial church planter, many of our people were pessimistic about a church plant, saying, "That poor new church. Who's going to want to leave Central Christian and Gene's preaching?" After people heard Mike preach for the first time, however, they were saying, "Poor Gene, who's going to stay at Central?"

Finding Mike didn't just happen overnight; it was the result of extensive prayer. We'd had a strong midweek service for a number of years, and one Wednesday night in January 1992, we asked for everybody to get on their knees, praying "Give us a name. Give us the name of the person you want to lead this work."

Although we had some name suggestions over the next month, none of them seemed to fit the profile of the person we were seeking. Finally, we heard the Spirit's calling. While I was in Houston and having a totally unrelated conversation with some other church leaders, Mike Breaux's name came up. At the time, he was leading a really exciting and thriving work in the little town of Harrodsburg, Kentucky. I had known Mike casually, but not very well, for over fifteen years. When I heard his name, something jumped in my spirit and I thought, "That's the guy. I know that's the guy."

A few days later, I gave him a call and shared with him our vision. He promised he'd pray over the possibility. That night he told his wife Debbie, "Hey, I got a call from Gene Appel today about coming to Las Vegas to plant a church. I told him I'd pray over the opportunity. It's not a real consideration, but I told him I would pray over the possibility anyway." The next morning, Mike found Debbie sitting at the dining room table crying. She asked, "We're moving to Las

Vegas, aren't we?" Although Mike disputed her comments, Debbie replied, "Yes, we're moving to Las Vegas. This is God's call for you. You love lost people. You're wired to do this."

Within two weeks of making the phone call to Mike and Debbie Breaux, we had a new pastor of our daughter church. I've never made a new hire so quickly in my life, but I was convinced of God's heavy involvement in the decision. Shortly after Mike's acceptance, Central Christian's financial commitment increased. We moved the Breauxs, started paying Mike's salary, set aside another $65,000 for start-up costs, and essentially conceived a church plant.

Pregnancy: Practicing Healthy Prenatal Care

Once you conceive, much has to happen before you are ready to give birth. Acts 13:2 reads, "One day as these men were worshiping the Lord and fasting, the Holy Spirit said, 'Dedicate Barnabas and Saul for the special work I have for them.'" Although unclear how the Holy Spirit communicated the message, God clearly selected specific people (Barnabas and Saul) to leave the church in Antioch and to move forward with God's ministry plans for them. God didn't call everyone to go and leave; three individuals of the leadership team stayed while two left.

When you're mothering a daughter church, how do you figure out who is called to go and who is to stay? Mike and I discussed the issue early on. Frankly, there were a few people I really wanted to send, as there were also people who wanted to send me. We decided early on, however, that we wouldn't recruit for these positions. Rather, we would follow the guidance and leading of the Holy Spirit. As we cast the vision of the daughter church—executing "tag-team" preaching over the next seven months and working as each other's biggest cheerleader—we waited for the Holy Spirit to recruit.

We waited for the Holy Spirit to recruit.

When you're preparing to mother a new church, you must be prepared to send the very best. If you were a member of the church in Antioch, enjoying the teaching and ministry of Saul and Barnabas, would you want to give them up and send them out to another church? Of course not; you'd want them to stay forever. Acts 13:3

presents a biblical response to the question of releasing a church's best leaders into this world. "So after more fasting and prayer, the men laid their hands on them and sent them on their way." Like the church in Antioch, I learned that practicing healthy prenatal care involves sending some of your most influential leaders, teachers, givers, and even staff members. After all, who would you rather send to communicate the gospel of Christ?

I learned that practicing healthy prenatal care involves sending some of your most influential leaders, teachers, givers, and even staff members.

As a mother church, you must also ask, "How does planting a new church cause us to face our fears?" Like all parents to be, we had numerous fears and anxieties about the unknown—"What if no one leaves? Or even worse, what if everyone leaves?"

I confess. I came face-to-face with much internal darkness at this point in the plant. Although natural to play comparison and competition games, both the parenting church and planting church must be honest with themselves and each other about their fears and anxieties. It's one thing to say that you trust the Holy Spirit to lead people to go, but there is a darkness inside you that emerges when certain individuals feel called to go. Your mind takes over, asking, "What did I do to make them want to leave? What didn't I do? Are they mad at me?" It might seem ridiculous, but it's real, it's dark, it's sin, and it must be faced. In fact, I'm convinced that an unwillingness to admit, face, and deal with this darkness often prevents Kingdom advancement from happening. We get more concerned about our kingdoms rather than *the* Kingdom.

An unwillingness to admit, face, and deal with this darkness often prevents Kingdom advancement from happening.

If you've ever heard Mike Breaux preach, you know that he is an awesome communicator. A gifted speaker, tremendous vocalist, and authentic worship leader, Mike Breaux allows his gifts of communication to interact warmly and personally with all people. Although I wish I could identify something dark and sinister about Mike, after hours spent at his side, I'm convinced that he is every bit as genuine in private as he is in public. In fact, I believe God took his hair just to keep him humble. Establishing a daughter church challenged me to look beyond my ego and instead look at what is necessary for Kingdom expansion. Every church leader and body in this same position must look beyond themselves, outside of selfish tendencies, and toward what is best for building strong communities for Christ.

The Final Stages before Birth

In preparation for the new church birth, a leadership team of called Christ-followers gathered to dream, pray, strategize, and plan over the new work. In addition, we placed an information table in the lobby of Central for publicity. A special section of the church newsletter highlighted the new church plant. Information meetings, socials, and picnics served as opportunities to share with interested people the vision of planting a new daughter church. We did everything in our power to share the vision, to excite potential leaders of the new work, and to pray over this God-sized growth project. It wasn't until over 400 people attended one of the information picnics, however, that we realized the magnitude of God's involvement in our plans.

Finally, a delivery date was established. We decided to induce labor and give birth on January 24, 1993. In order to prepare the spiritual climate at both Central and the daughter church, Mike and I delivered a series of messages from the book of Acts aptly named, "Do It Again, God!" We began the series by talking about an old pastor whose eyesight was failing to a point where he could no longer read his Bible or sermon notes. Each time he stood to preach, someone would open his Bible to the book of Acts, the old man would put his hand on the Scripture, and simply say, "Do it again, God. Do it again."

Quickly, this pastor's motto became our prayer, as we found ourselves repeating these words over and over again. Appropriately, the series ended with the passage in Acts 13 where the church in Antioch put their hands on Paul and Barnabas before sending them out. In our own emotional send-off, we joined hands around the nucleus of those who would be leaving us for a new adventure and prayed.

Birth: Trusting the Holy Spirit for Supernatural Results

Three fundamental results happen when you move beyond the comfort of the way things are, practice healthy prenatal care, and trust the Holy Spirit for supernatural results.

The Reach of the Kingdom Is Extended

Once Paul and Barnabas left the comfort of Antioch, the reach of the Kingdom was expanded. Until that time, the scope of Christian influence and church presence in the world had been limited to Jerusalem, Judea, and Samaria. As a result of the mission of Paul and Barnabas, however, the message went out in hopes of reaching the end of the earth. Because of their willingness to go, lost people were found, and new churches formed.

Canyon Ridge Christian Church was born in a YMCA gymnasium on January 24, 1993. It might have been the only church in America with an Olympic-size baptistery. Before the first Sunday worship service, we performed no mass marketing, no direct mailings, no radio announcements, and no TV advertisements—just extensive vision casting, word-of-mouth broadcasting, and prayer. We saw 725 people enter the doors of the church during the first Sunday worship. People just kept pouring in—lost people, seeking people, people who had never previously made the journey to Central Christian Church nor to the southeast side of Las Vegas. They started attending worship services at Canyon Ridge, however, and during their time in that new and joyous community, found hope and a church that cared. In the process, the reach of the Kingdom most definitely was extended.

Initially, we planned to financially support Canyon Ridge with $100,000 a year for the first two years of operation. They started with a staff of four full-time ministers, an intern, and three members on their support staff. They rented offices and two different locations for Sunday and midweek worship and devotion services. Their financial needs were great, but at just five months of age, they informed us of God's financial provisions and asked for our aid to switch from full-time financial support to full-time prayer support.

The Ministry at Home Was Multiplied

After the church at Antioch gave their best, the temptation to return to a state of comfort might have been high. Whether a struggle or not, the church at Antioch continued compassionate caring for all people, as illustrated by directly meeting people's needs and communicating God's love and concern for all people. Not surprisingly, scholars estimate that the church in Antioch grew to over 100,000 committed Christ-followers.

How was the ministry at Central affected by a new birth? With over 700 people pouring into the doors at Canyon Ridge the first week, it seemed natural that Central would display lower attendance numbers. On the same day that Canyon Ridge began services, however, our attendance shifted only forty people less than the week before the new church birth. Amazing! We couldn't figure it out; the math didn't add up. God had done something truly incredible, and all we could do was stand in awe.

Attendance at Central averaged at 2300, so Mike and I dreamed that within the next year, both Central and Canyon Ridge together would average 3000 in attendance. Amazingly, God chose the first week of both churches in action to validate this dream.

The Members of Both Bodies Were Energized

When Paul and Barnabas left Antioch, members of the body of Christ there stepped up to the plate to take their own positions in church leadership. While Central mimicked Antioch's changes in leadership, Canyon Ridge relied on people who had never led to take on new leadership and teaching roles. In both cases, new leaders emerged, bringing spiritual growth and healthy change to each community of believers.

Over the years, both churches learned from one another. Prior to Canyon Ridge's birth, Central held on to many traditions while still trying to navigate change. Canyon Ridge brought a fresh, new perspective to church that was inspirational to Central in pushing its creative envelope even more.

In addition, together we shared retreats, seminars, and social events. We volunteered to guest speak and teach at one another's churches. We partnered together on a new church plant, a plant that witnessed over 900 people at its first official worship service. Most excitingly, in this particular new birth, Canyon Ridge served as the church mother, while Central was the midwife.

In all my years of ministry, nothing has been as exciting as watching God mature daughter churches. Each time I visit a new church and see what God is doing there—how this infant church is meeting the needs of hundreds of people and offering their worship and praise to God alone—all I can say is, "God, thank You, thank You, thank You for letting me play a part in this."

All I can say is, "God, thank You, thank You, thank You for letting me play a part in this."

It's Still Hard . . .

Even for Paul and Barnabas, the conditions of their new mission were difficult. Along the way, they encountered and experienced beatings, rejections, imprisonment, and even stoning. In comparison, hardship and even labor pains mark conception, pregnancy, and birth. For example, there remains a sense of loss, especially during the first year of life when it's hard to look around at the empty seats that used to house friends and colleagues. It's hard when people come to their Sunday school classes and encounter unfamiliar teachers. As a church, we sent exceptional givers, servants, and leaders, leaving a vacuum in areas of our church. Similar to the case in Antioch, however, others stepped up to fill the voids, people who might not have ever accepted the growth challenge with other leaders already in position.

Even in the case of Canyon Ridge, new openings led to the advancement of courageous, new leaders within the church. Less than three years into this great adventure, for example, Mike and Debbie Breaux sensed God's calling to return to their hometown of Lexington, Kentucky, to lead Southland Christian Church. Although anxiety mounted in the church over Mike's decision to leave Canyon Ridge, Kevin Odor moved from associate pastor to lead pastor, rising to the challenge in front of him. He has since lead Canyon Ridge in building a $10 million campus, numerically growing to over 4,000 members, and encouraging the birth of another strong, daughter church. It's true—lives and churches experience incredible transformation when courageous leaders keep their lenses in the correct eye, never forgetting that God supports and encourages Kingdom building.

Future Family Planning: Looking Ahead with a Kingdom Mind-set

After all of these years, reality is becoming increasingly clear to me. New churches need not threaten existing churches. The opportunity to reach lost people still exists all around us. The Kingdom still needs expanding in our own communities.

New churches need not threaten existing churches.

Not surprisingly, Americans are the most traveled people in the world. One of my favorite stories tells of American tourists who visit a tropical island. On a tour directed by a native, they came upon a spewing volcano, a volcano pouring out intoxicating lava, smoke, and fire. At the sight, one of the American tourists said, "That looks just like hell." The native guide replied, "Man, you Americans have been everywhere, haven't you?"

I know Las Vegas might look like hell to many people. With between 5,000 and 7,000 residents moving in per month and with nine out of ten of these individuals having no previous connection, support, or relationship with the community, a tremendous need for thriving, Christ-driven churches exists in the city walls. This need is especially true of mother-daughter church plants. I believe that planned pregnancies giving birth to healthy babies might be the most effective means of reaching the city. I trust God to do something extraordinary in this valley that many refer to as hell on earth.

In an ever-expanding city like Las Vegas, even planting five megachurches per month wouldn't serve the extensive needs of the city. Every mother church is different, but when I was at Central, our hope was to plant or aid in the planting of ten to twenty strong, healthy, robust churches within the next ten to twenty years. It's the dream of rocking a city. And if it can happen in Las Vegas of all places, I just know that a ripple effect will take place, encouraging megachurches all over the world to become indefinitely impregnated. Do it again, God! Do it again!

[1] Gene Appel was pastor of Central Christian Church in Las Vegas from 1985 to 2003. Over this time, Central Christian Church was the mother and grandmother to Canyon Ridge Christian Church, the Crossing, and Apex Church.

[2] All Scriptures in this chapter are from the *New Living Translation* unless otherwise indicated.

[3] Editor's Note: Church planting strategists all agree that the most important decision made in the church planting endeavor is choosing the right leader.

[4] Mike Breaux joined the team of Willow Creek Community Church as a Teaching Pastor in September of 2003. After helping launch Canyon Ridge Christian Church in Las Vegas, he returned to his hometown of Lexington, Kentucky, and led the Southland Christian Church from 3,500 attendees to over 8,000. Mike and his wife, Debbie, have three children, one grandchild, and reside in the northwest suburbs of Chicago.

Dr. Rick Grover currently serves as the Lead Minister of a new church plant in New Orleans, Louisiana, called Journey Christian Church. This plant has been a cutting-edge new church implementing creative ministry opportunities in a difficult context. Rick is married to Laura, and they have three children—Will, Anna, and Luke. After completing his undergraduate degree at Manhattan Christian College (Kansas), Rick received an M.A. in Theology/Philosophy from Lincoln Christian Seminary (Illinois) as well as a M.Div. and D.Min from Emmanuel School of Religion (Tennessee). He served as the Pastor of Evangelism and Discipleship at Central Christian Church, Wichita, Kansas, which was followed by a growing ministry as the Senior Minister of Woodlawn Christian Church, Knoxville, Tennessee.

Urban Church Planting:
The Call to the City

"Listen! The Lord is calling to the city."
Micah 6:9a

You're going the wrong way!" I left a church of 2,000 and went to a church of 300. I left that church of 300 and went to plant an urban church with a small group of ten people. To some this would appear to be heading in the wrong direction. But to me, this has been the greatest adventure of my life!

Urban churches have the unique opportunity to build a ministry primarily among broken and hurting people

---

Reaching the Urban Unchurched—A Story

From Harley riders and racial diversity to drugs and gang violence, urban church planting is not for the faint of heart! All churches face challenges of ministering to broken and hurting people, but urban churches have the unique opportunity to build a ministry *primarily* among broken and hurting people—to people like Kourtney. Kourtney is an African-American woman who began attending our new church shortly after we launched. Soon after Kourtney and her husband began visiting Journey,[1] I asked her to share her testimony. Here's what she said:

Hello, my name is Kourtney. At the age of 14 my life changed drastically. When most little girls were enjoying dolls and middle school, I had my innocence taken from me. Between the ages of 14 to 16 I was a victim of incest. I found out I was going to give birth to a beautiful baby daughter, but I did not know if she was going to be born healthy or not. My body was prepared for the birthing process, but mentally I was only a child, and I had serious issues.

After not being able to cope with the incest and not having any professional counseling out of family embarrassment, I fell astray to drugs and the street life. I ran away from home. I became addicted to drugs and sex just to maintain the day-to-day process and whatever I had to do to survive. Jarred by the murder of a good friend, I decided to return home and get my life together. It wasn't that easy. After six abusive marriages and a failed career, one morning after a $600 drug night I turned myself in to a treatment center to get help for the addictions I had. You see, unlike the stereotypical addict, I was the most dangerous kind. I was a functioning addict. I went to work and partied only on weekends, until I hit rock bottom.

Treatment and counseling taught me about a Higher Power--a way to deal with addictions and emotional issues. They taught me that I had to make lifestyle changes and that I had to apply myself and work the program. There were no magic pills to help me overcome my addictions.

I was curious about this Higher Power concept. After intense therapy for being a victim of incest and surviving, I learned about God. I learned after one night of drugging that I wanted to be clean and to change, but being right with God meant (I thought) that you had to be boring—there was no laughter, everything was always serious, and there was no fun. I learned after being suicidal one night with a gun to my chin that when there is nothing left but God, that is when you find out that God is all you need. I was on my knees for the first time praying to a Man I knew nothing about, to a Man who was supposedly there with me at that moment, a Man who died for me so I could make it through this.

I removed the gun from my chin. I did not desire to do this; I wanted to live, but I was tired of the pain. I can honestly tell you that I was alone for the first time in my entire life. My family was fourteen hours away. The man I was in a relationship with was in another country. I knew no one here. I was lost, confused, and had no one but God. So I prayed.

For the first time in my life, I began to know God personally through Jesus Christ. I began to experience freedom. I then started to meet these people who were like 'angels' to me. They guided me to church, shared compassion with me, prayed for and with me, taught me to pray to God, to read my Bible, and to have a growing faith. I often wondered what brought me here to New Orleans. I can tell you now, that I found God here.[2]

Many suburban churches reach out to people like Kourtney, but the churches themselves consist of a *homogeneous* majority quite different from Kourtney. Likewise, urban churches also reach out to people like Kourtney, but these churches consist of a *heterogeneous* majority that allows for a greater diversity of people—ethnically, economically, and socially.

Suburban vs. Urban

Urban churches and suburban churches need each other. As the Apostle Paul wrote, "The eye cannot say to the hand, `I don't need you!' And the head cannot say to the feet, `I don't need you!'" (1 Cor 12:21).[3] We need to move beyond an either/or mentality in church planting. We should continue planting suburban churches in emerging communities, but we also need to develop stronger models of planting urban churches in the demographically changing urban centers of our country (and world).

Urban churches and suburban churches need each other.

Suburban churches can and should partner together to do urban church planting. For suburban churches this will provide a broader "Kingdom mentality," provide short-term missions opportunities for church members, and help extend the missions' ministry by working in evangelistic ministries in American cities. For urban churches these partnerships can provide financial support since most urban church plants take much longer to become self-supporting. This also will provide leadership training and healthy church leadership structures as examples to start-up urban churches. Urban churches need to be viewed as "missional outposts" for suburban churches, so that they are sharing in a partnership to reach cities for Christ.

Urban church planting must also be seen differently from suburban church planting. More extensive study needs to be done on the culture and context of our cities to understand more effective models and methods of reaching people for Christ in an urban milieu. As the ethnic and socioeconomic landscape of our nation changes, so do our churches. The following table illustrates some of the vast differences between urban churches and suburban churches:

Suburban Churches	Urban Churches
Homogeneous	Heterogeneous
Middle-class focus	Lower/middle- to lower-class focus
Larger campus/facility	Smaller campus/facility
Lower costs for property—land, buildings, utilities	Higher costs for property—land, buildings, utilities
Sunday mornings drive ministry	Ministry drives Sunday mornings
Evangelism precursor to social ministry	Social ministry precursor to evangelism
Educational needs: small group studies	Educational needs: "survival" studies
Counseling/therapy ministries	Support groups/substance abuse groups
Worship—professional quality emphasis	Worship—group participation emphasis
Children/youth—more outings, socials	Children/youth—more family-centered, getting kids off the street
Offerings support the church	Usually church needs supplemental income
Church members *go* somewhere for short-term missions	Church members *receive* others to help with short-term missions
Staff—specialists in ministry	Staff—generalists in ministry
"If you build it, they will come"	"If you go to them, they will come to you"
Preaching—more epistles	Preaching—more Gospels
Icon—Bill Hybels[4]	Icon—Martin Luther King, Jr.[5]

Obviously, the table above shares *general* insights to illustrate the point that urban churches have many cultural and methodological differences from suburban churches. Some of the comparisons ring truer than others, but the primary difference is that suburban church planting targets a homogeneous group and builds from there, whereas urban church planting targets a diverse community. Both approaches are necessary and good, because they can effectively reach their areas for Christ. Suburban churches will reach more mainstream, Caucasian, middle-class people, because those are the people who are generally in the suburbs. Urban churches, on the other hand, will reach more "edgy," racially and economically diverse people, because those are the people who live in urban areas.

My wife and I were at a biker hangout recently (as in Harley Davidson, not Schwinn), and as we were leaving, my wife (who is a gentle-natured Kentucky girl) said, "I never dreamed we would be hanging out with bikers!" Moving to the city to plant a church was not our idea. In fact, it was the furthest thing from our minds, but we knew of the incredible needs in the city, and somebody had to go. We prayed that God would give us a heart for people in the city, even if it meant inconveniencing ourselves for the sake of others. Randy White, who moved to the inner city to plant a church, once wrote, "Love of neighbor begins with the willingness to be inconvenienced."[6] The starting point for urban ministry should be the prayer, "Lord, let people get in the way."[7]

Urban Church Planting—The Need

According to the *World Urbanization Prospects* published in 1998:

> It is projected that just after the turn of the millennium . . . for the first time in history urban dwellers will outnumber those in traditional rural areas. . . . By 2006, half of the world population are expected to be urban dwellers. The urban population is growing three times faster than its rural counterpart. By 2030, three of every five persons will be living in urban areas.[8]

Others attest to the fact that today more people live in cities than in rural areas, and this trend is only expected to increase.[9] George Kurian states,

> By 2025 over two-thirds of the world's population will be urban dwellers compared with one-third as recently as 1975. . . . At the beginning of the 20th century, there were only 11 cities worldwide with over 1 million inhabitants. Now there are over 300. By 2025, according to U.N. Habitat II Conference, there will be 570.[10]

> **From a sheer numbers standpoint, we live in a time of the greatest need known to humankind.**

These statistics create a monstrous challenge for the church. Not only do we have urbanization reflected in the increase of medical needs, education, government structures, and resources, but also we have increases in spiritual issues. From a sheer numbers standpoint, we live in a time of the greatest need known to humankind. At the same time, however, when cities are burgeoning with social and spiritual issues, many churches have moved to the suburbs and left the cities behind.

Oddly enough, with all of the increases that come through urbanization, we also live in a time when people's interest in religion (not spirituality) is perhaps at an all-time low. Christianity has been marginalized and left outside the circle of social influence in most cities. Although denominations still pour millions of dollars into hospitals and benevolent programs, the *culture* of the city oftentimes remains untouched by the message of hope offered through Jesus Christ.

The trend in church planting within many denominations and churchgoers over the past twenty years has been a strategic focus on emerging communities. This makes sense. As people move into communities, they are generally more open to finding a church and making that a part of their social context. The challenge in suburban church planting is to uncover spiritual hunger when people do not *acknowledge* their hunger. Materialism, work, recreation, and the media all compete in offering satisfaction, and the church planter has to seek opportunities for inroads into the heart of the suburban person. The challenge in urban church planting is to validate that the gospel has immediate ramifications to meet the social, physical, *and* spiritual needs of people.

> **The challenge is to validate the needs-meeting ramifications of the gospel.**

A Theology for the Urban Church

When I was growing up, I always pictured God as "The Great Keeper of the Plains" (I grew up in Illinois and Kansas). Open land, rolling hills, farms, gardens—these were the pictures I had of God's domain. When I would visit a city, it seemed that God was absent. The hustle and bustle of city life seemed to be in stark contrast with the serenity and peace of the countryside. Thus, I assumed, God must be more present in suburban and rural areas than He is in the city. William Penn expressed in the eighteenth century what many people feel: "The country life is to be preferred, for there we see the works of God, but in the cities little else except the works of men."[11]

> Many of the 1,250 uses of the word "city" in the Bible deal directly with God's call to be in relationship with urban dwellers.

In my seminary years I began to search the Bible to learn more of God's heart for the city. What I discovered is that there are 1,250 uses of the word *city* in the Bible, and many of them deal directly with God's call to be in relationship with urban dwellers. Micah 6:9 says, "The Lord is calling to the city." In Luke 19:41 we read, "As (Jesus) approached Jerusalem and saw the city, he wept over it." God is a lover of the city, because God loves people. God longs to see people seek forgiveness in the city (Jer 5:1). He expresses concern over Nineveh (Jonah 4:11), and He calls for the city to be transformed into a place of righteousness (Isa 62:1-12). He calls us to pray for the city and work for its peace and prosperity (Jer 29:7). And Jesus sets the example for ministry by going "through all the towns and villages, teaching in their synagogues, preaching the good news of the kingdom and healing every disease and sickness" (Matt 9:35). With so many biblical passages that deal with God's love for people in the city, perhaps it's time for us to begin reading the Scripture through "urban eyes." If the masses of city dwellers are so valuable to God, then they should be important to us as well.

> Perhaps it's time for us to begin reading the Scripture through "urban eyes."

Urban Church Planting Principles

From Journey's experience in planting an urban church, we have discovered a number of principles that appear to be "workable" in most urban areas. Most of these (okay, all of them) came through our own trial and error, so anyone who can learn from our mistakes may be one step ahead when they begin their urban church plant.

Principle #1: Double or Triple Your Fundraising Efforts

Urban church plants will not become self-supporting as quickly as suburban church plants, and yet they still require the same amount (if not more) of start-up money.[12] Leasing space for worship, children's ministry, office, and counseling usually requires a much higher outlay of money than in a suburban context where church plants can move (and are often welcomed) into school auditoriums or gyms.

Principle #2: Extend Your "Ramp Up" Time before Your Launch

In many suburban contexts, a church planting team can move into an area three months before the launch date, do several weeks of mailings, conduct two or three outreach events, provide "preview services" and launch. This appears to work well where communities are experiencing 7% growth or more. In an urban context, however, churches are often planted in nongrowth or even declining communities.[13] In settings such as these it may take a full year to get established before the launch of the church. Trust is a major factor in an urban church plant, and people in the community will want to know that the leaders of the church plant are not trying to "get" anything out of them or use them in any way. Thus, just conducting some outreach events and sending out several weeks (or more) of mailers won't be sufficient to draw the large masses often seen in suburban start-ups.

It may take a full year to get established before the launch of the church.

Principle #3: Reassess Your Measurements of Success

In suburban life, everything just seems bigger. People even like to drive cars called "suburbans"! You can drive through the major streets of most suburbs and find sprawling shopping malls, new schools, and big church campuses. In most cities, however, the mainline churches who boasted of great accomplishments of brick and mortar have moved out and left a handful of senior saints sitting in the pews reminiscing of the "good old days" when the pews were full. In our area, for example, a church of 125 is considered a large church. Where I came from, a church of 125 was considered a struggling ministry. The important point in all of this is to know that in planting an urban church, other measurements need to be a part of the picture of the health of the church—and these need to be shared with supporting churches. What is the church plant doing in the community? How many people are involved in community service? What is the church doing to meet the needs of others? What is the church doing to teach and disciple new converts? These questions and many more need to be asked of all church plants, but additional emphasis needs to be placed on these issues in the urban church plant.

Principle #4: Develop Indigenous Leadership.

Urban church planters can learn a lot from missionaries. Our role is not to come in as a staff-driven machine and take over part of the city. Our role is to come in as servants and raise up local leaders who serve alongside us in leading others to Christ and meeting needs in the community. Ray Bakke, who has decades of urban ministry experience, gives us a healthy warning when he writes,

> People who come into urban communities from outside with timetables for church planting almost inevitably create the church in the image of the outside leaders. They usually require long-term sustaining funds as well. Nehemiah empowered the local people at the outset. . . . He understood that his call was public leadership for all the people. . . .[14]

Principle #5: Identify Needs and Begin Meeting Them . . . One at a Time.

The temptation we face in church planting is to have a full-service church overnight. Although it is essential for us to be ready on our launch day with quality worship, children's ministry, and hospitality/greeting, I recommend that the new urban church *begins* with a need-meeting ministry in the community prior to the first public worship service. The advantage to this is that, if that ministry is done well, it will help create a presence in the community which can only complement direct mail and other forms of marketing. When people hear about the church plant, they will say, "Oh, that's the church that does _____." Be careful, however, not to spread yourself too thin! Start with one need-meeting ministry that can grow and be done with excellence. It is far better to do one thing well than to do ten ministries that flounder and give the church a bad reputation.

I recommend that the new urban church begins prior to the first public worship service with one need-meeting ministry in the community that can grow and be done with excellence.

Worksheet:
Urban Church Planting Preparedness Guide

In an effort to help future church planters and churches considering a partnership for an urban church plant, the following guide is provided. Here are some key areas and a timetable that should be considered before planting an urban church:

Area	Questions	Time Before Launch
Prayer/Sponsorship	Who are the church planting agency or sponsoring churches? Have they committed to pray fervently for this project?	15 months
Team	Is the lead planter selected and is the staff team in place?	12 months
Target	Does the team have the specific target area selected for the new church and has it researched the demo-/ethno-graphics?	12 months
Vision	Does the team have a solid vision for this particular church plant in this particular area?	12 months
Plan/Strategy	Has the team developed a plan and strategy for all components of the church plant (outreach, worship, children, youth, discipleship, etc.)?	12 months
Fundraising	Is the lead planter committed and ready to raise support, and are the team members ready to assist? What are the budget goals and fundraising plans?	11 months

Community Ministry	What are the needs in the community and what is one area that the staff team can pick to begin showing the love of Christ in practical ways?	10 months
Launch Team	Out of the community ministry and through relationships, who are people we can recruit to be a part of our launch team (children's workers, instrumentalists/vocalists, greeters, etc.)?	9 months
Location	Do we have a location selected for worship/children's ministry?	6 months
Small Groups	What two or three small groups can we prepare to start for discipleship and connection purposes once the church is launched?	3 months
Outreach Events	What two or three outreach events could we conduct to give exposure to the new church and reach out to the community?	3 months
Marketing	What type of marketing should we use in our community and how much can we afford?	1½ months
Pre-launch Services	Are we ready to conduct two or three services as "trial runs" to make sure we have everything ready for our launch?	1 month
Follow-up	When people show up for our launch, are we ready to contact them and minister to them?	1 month
LAUNCH DAY	Are we ready to rumble??	Launch Date

For a downloadable version of this worksheet, visit **www.collegepress.com/churchplanting**.

Bikers. Gang members. Drug addicts. Alcoholics. Gays and lesbians. African-Americans. Asians. Hispanics. Muslims. Hindus. Buddhists. The city is full of people from all walks of life; all of them need to intersect with the path of Jesus Christ. If you are going to plant an urban church, be ready to reach urban people. Listen more than speak. Learn more than teach. Discover more than expound. Form teams more than going solo. Value the poor alongside the wealthy. Eliminate judgmentalism and grow in grace. Serve the people with the love of Jesus. Be committed to the long haul. Never give up. That's urban church planting. *That's the call to the city.*

[1] Journey Christian Church began October 6, 2002, under the leadership of Rick Grover and a launch team of thirty people. Prior to the launch, Rick and his family moved to New Orleans and began working with a Tuesday night Bible study that consisted of about ten people. Within a few months, an additional small group was added on Sunday nights until the church was ready for her "Grand Opening." Journey's mission is to help people experience a life-changing passion for Jesus Christ and His community. Journey focuses on community outreach and service, ministering to the needs of the poor and hurting, and building bridges to the unchurched through small groups and family ministry.

[2] I give a special word of thanks to Kourtney for allowing me to use her story.

[3] All Scripture quotations are taken from the *New International Version*.

[4] Bill Hybels is the Senior Pastor of Willowcreek Community Church in Barrington, Illinois. Hybels is most readily known for his innovative leadership and development of ministries under the umbrella of a "seeker-driven philosophy," i.e., providing ministries and worship services that target unchurched people. Hybels is listed here as an "icon" for suburban ministries because Willowcreek personifies megachurch structure and philosophy that reaches predominantly white, middle-class suburbanites.

[5] Dr. Martin Luther King, Jr. is listed here as an "icon" for urban ministry because of his emphasis on racial equality and ministry to African-Americans predominantly in urban areas.

[6] Randy White, *Journey to the Center of the City* (Downers Grove, IL: InterVarsity, 1996) 59.

[7] Ibid.

[8] United Nations, *World Urbanization Prospects: The 1996 Revision* (New York: United Nations, 1998) 2, 29. Quoted by Timothy M. Monsma in *Cities: Missions' New Frontier*, 2nd ed., ed. by Roger S. Greenway and Timothy M. Monsma (Grand Rapids: Baker, 2000) 13.

[9] George Thomas Kurian, *The Illustrated Book of World Rankings* (Armonk, NY: M.E. Sharpe Inc., 1997) 343.

[10] Ibid.

[11] William Penn, *Reflections and Maxims* (publisher and date unknown). Quoted in Randy White, *Journey*, 44.

[12] This is based on a high-impact model of church planting which utilizes a team approach and marketing.

[13] While there is an overall population growth in cities worldwide, many urban church plants find themselves in stagnant or declining communities.

[14] Ray Bakke, *A Theology as Big as the City* (Downers Grove, IL: InterVarsity, 1997) 110.

Greg Hubbard currently serves as the Co-Director of Apex Church located in Las Vegas, Nevada. There he assists on the pastoral staff team for new church start-ups, directs an organization that aids churches in reaching younger generations, and teaches courses for a local Bible Institute. Greg received both his B.A. (Biblical Studies, Christian Ministries Major) and M.A. (Practical Ministries, Church Growth Emphasis) from Cincinnati Bible Seminary in Cincinnati, Ohio. He married Rebekah in 1995, and together they welcomed their daughter, Tori, into the family just four years later.

Simple Churches

A "Simple Church" Planting Story

Jeremy worked as an electrician for a major hotel and casino on the Las Vegas strip. He and his wife Lori, both in their late twenties, became involved in planting a house church in Vegas. Jeremy and his house church have influenced many new daughter church plants. Each of these daughter plants has a unique story, but none as fascinating as the story of Jeremy's extended family.

One morning Jeremy was getting ready for work when his wife interrupted him with bad news. A phone call had come saying that Jeremy's grandfather was in the hospital and that the family should come quickly. Before Jeremy was out of the shower, news had come that his grandfather was in a coma and would not live much longer.

When they arrived at the hospital, the entire extended family was in the waiting room. Aunts, uncles, and cousins all awaited Jeremy's arrival. Together they entered the hospital room of the family patriarch. Twenty-five people gathered around the bed. Jeremy commented later how he felt a "spiritual authority" among his extended family at that moment. He led them in a time of prayer for his grandfather and in a time of caring for and encouraging one another. Once the final family members arrived, everyone tearfully circled the hospital bed one final time, and permission was given to pull the life-support system. The family remained circled around him as he died.

Jeremy's family gathered at an uncle's house for dinner, and the powerful time of encouragement and reconnection continued. Twenty-four hours later at the eulogy, Jeremy spoke of the family's need to gather around their grandmother and to ask God how this group could once again become a family.

One month later, the family decided to begin weekly meetings at the family's grandmother's house. At these meetings, the family came together to eat and to encourage one another. Many family members, whose spiritual stories were varied, began asking Jeremy questions about "that Christian faith." Jeremy and other believers in the room began openly sharing their walk with Christ.

The family went through two divorces and an abortion in the following months. Through all of this, they leaned on each other, and continued to seek to know more about Jeremy's faith.

One week Jeremy boldly turned the television off and began teaching the Bible to his family. On another week the family gathered together to figure out how they could help a hurting relative who was not there. Week after week went by. People who once were asking about "that Christian faith" began to share and ask about "their own faith." Somewhere in the midst of these weekly meetings, a house church was born.

More than a year later, one of the teenage cousins brought a hurting friend to the house church. She was seeking help for a marriage that was crumbling and a faith that had no answers. Soon a widow who lived on the same street started attending the house church and became friends with the family's grandmother, a widow in similar circumstances.

Not all house church plants have a story this dramatic, but in this case the availability of Jeremy led to a church being born at his grandmother's house. Soon after the start of this church, Jeremy left his job to become a full-time missionary in Las Vegas, starting and developing house church plants.

Foundations for "Simple Church" Planting

Description

Some call them *house churches*. Some call them *organic churches* or *relational churches* or *simple churches*. Perhaps it is best to just call them *churches*. Whatever label they carry, they are rapidly multiplying, simple communities of believers, meeting in homes, offices, campuses, or wherever God is moving. This is the pattern common to many parts of the globe, and is now becoming more and more common in North America as well.

In one region of China, a church planting movement grew from three churches in 1993 to 550 churches (reaching 55,000 people) in 1998. In one region of India, a church planting movement went from 28 churches in 1989 to 2,000 churches in 1998. In places like these, the church has grown faster than in North America in recent decades. This has happened through church planting movements, which allow small, simple churches to multiply rapidly.[1]

In recent years, simple church planting movements have begun to spring up in North America as well. Such movements have started in southern California; Austin, Texas; Las Vegas, Nevada; Cincinnati, Ohio; Denver, Colorado; and other places.

Theology of Church

Simple churches and simple church planting movements come to life when people clarify their understanding of church. As often said by simple church planters, one must "lower the bar of what it means to be a church and raise the bar of what it means to be a disciple." This is the attitude that allows simple church planting to flourish.

> Simple church planting movements come to life when people clarify their understanding of church, "lowering the bar of what it means to be a church and raising the bar of what it means to be a disciple."

Neil Cole and Paul Kaak of Church Multiplication Associates have expanded on this simple idea of church. They define church as "the presence of Jesus among his people called out as a spiritual family to pursue His mission on this planet."[2] From this definition they have developed the acrostic D.N.A. The letter D stands for *divine truth* (the presence of Jesus), N for *nurturing relationships* (his people called out as a spiritual family), and A for *apostolic mission* (to pursue His mission on the planet). Simply put, where there is D.N.A, there is church.[3]

This definition says as much by what it omits as by what it includes. The implication is that buildings, programs, and professional clergy are not essential elements of church. Such things are not wrong or necessarily detrimental, but they are not essential or even primary.

The Term "House Church"

House church is a term that has developed a negative connotation in the eyes of some people. For example, when a group of churchgoers angrily leaves a traditional church, huddles on their own in the name of Christ, and declares itself to be a house church, it often leaves a negative impression on the existing congregation. This is not the idea of house church that is promoted in this chapter.

In other cases, when a power-hungry leader oversteps healthy New Testament boundaries in order to control the people in his house church, this leader often leaves a negative impression, perhaps even raises the suspicion of being the manipulative leader of a "cult." This is not the idea of house church that is promoted here either.

Not only has the term *house church* developed a negative connotation in the eyes of some, but also the term is not even the best term to describe these churches. These churches may or may not even meet in a house. They can, in fact, meet almost anywhere. Thus the term, which intends to de-emphasize the building, can in effect backfire by emphasizing a house, which is another kind of building!

With this in mind, it is more helpful to use another term such as *simple church*, *organic church*, or even *relational church* in order to avoid the negative connotations that have been associated with the term *house church*. In fact, many house church members prefer to just use the term *church* among people who understand what they mean.

It is helpful to use a term such as "simple church," "organic church," or "relational church" in order to avoid the negative connotations of "house church."

A Very Old "New" Idea

Churches in the New Testament were often small gatherings that met in homes. Note the following examples:

> Greet Priscilla and Aquila, my fellow workers in Christ Jesus. They risked their lives for me. Not only I but all the churches of the Gentiles are grateful for them. Greet also the church that meets at their house (Rom 16:3-4).[4]

55

But when the Jews opposed Paul and became abusive, he shook out his clothes in protest and said to them, "Your blood be on your own heads! I am clear of my responsibility. From now on I will go to the Gentiles." Then Paul left the synagogue and went next door to the house of Titius Justus, a worshiper of God (Acts 18:6-7).

Most early churches met in homes and remained rather simple until the Roman Emperor Constantine changed Christianity from being commonly persecuted to being the state religion. In this environment the church quickly moved into a more institutional model. Elements of this institutional model have been passed down to today's church.

Questioning the "Place Where" Assumption

The Gospel and Our Culture Series published a book entitled *Missional Church*,[5] which describes how today's Protestants have inherited something from the Protestant Reformation that the reformers never intended to pass along: the idea that church is a *place where* certain things happen.[6] Today we hear examples in everyday church talk of this idea in statements like: "We don't go to church anymore," or "Where do you go to church?"

Church is better understood, theologically speaking, as a body of people, or a community, that has been sent on a mission. In contrast to the *place where* understanding of church, missiologist David Bosch defines church as "a body of people sent on a mission."[7] Church is understood as a moving people, not as a static place.

Practical Aspects of "Simple Church" Planting

An accurate theological understanding of church paves the way for simple church planting. Many practical issues, including evangelism, worship services, doctrinal standards, children's ministries, finances, and leadership need to be examined in light of this type of church planting.

Evangelism and Simple Churches

Rather than having programs for local evangelism or world missions, simple churches are missional in and of themselves. The word *mission* literally means *send* or *sent*.[8] Simple churches are able to understand themselves as *sent* into their neighborhoods on

Christ's mission. Each church understands itself as being the missionary in its particular neighborhood.

The exponential key to evangelistic growth is not in church growth, but is found in church multiplication. In his book, *Houses That Change the World*, Wolfgang Simson suggests a new growth principle. Rather than focusing on growing churches past the 200-barrier, Simson urges churches to keep beneath what he calls the "Twenty Barrier." He suggests that the key to church multiplication is to keep each church under twenty in attendance! The reason for this is that groups of fewer than twenty tend to operate as communities, where groups over twenty tend to organize and become less participatory.[9]

A church of twenty people meeting in a house has everything it needs to reproduce itself.

The concept of multiplication implies that a church of twenty people meeting in a house has everything it needs to reproduce itself. Simple math shows that a group of twenty that multiplies itself over several *generations* has the power to outgrow a church of several hundred that grows by 10% (or more) per year. It is the same principle that my seventh-grade math teacher once taught me when she said:

> If I offered you $10,000 this month for allowance, or you could take one penny on the first day of the month with the amount doubled everyday throughout the month, which would you take? All of those in the class quickly responded that they would take the $10,000. The teacher went on to demonstrate how foolish their decision was, because at the end of one month the doubling penny would have paid off millions of dollars![10]

This illustrates that the true growth potential in a church depends on how capable it is of reproducing itself, not necessarily on how large it is!

Some may doubt that this ideal example could really play out in church multiplication. However, in places like China and India this kind of church multiplication has led to unprecedented evangelism and church growth in recent years.[11] Unfortunately, sometimes in North America it is easy for the church to lose sight of successful church growth and church planting examples across the globe.

Simple Church Gatherings

In simple churches, gatherings do not necessarily follow the format of a traditional church service. Many churches pattern their worship services largely around teaching/preaching and singing. While these elements are certainly part of simple church life, they do not necessarily look the same as they would in other churches. In fact, the meetings often feel more like the reunion of an extended family than a programmed church service. Simson writes, "In many ways a house church is like a spiritual extended family, relational, spontaneous, and organic. For its everyday life a house church does not need a higher level of organization, bureaucracy, and ceremonies than any ordinary large family."[12]

> ### The only test is whether the group has D.N.A.

Simple church gatherings are open to many activities. No two simple churches meet in exactly the same way. The only test is whether the group has D.N.A. (divine truth, nurturing relationships, and apostolic mission), as discussed earlier. People frequently eat together, pray, share what God has taught them, sing, bless each other, study the Bible, share the Lord's Supper, and serve each other. Some simple churches follow predictable patterns in their meetings, but many have matured to the point where they come together and seek out what God's agenda for that day's gathering might be.

Simple church gatherings should allow people to truly use their spiritual gifts on a regular basis. Regardless of one's theological perspective on the supernatural gifts, it is still true that simple churches are able to function according to passages like 1 Corinthians 12–14 much more easily than more organized church services allow. Too often Christians get caught up in debates about the supernatural gifts when reading these Corinthian chapters. In doing so, they miss the main point of the chapters. Every person is gifted by the Spirit for the good of others (12:7). Every person is also part of the body of Christ (12:27). Love for one another, therefore, is the real goal of our spiritual gifts (Chapter 13). At a church gathering, everyone can use their gifts in love to build up one another (14:26).

Simple churches also get together with other simple churches for larger group gatherings on occasion. Though this is never the primary expression of church to these people, simple church movements often do larger-group gatherings monthly, quarterly, yearly, or sporadically.

Moral and Doctrinal Issues within Simple Churches

How do simple churches maintain control of their doctrinal and moral purity? There are two ways to respond to this question.

First, since each church is started by another church or by a church planter who has been trained, these relational/family lines often provide the best kind of accountability. D.N.A. is passed from generation to generation, much like in a biological family. Special training opportunities also exist to encourage high doctrinal and purity standards for church plants. The Greenhouse Retreat,[13] put on by Church Multiplication Associates, is currently one of the best in North America.

Second, if we are honest, only God controls His church. Moral failings and doctrinal issues have plagued some of the most structured and controlled church denominations throughout history. Control structures have not proven effective in eliminating problems. It seems that control structures may do more to limit the spontaneous expansion of the church than they have done to preserve its purity. Based on this, many who are committed to simple church planting would rather err on the side of freedom than err on the side of control.

Children and Simple Churches

If a church is thought of as a *family*, instead of as an institution, then healthy churches should deal with their kids in the same way that healthy families do. This means that kids are frequently included in the life of the church and in its gatherings. Families with small children often have to modify their lifestyles in order to deal with their kids. It is looked upon as a privilege rather than an inconvenience to do so. Church life should follow the same pattern. What better way to spend a church meeting than pouring life into the spiritual lives of the next generation?

Having said this, families occasionally need to get child care providers so that the adults can have some free time to relate on an intimate level. The church can practice this same pattern as well.

Finances and Simple Churches

How are finances handled in simple churches? There are many options for this. In the Apex Network[14] in Las Vegas, for example, the leaders encourage everyone to meet the financial needs of those in their simple church family first. Then, with whatever money is left, the leaders encourage them to give back to the church planting movement to help start new churches and network the existing churches. Each simple church then manages its own income, while the network manages the network's income. Other simple church movements around the country have used other methods, though. Some run all of the income through the network's books before distributing it back to the simple churches, for example. There seems to be no *one* right way to handle finances in simple church networks, just as there is no *one* right way to handle finances within a family. However, there are principles of accountability and stewardship that must be taught and modeled throughout the network.

Leadership in Simple Churches

The purpose of this section is not to debate leadership titles (such as *elder*, *deacon*, *pastor*, *apostle*, and *prophet*), but to simply describe the function of leadership as it has emerged in simple churches and their networks.

Two kinds of leadership *roles* emerge in simple churches: stayers and goers. Depending on one's theological and denominational background, various terms may be used to describe these leaders. *Stayers* are the spiritual fathers and mothers within a single simple church. They serve as the overseers of the family. They pastor the flock. Their leadership style is comparable to a father or mother in a healthy biological family. *Goers* are more apostolic (in that they are sent as missionaries) at heart. They go throughout the network planting new churches and networking the existing ones together. They often act as overseers of the network.

Both stayers and goers appear in the pages of the New Testament, particularly in the book of Acts. Though numerous examples could be cited, perhaps the most obvious is Acts 13:1-3:

> In the church at Antioch there were prophets and teachers: Barnabas, Simeon called Niger, Lucius of Cyrene, Manaen (who had been brought up with Herod the tetrarch) and Saul. While they were worshiping the

Lord and fasting, the Holy Spirit said, "Set apart for me Barnabas and Saul for the work to which I have called them." So after they had fasted and prayed, they placed their hands on them and sent them off.

In these verses, we see Barnabas and Saul as goers and we see Simeon, Lucius, and Manean as stayers. The same leadership roles emerge in modern-day simple church networks.

Conclusion

It is hard to deny that rapidly multiplying, simple churches are responsible for some of the fastest church growth and evangelism on the planet in recent decades. Church planting movements in China, India, and Latin America prove this point.[15]

The question still lingers, however, as to whether this method of church planting can play a prominent role within the North American context. North American culture continues to experience rapid change, as evidenced by recent writings about the postmodern culture shift. Some argue that the ideal soil for these simple churches generates from the more tribal, relational, postmodern culture. While past North American culture has not been receptive to these ideas, future culture may depend upon them.

For now, we are only able to cite various examples of simple churches and simple church movements that have begun to emerge across North America. However, in the end, only time will tell what impact these simple churches will have on the fulfilling of the Great Commission in North America.

"Soil Analysis" Worksheet

These questions can be used by a simple church planter or team to evaluate the soil of a given field in anticipation of simple church planting. These are adopted from questions created by Neil Cole and Paul Kaak in the *Greenhouse Retreat*.[16]

1. What is the culture of this place?

2. What is the political, economic, and spiritual status of the people here?

3. What is the history of this place?

4. What "strongholds" are working against sowing the gospel here?

5. Who might be "receptive people" in a place like this? (Hints: *bad* people make good soil, young people often more receptive than old, crisis is often a breaking up of hard soil)

6. What other spiritual groups might already have an influence here?

7. How might we be able to serve this place or these people? (Random acts of kindness? Making peace with those who are normally oppressed?)

8. How should we pray specifically for the needs we see here?

9. How would the gospel be worded to this place/these people (we affirm in you this: _____, followed by we confront in you this: _____)

10. How can genuine friendships be made here?

For a downloadable version of this worksheet, visit **www.collegepress.com/churchplanting**.

---

[1] David Garrison, *Church Planting Movements* (Richmond, VA: International Mission Board of the Southern Baptist Convention, 2000) 11-32.

[2] Neil Cole and Paul Kaak, *The Organic Church Planter's Greenhouse Intensive Training Event Participants Notes* (Signal Hill, CA: Church Multiplication Associates, 2003) 1-2.

[3] Ibid., 1-7.

[4] All Scripture quotations are taken from the *New International Version*.

[5] This book is a part of a series entitled, *The Gospel and Our Culture Series*. A Network has also emerged, known as The Gospel and Our Culture Network. This Network has led the way in helping churches and Christians understand how the gospel interacts with North American culture, especially as expressed in the Church. The Network's web site, **www.gocn.org**, contains additional information.

[6] Darrell L. Guder, ed, *Missional Church: A Vision for the Sending of the Church in North America* (Grand Rapids: Eerdmans, 1998) 79-80.

[7] David J. Bosch, *Transforming Mission: Paradigm Shifts in Theology of Mission* (Maryknoll, NY: Orbis Books, 1991) 1.

[8] Guder, *Missional*, 81.

[9] Wolfgang Simson, *Houses That Change the World: The Return of the House Church* (Waynesboro, GA: OM Publishing, 2001) 20-21.

[10] The author remembers his seventh-grade math teacher, Miss Rose, making this offer in class.

[11] Garrison, *Church*, 11-32.

[12] Simson, *Houses*, 80.

[13] The organic church planter's greenhouse is a relational context for leaders from a city or region to gather together in a supportive environment and learn more about church and church planting from one another and the Scriptures. Greenhouse weekend intensive training events are held across the nation and around the world. To learn more, please visit **www.cmaresources.org**.

[14] Apex is a network of churches that meet in homes and other places around the Las Vegas Valley. Apex began in 1997 as a "Generation X" targeted outreach within Canyon Ridge Christian Church in Las Vegas. Apex has gone through a radical transition to become an independent simple church network. To learn more about Apex, please visit **www.apexchurch.org**.

[15] Garrison, *Church*, 11-32.

[16] Cole and Kaak, *Organic*, 2-3.

Dave Ferguson and five friends launched Community Christian Church in the west suburbs of Chicago in 1989. This church has grown to over 500 leaders, with more than 3,500 in attendance at four sites every weekend. Dave serves as a resource for other churches and leaders seeking to expand through multiple church sites and provides visionary leadership for the NewThing Network, a catalyst for a movement of reproducing churches. Dave can be e-mailed at **davef@communitychristianchurch.org**.

The Third Option: Multi-Site

*"Forget the former things; do not dwell on the past.
See, I am doing a new thing! —Isaiah 43:18*[1]

Leaders will always look for a third option. By definition, the role of a leader is to look beyond the first option of where he or she is and the maintenance of the status quo. A true leader will never retreat and head back to what he or she has known—the second option. Our role as leaders is always to look for a third option.

It was about 300 B.C. when Alexander the Great was marching across Asia Minor. He was the leader of the greatest army ever put together. Alexander and his men had conquered every enemy and the entire known world, but even the greatest armies had times of uncertainty. When they reached the Himalayan Mountains, the advance scout, who was responsible for giving strategic directions, returned to Alexander with his report. Full of concern and dismay, he said, "Sir, as best I can tell, we have marched off the map." They literally had marched off the map of the known world at that time! Then the scout added, "Sir, we should go back to where we know."

Alexander listened and responded, "Mediocre armies always stay within the known territory. It is the great army that will march off the map!" In that moment Alexander had three options: stay in place, go back to familiar territory, or march off the map.

The third option concept was introduced to me during a conversation with Dr. Daniel Reeves, church consultant and past President of the American Association of Church Growth. Reeves said, "Dave, multi-site is like a third option. Up until now the church has had two options: church planting and church growth. But now we have a third option, multi-site." During that talk, a light went on for me!

Since the days of Donald McGavran and his groundbreaking book, *Understanding Church Growth*, churches have essentially had two options or strategies for accomplishing the great commission: church planting and church growth. These are still important strategies for churches. We need to continue growing the local, single-site church. We also need to continue planting more new churches. I believe in both options (We actually practice each at Community Christian Church.). God, however, is doing a "new thing"; He has given us a third option called the Multi-Site Church.

God, however, is doing a "new thing," a third option.	• 1st Option: Church Planting • 2nd Option: Church Growth • 3rd Option: Multi-Site Church

The Community Christian Church Story

Why do I believe this multi-site movement is an Isaiah 43 "new thing" that God is doing? Let me tell you our story. From the day four college friends and I moved to Chicago to start Community Christian Church, we had a three-phase vision: Phase 1—Become an Impact Church; Phase 2—Become a Reproducing Church; Phase 3—Become a Movement of Reproducing Churches. In the last five years, God has fulfilled that vision in ways I never imagined! In 1998, we became a multi-site church, one church with two locations. That wasn't a part of our original vision, but since the second location was so successful, we have now launched a third and fourth location. Since becoming a multi-site church, our outreach has more than quadrupled from an average attendance of 800 people to more than 3300 people, with the majority of these new attendees being people who are unchurched and far from God.

When we considered starting our second campus, the decision was easy because it was so evident God was at work. Imagine this: you have a real estate developer who wants to build a 35,000-square-foot community center to be used by your church. Imagine the same developer wants the direction for the architectural design to come from focus groups comprised of your church leadership. Imagine he wants to partner with the church to establish a communal social capital in the middle of a brand new real estate development.[2] Finally, he wants to financially support the start of the new campus. A friend of mine who became a Christ-follower at CCC made that offer to us. God was so obviously at work that all we could say was "yes."

We really weren't intentional about starting our third campus either. Again, God made Himself obvious when we started our West Campus. An existing small church offered to give us their five acres and facility to use however we wanted. It was a $1 million asset they offered to hand over to us. This little church knew one thing for sure. They wanted to join in our mission to "help people find their way back to God," and the rest we could figure out in time.

I kept it very quiet, telling only our lead team members so they could pray and process this decision. I will not forget the day I told the rest of our staff about this possibility. Prior to this meeting, no one outside our lead team knew about this potential new campus in Montgomery. When we finished our all-staff meeting, I went back to my desk where an e-mail awaited me. Sherry, one of our key staff members, wrote:

Dave,

Weird thing—I had a dream last night. It was weird, but what stood out to me was this little old lady standing there telling me that I needed to go and find this church in Montgomery. I kept asking her how to get there and she told me to go down Montgomery Road so I could see the signs that would tell me where to go. She said I couldn't miss it, but it was important I check it out. Then I hear about this church thing today with that property someone wants to give us in Montgomery? On Montgomery Road? Weird, isn't it?

Weird? Yes! God was confirming through a dream that we were supposed to start this new location on Montgomery Road in Montgomery, Illinois. Again, God was so obviously at work that we could only say "yes."

The next thing we did was something unusual; we had a funeral service for that small group of people that had called the building in Montgomery their church home. We celebrated their 163-year history, and they gave me a compass representing a new direction for all of us to "help people find their way back to God." After six months of renovation, we reopened the doors as Community Christian Church West Campus. On the first Sunday, God brought 606 people into that little building that had never seen more than 75! The most amazing event of the day occurred when the elderly couple who had given us this facility gave up their seats because we had more new people than chairs. They stood in the back with tears of joy streaming down their face as that facility was packed with people who had not been to church in years.

They gave me a compass representing a new direction for all of us to "help people find their way back to God."

I believe that God is doing a "new thing" and giving us a third option to grow His church and expand His Kingdom. At Community Christian Church, we are going to be a part of this "new thing." As I write this, I can see a giant Post-It on the wall of our offices describing how we will become a church of 26 congregations in the next few years. Ultimately, we dream of becoming a church with at least 10 campuses, 200 congregations, and 100,000 Christ-followers.

Multi-Site Church Movement

A movement of multi-site churches is emerging around the globe. In 1999, Lyle Schaller told me he estimated that there were about 100 multi-site churches in North America. In 2003, just four years later, Leadership Network[3] estimates there are now over 1,200 multi-site churches in North America, and that number is increasing every week.

There are now over 1,200 multi-site churches and the number is increasing.

In November of 2003, I spoke at Onnuri Community Church in Seoul, Korea, for their first evangelism conference. While there are some churches in Seoul that are larger, this 18-year-old church of 40,000 people is setting the pace for churches in Asia. Onnuri had "accidentally" become a church of four locations with 36 worship services every weekend. The founding pastor looked at what God was doing around the world and became convinced that the single-site megachurch is not the church of the future; the church of the future is the multi-site church! Unfortunately, other churches in Korea were intimidated and threatened by this strategy. Some of the more traditional churches that didn't want Onnuri "on their turf" went to Onnuri and picketed their worship services. Although only 25% of Koreans are Christ-followers, they couldn't see this "new thing" God was doing to bring more people into His kingdom. So, at this conference they asked me to speak on "The Third Option: Multi-Site" before 10,000 Korean church leaders. As I spoke, for the first time church leaders began to see that there are not just two options, but three.

Types of Multi-Site Churches

Multi-site churches are not just one type of church in one type of setting or in one part of the world. Many types of churches in many different settings and in many parts of the world are now choosing the third option. The following are some of the different types of multi-site churches.

New Churches

In 2001, Dave Richa and thirty people from Community Christian Church moved outside of Denver to Thornton, Colorado, to start Jacob's Well Community Church. Dave and his team knew from the beginning their dream was not to start a single-site church, but a church with multiple locations. This is also true of Life Journey Christian Church in Bakersfield, California. Dave Limiero, the Lead Pastor, and about twenty people from our area moved to California to pioneer this church in 2002. They knew reaching the greatest possible number of people would require a multi-site church. Jacob's Well and Life Journey are just two examples of new churches planted with a vision of becoming multi-site.

Community Christian Church, along with these two apprentice churches (Jacob's Well and Life Journey), have birthed the NewThing Network whose mission is to "reproduce networks of multi-site churches that are relentlessly dedicated to helping people find their way back to God." The NewThing Network is coaching new and existing churches that want to go multi-site. One of the church planting teams we are coaching is set to launch a church that will have two locations on the very first weekend. Definitely a new thing!

Megachurches

On the other end of the spectrum are a large number of megachurches that are now going to multiple sites. Willow Creek Community Church, one of the largest churches in North America, adopted a regional strategy and went from a single-site megachurch to a megachurch with three locations. Willow Creek now has plans for a fourth and fifth location in the next two years. Another well-known megachurch that is making a move toward multi-site is North Point Community Church. They have their first location in Alpharetta, Georgia, and their second location in Buckhead, Georgia. The list of megachurches is growing and includes: Life Church in Oklahoma City, Oklahoma; Fellowship Bible Church in Little Rock, Arkansas; and North Coast Church in Vista, California. All of these churches choosing the third option are over 5,000 in average weekend attendance and are seeing that God is doing a "new thing."

The list of megachurches is growing.

Center-City Churches

St. Paul's Lutheran Church in Aurora, Illinois, represents another category of churches that are becoming multi-site, center-city churches. St. Paul's is located in the downtown area of a city marked by significant demographic change in the last 30 years. Here is the challenge: St. Paul's is located in a neighborhood identified as a "port of entry" community for Mexican immigrants. The leadership and a large part of the church are Anglo. At the same time, on the west side of town, large numbers of new families who match the demographic of the leadership are moving in. The struggle they face is "do we stay here and serve this changing community, OR do we relocate to the west side of town where we know we can be more effective in reaching people like us?" I love St. Paul's decision. They didn't take the first option of staying where they were. They didn't choose the second option of relocating the church. They chose the third option. They kept a site in downtown Aurora AND built a new site on the west side of Aurora. Today they have one church with two sites that are each reaching 350 people for a total weekend outreach of 700 people.

They kept a site in the downtown AND built on the west side.

Missional Churches

I would categorize Community Christian Church in this last type of church that is choosing the third option—missional churches. I didn't say missionary churches, but missional churches. Missional churches see themselves on mission with God and understand the church exists for mission. These churches do not use multi-site as a strategy; it is a natural outgrowth of their theology and philosophy of ministry. These churches understand God is in motion, and they move where His Spirit takes them.

> These churches do not use multi-site as a strategy; it is a natural outgrowth of their theology and philosophy of ministry.

Mosaic Church in Los Angeles is a good example of a missional church. In 2002, they sold the only facility they had in East Los Angeles. Today, they are meeting in three temporary locations with no permanent facilities. They meet in two high schools and one nightclub, reaching 1,500 people of fifty different nationalities every weekend. They didn't choose multi-site as a strategy. They just continually asked two questions: "Where is God at work?" and "Where is God still dreaming?"

Remember Onnuri Community Church I mentioned earlier? It's true that they "accidentally" became a multi-site church. They were already meeting in four locations with 36 services every weekend before they discovered the multi-site strategy. This Korean church simply followed the activity of God's Spirit. At Community Christian Church, we didn't have the vision for becoming a multi-site church. If you understand our story, the God-thing came first, and then we had the vision. It was very clear God was at work; we just followed Him. Missional churches are churches that are looking for proactive ways to fulfill God's dream and join Him when they see He is at work.

> Missional churches look for proactive ways to fulfill God's dream.

Advantage of Multi-Site Church vs. Church Planting

Before I talk about an advantage of multi-site over church planting I want to say again that I'm all for church planting! We have planted two new churches in the last two years, and we hope to plant hundreds more in the future. However, we have discovered that within a close geographical distance there are some very real advantages to the multi-site strategy over church planting.

	1st Service	Average at 1st Quarter	Retention Rate
CCC Church Plant	465	180	39%
CCC South Campus	552	360	65% (+26%)
CCC West Campus	606	350	58% (+19%)

When we started Community Christian Church in 1989, we had a big first Sunday with 465 attendees. We were thrilled! Then, like any church plant who uses a lot of marketing, we began to free-fall for the next four to eight weeks. About three months later our attendance leveled off at 180 people, with four of five people being unchurched. The fact that we were reaching the unchurched was awesome! However, we only retained 39% of our attendance from that first Sunday.

When we started our second and third locations, eight-years later, the result was different. The first Sunday at our South Campus was another thrilling day with the majority of the 552 people being unchurched. However, the fall after the first weekend was much less; we leveled off at 360, a 65% retention rate. This was a 26% increase in our retention rate and 70% better than our launch as a church plant. We found it wasn't a fluke when we started our West Campus. On the first weekend at our West Campus we had 606 people attend, and the average attendance leveled off at 350 for a 58% retention rate.

When we discussed our plans to go multi-site with consultant and friend Lyle Schaller, he said, "The most important thing that you offer this new work is the Community Christian Church culture." At first, I was not sure what he was talking about. In retrospect, I think Schaller was talking about two parts of our church culture—expectations and quality. In the eight years between starting a church and adding new campuses, we developed an ethos of high expectations and quality experiences. So when we started these new locations, the first-time attendee came on opening day to a place with high expectations and a church that understood how to create quality experiences. The bottom line: a new site can offer a higher level of quality than a new church, thereby retaining a much higher percentage of new attendees.

We developed an ethos of high expectations and quality experiences.

Advantage of Multi-Site Church vs. Church Growth

We are discovering that in our community the people who live more than a twenty-minute commute to a church campus will never reach their evangelistic or serving potential. Our experience has been that people who live more than twenty minutes away will continue to come on weekends to worship services and will continue to give their money, but the chances of them inviting non-Christian friends dramatically decreases. They just don't think their friends will want to be a regular part of something so far away. We have also noticed the percentage of people who serve in their area of giftedness dramatically decreases if they live more than twenty minutes away from the church campus.

The converse is also true. When we became a multi-site church, we discovered that starting new locations near the previous commuters helped dramatically increase their evangelistic effectiveness. These same people who were only attending and not serving have begun increasing their service in the church since they have a location in their neighborhood.

Willow Creek Community Church has done research showing the effects of proximity to the church facility on an attendee's level of commitment. At Willow Creek, they want people to live out the Five Gs—Grace (evangelism), Growth, Groups, Gifts (serving), and Good Stewardship. Their research revealed that people who lived more than thirty minutes from South Barrington very rarely practiced two of the Five Gs. The two missing Gs were Grace and Gifts.

As a leader, don't be content with the first option. And don't retreat to what we have done in the past, the second option. Our role as leaders is to always look for a third option. Remember, "Mediocre armies always stay within the known territory—it is the great army that will march off the map!" God is doing a "new thing," and it's the third option of multi-site churches.

---

[1] All Scripture quotations are taken from the *New International Version* unless otherwise noted.

[2] See my brother Jon's chapter on building community in this book.

[3] Leadership Network is recognized as a primary source to which 21st-century congregations and church leaders turn for information, innovation, and networking. The mission of Leadership Network is to accelerate the emergence of effective churches (**www.leadnet.org**).

Mont Mitchell is the Senior Pastor of Westbrook Christian Church in Bolingbrook, Illinois, which is a southwestern suburb of Chicago. Mont and his family moved to the Chicago area in February of 1996 and planted Westbrook in October of 1996. Westbrook is a multicultural church committed to reaching all people of all ethnicities in their region as well as planting additional church planting churches. Mont and his wife Christie have three sons. Visit Westbrook at **www.Westbrookchurch.org**.

Starting or Restarting the Church:
Call It What You Will!

I remember the day that I sat with my wife's family at the graveside of her grandfather. His passing was a bittersweet event. He was a godly man, full of energy and vision. His heart for the Lord and his love for the church was evident. He lived a full long life, selling out from underneath his business in a timely manner which allowed him to enjoy many wonderful years of retirement. As happens in the normal course of life, his time to spend eternity with his Creator came after a brief illness. His passing was marked with vivid reminders of his goodness. Hundreds of people came to his funeral and, as we laid him to rest, there was no small amount of tears. However, the most touching thing about his service came near the end. As the minister was expressing sympathy from God's word, our infant son Reid began to cry. In this moment, tears of life interrupted tears of death and sorrow.

A Premise

That's my perception on church plants that stem from the death and life of other churches: let's celebrate both! Often when a church has experienced a descent, or a trial, or even a tragedy that has brought the church nearly to nonexistence, the subject of restarting the congregation is brought up. Memories of the good old days evoke a desire to do something to bring those pleasant thoughts back. "Remember when our church had an attendance of . . . ?" "Remember when Preacher so-and-so loved us . . . ?" "Remember that meeting where we said we were going to do . . . ?"

All too often it seems that our thoughts and desires for how it used to be hinders us from even visualizing what can become.

Past memories and pleasant thoughts of days gone by are wonderful, but may they never keep us from preparing for and celebrating the new things that God can bring. Even the Scriptures that paint the glory and splendor of the heaven of our eternity tell us, "God will make all things new" (Rev 21:5).[1] All too often, however, it seems that our thoughts and desires for how it used to be hinders us from even visualizing what can become. This is, in my estimation, the reason that Jesus has John include a picturesque description of heaven:

> Then I saw a new heaven and a new earth, for the first heaven and the first earth had passed away, and there was no longer any sea. I saw the Holy City, the new Jerusalem, coming down out of heaven from God, prepared as a bride beautifully dressed for her husband. And I heard a loud voice from the throne saying, "Now the dwelling of God is with men, and he will live with them. They will be his people, and God himself will be with them and be their God. He will wipe away every tear from their eyes. There will be no more death or mourning or crying or pain, for the old order of things has passed away." He who was seated on the throne said, "I am making everything new!" Then he said, "Write this down, for these words are trustworthy and true" (Rev 21:1-5).

Yes, death is painful, but Christ can bring life and joy even from ashes.

Our Process

The above-mentioned premise was the abiding force in our locating to a fast-emerging community to plant a *new* church in a similar location where a church had recently died. Just like that day in the cemetery God would use us to bring tears of brand new life where only months before there had been tears of death and sorrow.

When employees at the Chicago District Evangelistic Association (CDEA) contacted us,[2] they had been working with a small, established church in a southwestern suburb. This congregation had been a troubled group and had endured much heartache and pain. With praise to God, several people had come to Christ through that ministry over the years, but evidently this good was overshadowed by the bad. Leadership struggles ensued, theological differences brought challenge, and overall feelings of inadequacy prevailed. God had used this church, but it seemed obvious that it was time to submit to drastic change. In short, they maturely observed that they weren't being faithful to what God called them to be. They knew their current church wasn't an effective church. They told the CDEA that they wanted to "restart" the church. They reasoned, "Let's use all of these new methods of modern-day church planting and do this over again." The problem was they really didn't mean that, nor did they know what they were requesting. The answer to us was obvious: they needed to shut down and pray that God would raise up a new church planter and a new vision. To their credit, that's what they did.

Sometime after this official funeral service for the church, my wife Christie and I arrived on the field, ready to start a new work. In the minds of the twelve people, they were starting "anew." And in our minds we too were starting "new." Either way, the old was gone and the new life was about to arrive. With a built-in core of twelve to fifteen people, we rolled up our sleeves and proceeded to plant a church. The CDEA had laid the groundwork, thankfully. The analogy of "driving the bus" is to be credited to them. For quite some time before our official call to this area, they had been telling these folks that a new work would require a new vision and new leadership. In other words, "we're driving the bus! You can't slow us down; you can't change direction. Sure, you can ride, but we're the drivers."

When we arrived, we clearly established ourselves as the new drivers, and challenged any and all who shared our vision to fasten their seat belts for the ride of their lives. And off we went. We did all the standard things to start a new multistaff, high-impact church. We prayed earnestly, developed a relationship with the school district, hired staff, raised money, developed a marketing approach, held vision-casting sessions, and designed special outreach events. We worked hard, and as we met together with our staff and launch team, always prayed to the Lord for anointing and blessing. Nine months and one practice Sunday later we held the grand opening service of Westbrook Christian Church.

In the minds of some people we *restarted* the church. For others—and frankly for us—we *planted* a new church. It was a new engine in a brand new car. But, whatever you want to call it, a new life began and for years has grown and impacted our community in ways that the "old" church did not. We are in no way overly proud of what we have done or disdainful of what they didn't do. On the contrary, we are honored that those who had forged a ministry in our community in earlier days had enough foresight to let the kingdom be expanded in a new way. From the death of an existing, feeble work came a new living organism that has greatly impacted our region.

Some Practicality

So, you're thinking of restarting a church! Are there right ways to do this? Are there wrong ways to do this? There probably are. Did we do it right in our area? Only time and eternity will tell. While we wait for time to pass and our ministries to develop, allow me to share some of the things that we learned that might help you.

1. **Make every effort to ensure that the old is gone and buried.**

In our situation, the previous congregation literally had a celebratory funeral service as they closed their doors for the last time. In this funeral service, they celebrated their past, encouraged each other in their present pain, and prayed about the future work that might be established in their community. To be honest, this was a very important step in the process of releasing the old and allowing the new to come. Had they not been willing to completely relinquish all life, there would have been no finality to the situation. In grief terminology, there needed to be closure for the reality of the death to be accepted fully.

2. **If there are people who are willing to join this new work, be certain that they know that this is a new direction and someone else is leading the way.**

We told the twelve people from the deceased church that we were going a new direction—on a new bus—and if they attempted to change directions or slow things down, we would ask them to get off the bus. For sure, that sounded quite direct and maybe even a bit obnoxious, but we felt that it was important that they understood this was a new church and that they accepted our leadership and vision.

3. Make every effort to ensure that all involved understand the mission and direction of the new thing being started.

Communicate what I call "The Big Four": who we are, why we're here, where we're going, and how we're going to get there. Explain the mission, vision, and values that will drive the ministry. People need to know where the bus is headed, and unless you are an amazingly winsome leader whom people will follow blindly, you must communicate your vision early in the process. In our church plant, we insisted that every person who expressed a desire to be a part of the church plant go through a formal "Launch Team Informational Appointment." We went out of our way to communicate our plan, especially to those who had been involved in the old church. Even now, no new person escapes the "spiel." We articulate our vision regularly, so that no one will be uninformed.

> We articulate our vision regularly,
> so that no one will be uninformed.

4. Celebrate the past efforts in ministry and evangelism and express appreciation to those with the ministry foresight to relinquish what they cared about for so many years.

For most dying or deceased churches there are a few people who have worked their fingers to the bone to keep the doors of the church open. They laid awake at night fretting over "their" church. Many of these people have contributed countless dollars to the previous place in an attempt to keep it afloat. If you are the new church planter, be certain to recognize their labors of love and the financial sacrifices made. The chances are quite high that these folks will end up being "scaffolding" people. But remember, had it not been for their passion for the church and their passion for the kingdom of God, this opportunity might never have materialized.

5. Be OK with the fact that residual people from the deceased ministry may not be with you very long.

Our experience taught us that while the excitement of the work initially drove the people to get on the bus headed in a new direction, there were elements that eventually caused them to jump off. For instance . . .

- They did not accept the new direction.
- They resented not being in immediate leadership positions.
- They were overwhelmed by the success of the new work.
- They were frustrated at their lack of involvement.
- They did not like the fact that the new place didn't look or feel like the old church they loved for many years.

These are just a few of the reasons that these people got off the bus of their own initiative. We welcomed their involvement, were grateful for their support, and knew that we needed to accept the reality that some would just never be able to completely embrace the new vision.

6. Have the fortitude to stand your ground on the new direction and new vision.

One of the greatest pieces of advice that we heard in the early days of our work was this: "Be prepared for those who will come into your infant congregation attempting to change it to the way that they want it to be." The advice continued: "When they come, stand your ground and stay focused on your God-given direction and vision."

This was great advice! Just as we were told, the change agents showed up. They were cloaked in talent, passion, desire, and experience. But they were also driven by their own agendas. Since we had been forewarned, we proceeded to interact with these people cautiously. In time, they made every effort to change our direction. With firm conviction we drew the line and stayed on track.

7. Prepare yourself for criticism.

Gird yourself for inevitable attacks. This caution is not reserved for the church planting world; it applies to all ministry in this world. Critics, some vicious, will emerge. People will criticize your vision; there will be those who criticize your technique, even your morals and integrity. Arm yourself; for criticism will come. I have heard of church planters who have received criticism from their launch team, from their supporters, and even from the community at large (who may or may not even understand what is going on). If your new church is going to meet in a school, parents will criticize the effort. If you're planning to meet in a theater, patrons will be vocal. And no matter what form of outreach and marketing you do, you'll be sure to get an earful. Without a doubt, your slick, creatively designed outreach pieces will offend someone. So get ready and just let the harsh words roll off your back.

8. Don't think, "If we do the things of a new church plant then we will be successful."

Don't get caught in the trap of thinking, if we do what that new church did in a certain area, then we will be as successful as they were. In simple terminology: The trappings of a new church plant do not make for a new church; you can't simply:

◆ Change locations to a school or a theater

◆ Change the name of your place from First Christian to something cool and trendy

◆ Unveil a new logo

◆ Change service times and service formats

◆ Have a hot worship band that plays cutting-edge music

◆ Switch from using hymn books to songs on PowerPoint

◆ Change your dress code from a suit and tie to Dockers and Hawaiian shirts

---

Making external changes won't make you a new church.

Making external changes won't make you a new church. I've seen churches that tried to do that. They did everything right. They made all the adjustments; they put on the "New Church Plant" face. They didn't miss a detail on the outside, but they weren't prepared from a vision perspective. They didn't have their people on board. They didn't have "their house in order." Unfortunately their efforts were nearly in vain. The mass changes really didn't result in church growth. Instead, they alienated good people and further damaged the body. For this type of transition to be successful, the internal change is much more important than the external. Building the structure of the house is much more important than the color of the siding and trim. You wouldn't put a new car engine in a rusty car body with dented bumpers. To take what is old and create the new requires new life, new direction, new vision, and a new passion!

I grew up around death. I know that sounds odd, so let me explain. My earthly father owns a greenhouse, floral shop, and landscaping business in east central Illinois. The business has always been a part of our family's daily life. A major component of the business is the funeral business. In fact, I'm sure there have been times when the funeral work kept things afloat. Never in my life have I observed such amazing design work and creativity as in the floral part of my dad's company. Why does a family go to the expense to memorialize a deceased person? It's not to bring the dead back to life—that's only happened a rare few times (in the Bible!). It's purely to bring honor and peace to the memory of the life of the one who has passed. For life goes on, and every family and person must have a way to memorialize the death of a loved one while coping and carrying on with life.

I, for one, am grateful that a remnant of faithful Christ-followers had enough kingdom passion to let a tired, diseased body pass from this life. The body was memorialized and from that act came new life, a new start, a new church. Life can come from death!

Life can come from death!

---

[1] All Scripture quotations are taken from the *New International Version*.

[2] The Chicago District Evangelistic Association is a church planting agency among the independent Christian Churches in the greater Chicago area.

Laura Buffington serves as the Young Adult Discipleship Leader at SouthBrook Christian Church in Centerville, Ohio. She started life out in Columbus, Ohio, and spent a good long time in East Tennessee earning a B.A. from Milligan College and a Master of Divinity from Emmanuel School of Religion in May 2003.

John Emmert serves as the Shepherding Minister at First Christian Church in Johnson City, Tennessee. John and his wife Brooke met at Carson-Newman College, where John earned, a B.A. in Religion and Psychology. John graduated from Emmanuel School of Religion in May 2003 with a Master of Divinity. John grew up in Jefferson City, Tennessee, at Jefferson City Christian Church—a church started by his family.

Erin McDade graduated from the Georgia Institute of Technology in 2000 with a B.S. in Industrial Design. After completing her degree, she served as an intern for the Georgia Tech Christian Campus Fellowship, a thriving and dynamic campus ministry. Erin earned her M.A.R. in Christian Doctrine from Emmanuel School of Religion in May 2003, and now, along with her husband Nathan, is preparing to plant a campus ministry in Puebla, Mexico, with Christian Missionary Fellowship (Globalscope).

Chris Smith serves as the Associate Minister at the Christian Church of Buckhead—a new church plant in Atlanta, Georgia. Originally from the Atlanta area, Chris completed his undergraduate work at the Georgia Institute of Technology, earning a B.S. in Management and specializing in Finance. He will graduate from Emmanuel School of Religion in May 2004 with a concentration in Church History.

Postmodern Issues in Church Planting

*I*n the morning, we sit at our laptops and catch the latest news—from Bangkok to London to L.A. In the late afternoon, we spend time at a local diner on the corner of Roan Street and Walnut, or maybe at an old bookstore full of both bestsellers and classics. We may bump into a buddy from high school, rub elbows with a Hispanic man who has come to the area to find work, meet a Muslim doctor who works at the local V.A. hospital, or chat with a math professor from an area university who grew up in Sydney, Australia. In the evening we flip on the television. Our choices include a documentary on the birth of civilization in the Far East; a televised sermon from a screaming and sweating Southern Baptist minister; or a reality show starring a forty-year-old homemaker, a twenty-two-year-old accountant, and a thirty-year-old homosexual. A typical day takes us around the world to gather information, into the company of strangers just trying to make it to the weekend, and before a smorgasbord of enlightenment and entertainment. The proximity of information, strangers, and entertainment forces us to absorb bits and pieces of the world around us. In theory, this puts us in touch and keeps us connected. But the reality is this: At the end of the day, we still go to bed alone.

When we drag ourselves out of bed on Sunday morning and darken the door of a church, we go to hear words. We're told that Jesus is God's Son and that He loves the whole world, including us. We are ever-hearing, but we're having a little trouble perceiving. Our minds are preoccupied with wars and disease, with prejudice and suffering, and with a preacher who quotes the seventh commandment while his secretary's perfume lingers upon his necktie. We admit it. When it comes down to it, we're sick of hearing words. Really, all we want to know is this: What does faith *look* like, and how do we *live* it? That is our concern. "Love thy neighbor" is poetic, but we're a bit confused about who our neighbors are. Is the Hispanic man looking for work our neighbor? What about the Muslim doctor from the V.A.? What does "love your neighbor" look like with them? We need clarity about Jesus. We are desperate to know who He was and what He wants. We know that Christian faith has something to do with "others," and that is a direction we might be willing to go. Maybe loving others can help us define who we are, and maybe when it is time to be heard, we'll have something to say. Maybe Jesus can teach us a little about life in a world full of strangeness and strangers. Perhaps, along the way we will feel a little less alone.

We are the people that you are trying to figure out. We are those you like to call "postmodern." (By the way, we hate that.) At times, we've been called "birds of a feather." But we're not "birds of a feather" at all. We may be birds, but we're all different and strange. Certainly these are changing times. For the sake of argument (and for a "modern" audience) we'll agree to be "birds." For now, that's better than "postmoderns" or "PMs."

So what do we know about birds? Did anyone else have a grandmother who told you it's easy to catch a bird by pouring salt on his tail? If you were "postmodern" at birth, you were too cynical to try it. For even the naïve among us realized it's impossible to pour salt onto a bird's tail. And if you could get salt on its tail, what good would the salt do? Perhaps, the old-wives'-tale simply provided exhausted grandmothers another way to entertain us.

As churches try new methods to capture the postmodern spirit, it is like they're trying to catch birds with salt. At times, their strategies relate more to the strategists than they do to the flocks they're trying to attract. In the end, birds are attracted by worms and birdseed, not salt. So the Church continues its search for the bait that will lure the elusive "postmodern." Allow us to offer some "bird's eye" perspective.

The Church is under tremendous pressure to change with the times and to adjust in ways that will not compromise the integrity of God's kingdom. Issues of style, strategy, and survival consume us. For the Church, change is often intimidating. All of us are concerned with the state of truth, and this change seems to be accompanied by a deterioration of morals and a growth of relativism. But let us be very clear about one thing: Postmodernism stands outside of the simple notion of "change." Contrary to popular belief, postmodernism and change are not synonymous.

In fact, where modernism has emphasized "newness" and innovation, postmodernism asks us as Christian people to reevaluate, reconsider, renew, regenerate, and rehearse what it means to be the Church. We do not think that old is necessarily bad, or that new is necessarily good. What matters to us is how old or new is lived out from day to day. Our culture presents both challenge and opportunity to the Church. It demands new paradigms consistent with eternal truths and an ancient identity.

How do we know this? What qualifies us to say what postmoderns run to or run from? We are among the fleeing birds. Our peers, our teachers, and our children are among those who are walking out of your doors. For the Church, the postmodern no longer exists "somewhere out there." We are everywhere. We write because we are in the Church. Yet, we are entrenched in educational systems and neighborhoods that have crafted us into postmodern people. We plead to the Church to respond to our deep desire for a place to roost . . . and a place to which we can invite our hurting friends to roost— hence our infatuation with church planting. Why are we excited about church planting? Because church planting is for the birds.

Church planting is for the birds.

The challenge for today's church planter is to pay attention to the shifting seasons: Where are we as birds flocking? How do we relate to one another? How do we understand the world? In a world where people are exposed to different cultures at an unprecedented level, the church plant has a chance to celebrate diversity with their building and programming. In a world where truth is difficult to pin down, the church plant offers truth a place to land—that is, in lives carefully lived. In a world where people are increasingly isolated from one another, the church plant has the opportunity to remind people of a call to live alongside one another. In a world where uncertainty seems to prevail, the church plant can provide stability and security. The call to the postmodern church plant is to redefine what it means to live an abundant life alongside others in a way that demands and directs the attention of distracted, disintegrated people towards God. The call to the postmodern church plant is to be for the birds. First, you must find them.

Bird Watching

Your eyes squint as you scan the sky for your target. You survey the ground and the treetops to look for an unaware spectacle. Where are the birds? Who are they? As a church planter, you've been taught to "know your context."

We have yet to establish our own neighborhoods. We may not have signs on our doors that label us "postmodern." In fact, we detest labels. Honestly, it is difficult to determine where exactly we live and what we look like. Because society is amidst the shift, it may be assumed that we come in any age, color, or shape. We may be rich, poor, young, old, suburban, urban, or anywhere in between. It is reasonable to say that, in time, we will grow in number and in influence. Soon, every church in every neighborhood will be forced to deal with a postmodern infusion.

As you set your sights on the postmodern target, you notice that we place a very high value on the coexistence of diverse groups of people. With this in mind, a challenge and opportunity for the church plant is to address and break down racial and economic barriers. From the onset, the church plant has the ability to establish itself as "uncommon ground," a place where anyone is welcome and all are valued. The church plant can lead the way for the church to truly be the Church through the fellowship of Jews and Gentiles, Barbarians and Scythians, maintenance workers and executives.

Choosing a target group, on the other hand, invites a nonpostmodern church, perhaps a church with an expiration date. Adding a "Postmodern Service" to your schedule is not sufficient. Your target is too narrow. New music and high tech lighting will repulse us if not accompanied by a genuine push for serious discipleship throughout the week. Relying exclusively on a new, innovative service to reach the postmodern is like using salt to catch birds.

> ## The church plant has the ability to establish itself as "uncommon ground."

It is not enough to be innovative. In fact, we are exhausted by innovation. We are skilled at discerning your motives and intentions. We will not settle for only the appearance of a transforming community. We want to be a part of something that will change us and change the world in a way that is unapologetic. We do not want to be lured in by marketing that is inconsistent with the radical call of what it means to follow Christ in this world and to be a part of the Church. The redesign of corporate logos into "Jesus" slogans are cute, but they are not postmodern. We don't buy cute. We buy rootedness and time-tested experiences. Anything less, from our perspective, is plain silly—or maybe we should say "salty."

So many new and innovative experiences are offered to us each day that we have reached a point of an identity crisis. We are pleading with the Church to tell us who we are, to tell us who we can be. When we turn off the TV, we wonder if we were not created for something more. We are poking around for something that takes us beyond ourselves, something that gives us a larger purpose, a greater hope. That something is what you, the church planter, have to offer. And with a fresh entrance into a neighborhood or into a person's life, the church plant has the opportunity to redefine the direction of life. We are looking for truth to be illustrated, rather than dictated, demonstrated rather than defended. We are asking you to shape our perspective through a new life—through living truth instead of absolute truth.

> ## We are looking for truth to be illustrated, rather than dictated, demonstrated rather than defended.

The postmodern reaction has not been against absolute truth as much as the way it has been manipulated.

And so we've struck one of the primary concerns with postmodernism. Postmodernism has become infamous for its supposed rejection of absolute truth. The postmodern reaction, however, has not been against absolute truth as much as it has been against the way it has been manipulated. The Church employed absolute truth to defend its message against modernity—against Darwin's "survival of the fittest" or Nietzsche's "God is dead," for instance. But Christians unknowingly succumbed. They allowed modernity to choose the battlefield. "If we can provide rational, scientific proof for our beliefs," Christians concluded, "we can refute the liberals and win!" To keep fighting on that field of battle is to never reach the postmodern. This battle has taken the Church nowhere. As for postmoderns, we're over it. Already we soar far above the limits of secular science. We are not bound by it. And we care far more about how to live than about how to prove.

As Christians who are postmodern, we believe that this concern for living resounds more with what Christ was preaching when He said, "I am the Way, the Truth and the Life" (John 14:6).[1] Jesus is truth, but He spent far more time teaching people how to embody truth than He did teaching people what set of propositions they needed to believe.

The church plant has the opportunity to be a living model of truth. Rather than preparing and organizing propositions, the Church must be willing to engage itself in the lives of people and to provide an example of what a God-honoring life looks like. In other words, the Church must illustrate life lived in the Spirit. The church plant must be ready to make discipleship a HUGE priority from day one. We are far more likely to accept truth when it is revealed to us in the context of relationship than when it is dictated doctrinally. Whether through small groups, life groups, coffeehouse gatherings, or sports teams, you reach us by offering what we crave—relationships. If cute T-shirts are like salt, relationships are like seed. Salt? We run from it. Seed? Mmmm.

Building the Nest

Now that it's been established that postmoderns crave authentic, no-gimmick relationships, we must now discover how to prepare a place for us to reside. For many communities, a church becomes the center of life: a place of protection and fellowship, a place where people find life partners and where education is readily available to all. Here we find the postmodern Church in waiting. In many ways, these circumstances parallel those confronted by the Church in the Middle Ages. At no time was as much attention given to setting as in this era of the architectural and symbolic advancement of the Gothic cathedral.

As we reflect upon the past, postmoderns marvel at medieval architects and their daring use of materials and mathematical proportions. They were flexible and considered outside material developments before constructing their own buildings. They had a knack for transforming traditional edifices into symbolic expressions of divine longing.

The medieval architects understood the significance of a place—particularly of a spiritual place. The Church was the most prolific builder of the Middle Ages, providing the widest scope for the development of architectural ideas. During medieval times, Gothic cathedrals were often centers for urban life. Warren Hollister and Judith Bennett note, "Cathedrals themselves were central gathering places, not only for religious services but also for civic festivals, victory celebrations, assemblies of nobles and princes, and even public meetings of town councils."[2] At any given time, cathedrals housed traveling pilgrims, local beggars, drunks, and prostitutes; they were homes to people of all social strata. Gothic cathedrals were safe havens where people retreated for both spiritual and physical support. Towering structures of stained glass and concrete communicated the power of the Church to protect and grow.

> As planters of new churches, we cannot afford to neglect the design of a building—how it will look, how it will function, and what it will communicate.

In a ministry that seeks to bring people of every social class, ethnicity, and gender into a right relationship with God and into communion with other believers, postmodern church planters should never underestimate the power setting has for community development and for inviting all people inside regardless of their present physical or spiritual state. Carefully designed, the meeting place can help lead individuals along a spiritual journey with God and others. As planters of new churches, we cannot afford to neglect the design of a building—how it will look, how it will function, and what it will communicate.

The meeting place must also reflect postmodernism's concern with authenticity and integration. It must paint a real picture of the church's personality by drawing people in. Church buildings articulate the fabric of society as well as provide meaningful settings for daily social and spiritual interactions. For people who are concerned with the restoration of beauty and creativity in everyday life, the church building ought to inspire and invite them closer to God and one another.

Never forget that postmodern culture suffers from a communal loneliness. Despite the interconnectedness of the world, each night we still go to bed alone. The new church space, therefore, ought to reflect the priority of "togetherness" in the church. The layout and aesthetics should create an atmosphere conducive to fellowship *and* intimacy. Flexibility should be built into the design plans as well (e.g., a room that can host large meetings but can also be transformed into a place for casual conversations). Why bolt down chairs or pews when we want to send the message that we serve multiple purposes and needs in people's lives? Why not reflect that worship is a way of life, rather than something that we only do in rows on Sundays?

In an urban area, for example, there is opportunity to connect people to the past by reinvigorating an old building, giving people a sense of "rootedness." To build a brand new facility in the city requires a bottomless building fund—something most new churches do not have. In addition, land in crowded cities is difficult to obtain. By working with existing abandoned buildings, the church planter's transformation of an abandoned space can also symbolize the hope for a spiritual transformation of the city and its inhabitants.

Whether renewing existing buildings or designing an entirely new church structure, all principles of religious design apply. Issues to be considered include external style and physical location, the church's ability to extend hospitality through design, and the place's suitability for focusing worship and encouraging fellowship.

Relearning to Fly

All birds must eventually venture from their nest. As postmodern birds, we must relearn how to fly. What prepares us? The fact that we yearn for something authentic, something that exposes our shortcomings but captivates our hearts, souls, and minds for a greater purpose means that, essentially, we yearn to be part of a story.

> We yearn for something authentic—
> essentially, to be part of a story.

Here, a renewed (as opposed to a new) understanding of Scripture is crucial to a church planter's attempts to reach the postmodern. Scripture is the very strand that connects people to an ancient story. Our mysterious participation in the story of Scripture inevitably transforms how we share the gospel. Instead of accepting Scripture as a system of logical proofs, we must begin to view Scripture as a *script*—one that details for us a way of life. (Again, the postmodern cares more about how to live than how to prove.) We become players—participants—in the story of Scripture; the life of the church becomes a life of rehearsal.

N.T. Wright compares our rehearsal of Scripture to the working out of a Shakespearian play "whose fifth act has been lost." In Wright's analogy, the first four acts provide "such a wealth of characterization" and "such a crescendo of excitement" that everyone knows where the final act is headed. Assign the key roles to "highly trained, sensitive, and experienced Shakespearian actors" who "immerse themselves in the first four acts and in the language and culture of Shakespeare" and the final act will be acted out with amazing consistency. Just as Shakespearean actors would be guided by a sense of the Shakespearean identity and the first four acts, believers work out "something between an improvisation and an actual performance of the final act" of the story of Scripture.[3] The image is of players trying over and over to get the performance just right—to nuance it for the purpose of reaching its audience. Players who immerse themselves in the role—who *become* the role—make the play seem real. They do not merely play the part; they *become* the part.

Scripture is dramatic in character and guides the eternal performance of the gospel. The sharing of the gospel has always taken on a dramatic form and reaches its fullest power as a story—a story of God's initiative in God's relationship with humanity. Scripture is not exclusively a body of truth. It is expressive, not only of truth, but also of the life by which men and women came to be mysteriously captivated by the gospel of Jesus Christ. Scripture is also more than a treatise. It is God's answer to the Church's felt need to rehearse its story with God in worship. Scripture is, in fact, more of a *script* than a systematic exposition of truth. If you want to reach postmoderns, show us how to participate in the story.

Overall, story is important because it captivates people universally and is an essential element of the human experience. Story breathes life into propositions and doctrine. Story uncovers the postmodern version of truth—namely, that which is authentically experienced. Story transforms text into experience. "The *good* which God does to us can only be experienced as the *truth* if we share in performing it," according to Hans Urs von Balthasar.[4] For the postmodern, it is not enough to translate the words of Scripture into propositional truths. The truth must be conveyed through performance. To win hearts, therefore, the gospel must be performed. For us to relearn how to fly, we must watch those who have flown before us.

To win hearts, the gospel
must be performed.

Conclusion

Our call to the Church and to church planters is to understand that postmodernism does not demand innovation as much as renovation. Postmodernism does not signify the end of anything but, rather, the beginning of a new cycle. This new cycle offers a way for modern and premodern to share the stage. For this performance, our prefix of choice is "re." As postmoderns, we remember. We rehash. We recite. We relive. We rehearse. What you have heard about us is true. We find meaning in experience. But hasn't God always conveyed meaning via experience? In fact, experience is the dust into which God breathes meaning. Ashes to ashes, dust to dust. As soil is recycled, made richer with each succession of life and death, so are the experiences of God's people fulfilled as they are rehearsed, retold, and replanted.

Postmodernism does not demand innovation as much as renovation.

Perhaps we are elusive birds—ones that you will not catch with salt. Above all, however, we're people. And people need to be loved. We need somewhere to belong. We need to know how much God values us, what Christ did for us, what the Spirit can recreate in us. Tell the story. Trust the Author. Show us the picture. And we will fly.

---

[1] All Scripture quotations are taken from the *New International Version.*

[2] C. Warren Hollister and Judith M. Bennett, *Medieval Europe: A Short History* (New York: McGraw Hill, 2002) 307.

[3] N.T. Wright, "How Can the Bible Be Authoritative?" *Vox Evangelica* 21 (1991) 18-19.

[4] Hans Urs von Balthasar, *Theo-Drama: Theological Dramatic Theory*, vol. 1, trans. by Graham Harrison (San Francisco: Ignatius Press, 1988) 20.

Marcus Bigelow is the president of Stadia: New Church Strategies. Prior to that, he led the Northern California Evangelistic Association and also planted and pastored a church in Northern California. Since 1996, Stadia has proudly assisted in the planting of 45 churches. The development of assessment, coaching, mentoring processes, and a business model that provides strong financial stability have all been keys in Stadia's successful church planting movement. Currently, Marcus and his coworkers at Stadia are working toward 30 new church plants in 2004. Marcus lives with his wife, Jan, in Vacaville, California. He is the father of three Christian daughters and four grandchildren.

It Takes a Movement

*T*he turn of the twenty-first century seems to be ushering in a golden age of church planting in North America. In the twentieth century, there were two successful eras of church planting in the United States. This was verified by Carl George and David Mobel who conducted a study of the Nazarene churches from 1908 to 1986. They discovered a relatively consistent, high level of church planting efforts from 1921 through 1955. From 1955 through the mid-1980s, however, there was a notable decline in church planting. Then, around 1986, a renewed interest in church planting emerged, and this movement of rapid church planting has continued into the twenty-first century.[1]

What Is a Church Multiplication Movement?

David Garrison says, "A simple, concise definition of a church planting movement (CPM) is *a rapid and multiplicative increase of indigenous churches planting churches within a given people group or population segment.*"[2] The operative words are rapid, multiplicative, and indigenous. Garrison's excellent primer entitled *Church Planting Movements* cites numerous examples of church multiplication movements around the world. These impressive statistics show that throughout the world, excluding North America and Western Europe, the church is growing faster than the population rate due to the multiplication of new churches.[3]

Garrison adds that a church planting movement occurs when the vision of churches planting churches spreads from the missionary and professional church planter into the churches themselves, so that by their very nature they are winning the lost and reproducing themselves.[4]

Neil Cole, leader of Church Multiplication Associates[5] in Long Beach, California, defines multiplication as

> church planting with multi-generational reproduction. In other words, it is where daughter churches have granddaughters who have great granddaughters who have great great granddaughters and so on. If all you do is spin off daughter churches, if those daughter churches don't have daughters, no matter how many times you do it, it's not multiplication.[6]

The ultimate key to a church multiplication movement is the momentum that builds as God brings a revival of discipleship and obedience. This momentum results in a large number of new churches and an even larger number of new believers.

Why Multiply?

Church multiplication is biblical. The biblical mandate is to be fruitful and multiply. The Great Commission in Matthew 28 says, "Make disciples of all nations" (Matt 28:19).[7]

Church multiplication is biblical.

At creation, God established the principle that every living thing should multiply after its own kind. Sheep give birth to sheep, apple trees produce apple trees (not apples, which are only a means for making sure the seeds of a new apple tree are planted), and humans reproduce humans. Spiritually, this principle means Christians multiply Christians, leaders multiply leaders, small groups result in more small groups, and churches give birth to churches. A recent study of Southern Baptist Churches reveals that only four percent (4%) of existing congregations ever give birth to a daughter church.[8]

Acts records multiplication occurring as a result of persecution (Acts 8:1), intentional church planting (Acts 13ff.), apostolic mission trips, and converts taking the gospel back to their homeland (Acts 8:26-40). These examples invite the question, "Can a church fail to reproduce and still be biblical?"

Church multiplication is healthy. After recently studying 22,000 congregations, Christian Schwarz confirmed healthy churches are multiplying churches, making more and better disciples in loving obedience to Christ. His study also showed a clear, positive correlation between the quality of a church and the number of churches it had planted within the last five years.[9] This author's experience indicates birthing a daughter church is a contributor as well as an indicator of church health. Multiplying gives fledgling or dormant leaders who are underutilized a chance to fulfill their giftedness. Healthy practices such as sacrificial giving of time, talent, and treasure are raised to new levels among a wider group of members when a daughter church is on the way.

Church multiplication is important because too many people are going to hell. Tom Clegg and Warren Bird, in their book *Lost in America*, highlight some alarming facts pertaining to church planting in North America, namely:

- We are closing more churches than we are opening by a 3:1 ratio.

- We are not keeping up with the population growth. For example, the United States' population increased 24,153,000 while the church decreased by 4,498,242 in the last decade.[10]

If, as Peter Wagner has written, church planting is "the single most effective evangelistic methodology under heaven,"[11] then rapid church planting should yield the most effective results in terms of reaching our population.

Church multiplication is also important because new churches reach more people for Christ. According to research from Will McRaney at the New Orleans Baptist Theological Seminary, "In a newly planted church there are 14.4 baptisms per year for every 100 people in regular attendance in worship. When a church has been in existence sixteen years or more, the baptism rate is half that: Only 7.3 baptisms per year for every 100 people in attendance."[12] Carl George adds that around the twenty-seventh year of existence, churches usually begin a period of lower efficiency and consequent decline. Peter Wagner remarks,

> Church planting means denominational survival. While some may not consider institutional survival a worthy motive, deep down in their hearts most church leaders do. Most of us rightly feel our denomina-

95

tional emphases contribute something important to the wholeness of the universal body of Christ. But if the present rate of decline in many of the denominations continues for another 25 or 30 years, given the steady rise in the age profile of present membership, the future is bleak to say the least. One of the essential ingredients for reversing the decline is vigorously planting new churches.[13]

William Easum adds, "The longer I consult, the more I realize the importance of starting new churches. Studies show that if a denomination wishes to reach more people, the number of new churches it begins each year must equal at least 3% of the denomination's existing churches."[14]

How Are We Doing?

Presently, there are only a few church multiplication movements in North America. Even Church Multiplication Associates, a movement dedicated to multiplying "organic" church networks, admits they are still adding rather than multiplying.[15] The rate of church planting in North America is increasing, but for the most part, we have not truly practiced multiplication. Only since the late 1990s have congregations been giving birth to daughter churches with any regularity. Until recently, church planting has been the domain of parachurch organizations, denominational task forces, or brave individuals who pioneered on their own.

> The rate of church planting is increasing, but we have not truly practiced multiplication.

One example of a North American church multiplication movement is Ralph Moore and the Hope Chapel Movement. Currently, Moore pastors Hope Chapel in Kaneohe on the north shore of Oahu. Over the past quarter century, Ralph has personally pastored two churches, one in California and one in Hawaii. Under his leadership, however, over 200 Hope Chapels have been started on six continents.

Another leader is Dr. Rob Roberts of the NorthWoods Church.[16] Since 1985, the NorthWoods' Church Starting Center has planted over seventy new churches. They gave birth to fifteen new churches in 2003 alone. Many of these are now giving birth to granddaughter churches. These churches are found in Keller, Texas (the mother church), as well as other locations across the United States, Mexico, and Vietnam.

Tim Keller, pastor of Redeemer Presbyterian Church in New York City, is another catalyst of a church multiplication movement.[17] Redeemer has partnered with Concerts of Prayer Greater New York to multiply churches in that metropolitan area. One key covenant each member agrees to is: "Every church will birth a new church in the next three years." They have also founded the Redeemer Church Planting Center to help facilitate the movement.

Dave Ferguson of Community Christian Church (CCC) in Naperville, Illinois, is approaching multiplication from another perspective. CCC is actively helping congregations across the U.S. establish multiple sites for the same church.[18] While still in the beginning stages, this strategy holds promise for many congregations. Some of these multiple-site congregations are now approaching a second generation.

East 91st Street Christian Church in Indianapolis, Indiana, began planting daughter churches almost twenty years ago. Their contribution to the church planting movement has been as a catalyst involving other existing churches in planting daughter churches. Their guiding principle is that they will not start a project without another existing church participating as an additional mother church. This technique has brought over twenty new churches into existence, and has led many new mother churches into church planting. Their goal for 2001 to 2010 is to plant 136 churches. The breakdown of how that will happen is:

- East 91st Street will plant 65 new daughter churches.
- Their daughter churches will plant 51 granddaughter churches.
- Their granddaughter churches will plant 18 great-granddaughter churches.
- Their great granddaughter churches will plant 2 great-great-granddaughter churches.
- Throughout this process, they will involve 25 other megachurches.[19]

They will not start a project without an additional mother church.

Stadia: New Church Strategies has also begun the multiplication cycle across the United States. Their key principles are: 1) Every church should give birth to a daughter congregation every three to five years; and 2) taking care of the church planting couple or team will result in better and sustained multiplication.

Dr. Bob Logan of CoachNet also teaches that healthy congregations reproduce at least every three years. He cites examples of churches as small as forty-five people who are reproducing regularly and giving birth to daughter and granddaughter churches bigger than the mother. Additionally, he mentions congregations such as Saddleback Community Church who have planted a church every year of their existence while growing in attendance to over 10,000 people. The issue is not size, but health.[20] The issue also involves an external focus on the mission field rather than an internal focus on maintenance.

What Are the Essentials of a Church Multiplication Movement?

Logan lists five essentials to a multiplication movement.

1. Passionate commitment to reach lost people—Without this commitment, there will not be the willingness to sacrifice ecclesiastical creature comforts for the good of those who have not heard. The heart of God expresses itself in a love and compassion for lost people.

2. Comprehensive prayer strategies to catalyze and empower healthy church development and multiplication movements—The North American church is just now beginning to understand the spiritual dynamic involved in multiplication. No amount of "scientific" or church growth methodology can substitute for God. Thinking we can do it ourselves is shortsighted and sinful. Unless the Lord of the harvest is leading the harvest, we will not see the fulfillment of our vision.

3. Culturally relevant methods so that more and more people are experiencing the transforming power of the gospel—As culture rapidly changes, the wineskins of yesterday become brittle and unable to hold the new wine of the gospel. We must learn to communicate the gospel in accurate and culturally relevant ways. The methods of the '50s were not sufficient for the '90s, nor are the models that communicated to modernity sufficient for a postmodern context.

4. **Leadership development systems that raise up an increasing number of leaders for cultivating and multiplying healthy churches**—Dr. Logan loves to say, "We must raise up leaders *for* the harvest *from* the harvest." Along with Neil Cole, Logan has written an excellent manual called *Raising Leaders for the Harvest.*[21] Jesus commands us to pray for harvesters in Matthew 9:37-38. This guide helps give practical steps for training and deploying leaders.

5. **Reproducible processes for cultivating and multiplying healthy, multiplying churches**[22]—Any process used for planting must be evaluated for its reproducibility. If a method or system for planting is too expensive, personality driven, or dependent upon onetime factors, it will not result in multiplication. It is tempting to use means that promise immediate results without thinking about the long-term implications. Modern missiologists have learned that what is external to the culture and nonreproducible is not good for the harvest. We need to learn this lesson as well.

Any process used for planting must be evaluated for its reproducibility.

Stadia: New Church Strategies has developed a process for church multiplication illustrated in the chart below. It incorporates a systems approach that is reproducible by churches and church planting organizations.

Stadia New Church Process:
L4: Look – Lab – Launch – Launch Again

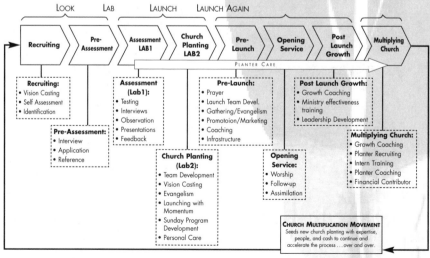

99

The key elements in the Stadia model of multiplication are:

- Careful selection of church planters through a process of interviewing and assessment
- The resourcing and training of church planters
- Incorporating planters into a community of other planters for peer support
- Providing a coach, mentor, and business advisor in a team approach to planting
- A systems approach to start-up that provides clear action steps
- The explicit commitment by the planter and the new church to not settle for anything less than planting a daughter church committed to the same process

Only when such a commitment is made and followed does a multiplication movement form. As part of that process, a planter is asked to commit to planting a new daughter church within three to five years.

What Will It Take for Church Multiplication Movements to Continue in the United States?

First, it will require a firm conviction that people separated from Jesus are going to hell. This must become more than an intellectual assent to a theological proposition. It must become a soul-gripping reality. If we truly believe this, every Christ-follower who is truly listening to the Spirit will be moved with compassion for the lost. New churches also bring hope and healing to people who formerly had none. Marriages are restored, addictions are broken, and guilt is truly relieved through the forgiveness offered by Jesus.

When this compassion for the lost is coupled with current scientific study of what it takes for the church to reach the most people, the conclusion must be to plant churches that will plant daughter churches that will give birth to granddaughter churches.

This author has two suggestions for churches and planters. First, every planter who starts a new church should include in their vision steps to starting multiple generations of new churches. Let us not be satisfied with starting a church, nor with starting a church that starts a church. Rather, let us work with all our being for multiplication. Second, every church should remember that it also has a life cycle. Therefore, every congregation should strive for continued health and purpose. Give birth to at least two daughter churches—one to replace the mother church and one for kingdom growth.

It will take a movement for the church to reach North America. It will take a movement of God to empower a revival. Before new churches can share the gospel with the unreached, our hearts must be moved to a place of concern, and action must be taken to create a multiplication movement that encourages continuous church planting. As a billboard near my house reads, "It is good to have compassion; it is better to do something about it."

---

[1] Kenneth Crow, "The Life Cycle of Nazarene Churches," published by the Association of Nazarene Sociologists and Researchers, 1998. Available from http://www.nazarene.org/ansr/articles/crow_88.html.

[2] David Garrison, *Church Planting Movements* (International Mission Board of the Southern Baptist Convention, P.O. Box 6767 • Richmond, VA 23230-0767) 7.

[3] The International Mission Board of the Southern Baptist Church maintains a web site dedicated to church planting movements. This web site can be accessed from http://www.imb.org/CPM/default.htm. Videos and presentations on this subject are available from this same source.

[4] Garrison, *Church Planting*, 9.

[5] Information concerning the operations and purpose of Church Multiplication Associates can be found on their web site, http://www.cmaresources.org.

[6] Neil Cole quote available on the Dawn Ministries' Web site at http://www.dawnministries.org/old_home/2003/index_oct08.html.

[7] All Scripture quotations are taken from the *New International Version* unless otherwise noted.

[8] North American Mission Board Webzine, *On Mission* [updated March/April 2003], available from http://www.onmission.com/webzine/mar_apr03/assisting.htm.

[9] Christian Schwarz, *Natural Church Development: A Guide to Eight Essential Qualities of Healthy Churches* (St. Charles, IL: ChurchSmart Resources, 1996) 46-48.

[10] Tom Clegg and Warren Bird, *Lost in America: How You and Your Church Can Impact the World Next Door* (Loveland, CO: Group, 2001) 30.

[11] C. Peter Wagner, *Church Planting for a Greater Harvest* (Ventura, CA: Regal Books, 1990) 11.

[12] Will McRaney, *Church Planting as an Effective Evangelistic Strategy* (Alpharetta, GA.: North American Mission Board, 2003) 23.

[13] Crow, "Life Cycle."

[14] William Easum, "Eastland Report: Church Planting" (accessed 11 December 2002) available from www.easum.com/church.htm.

[15] Neil Cole, *CMA Resources* (August 2003) available from **http://cmaresources.org/ articles/cma_movement.asp**.

[16] For detailed information on NorthWoods Church, visit their web site at **http:// www.northwoodchurch.org/**.

[17] Information on Redeemer Presbyterian Church can be found at **http://www. redeemer2.com**.

[18] You can read this expert church planter's wisdom on multi-site churches in his chapter (6) of this book.

[19] East 91st Street Church, *Church Planting Plan*, available from **http://www.east91st. org/church%20planting%20brochure%20may%202002.pdf**.

[20] Dr. Robert E. Logan, "Church Planting—The Most Successful Form of Church Growth," *Enrichment Journal*, available from **http://enrichmentjournal.ag.org/200004/ 012_most_successful.cfm**.

[21] Robert E. Logan and Neil Cole, *Raising Leaders for the Harvest* (Carol Stream, IL: ChurchSmart Resources, 1995).

[22] Dr. Bob Logan, "Cultivating Church Multiplication Movements," an article posted on the CoachNet web site at **http://www.coachnet.org/admin/files/upload/ C2M2ResourcesForSite.pdf**. CoachNet is an on-line coaching and mentoring community dedicated to church planting and church multiplication. Similar information may be found at **http://www.crmnet.org**. Dr. Logan and Dr. Steve Ogne worked on this material together for several years. Training is available in the dynamics of church multiplication movements from both of these organizations.

Greg Marksberry is the founding pastor and senior minister of the Heritage Christian Church in Peachtree City, Georgia. This dynamic congregation has grown from 77 to 800 in attendance in six years. Greg also serves as the Southeast Area Director for Stadia: New Church Strategies. He is a graduate of Cincinnati Bible College. He and his wife, Eliana, have two children.

The True Value of Partnership

*T*he Lusby brothers, Hubert and Delbert, along with their father, operated the local hardware store in our small midwestern town. It was called "Triple L True Value Hardware." You could find everything from stoves to screwdrivers at this hardware store. In fact, some of the first television sets sold in our town in the 1940s were sold by "Triple L." As kids we often stopped by the store on hot summer days for colas and candy bars. Each of the Lusbys had their specialty, from tools to appliances to plumbing. Their combined energies created a reputation of quality customer service. The true value at Triple L was not in the "True Value" brand name, but in the partnership that existed between these men. Together they were able to offer a wide range of merchandise, without compromising their product knowledge or customer care.

Partnership is a joining of individuals or organizations in a shared activity with joint benefit.

Partnership is defined as a joining of individuals or organizations in a shared activity, resulting in all partners benefiting from the union. The concept of partnership was initiated at creation with Adam and Eve. God demonstrates an ongoing commitment to partnership by joining with every believer to accomplish His work in the world. Ephesians 3:20 describes how God partners with His people,

"Now unto him who is able to accomplish more than all we can ask or imagine according to his power at work within us."[1] God chooses to partner with us in order to accomplish what we could never imagine doing on our own. What an incredible partnership—God and you! The ancient wisdom of Solomon echoes this biblical principle as he writes, "Two are better than one, because they have a good return for their work" (Eccl 4:9).

The idea of individuals, churches, and organizations joining together to accomplish a common goal is well documented in Scripture. Even in nature we find that every higher species propagates itself through reproduction, which requires a partnership of two in doing so. Should anything less be expected in the reproduction of Christ's church? The church multiplies itself by birthing new congregations. Partnering together to accomplish this end is a fundamental principle that gets God's work done. There are three basic reasons why forging strategic partnerships to accomplish God's will on earth, specifically in the work of church planting, is not only wise, but also vital.

Grander Vision

One reason partnerships are vital is because they produce a grander vision. God's partnership with His people, as Paul points out in Ephesians, raises the vision level to "more than we can ask or imagine." When working alone, the vision for what can be accomplished is limited, but joining forces with others enlarges the possibilities. A.W. Tozer highlights this reality by writing, "God is looking for [people] through whom He can do the impossible—what a pity that we plan only the things we can do by ourselves."[2] Working together gives us a new perspective on how much can be accomplished. Partnership inevitably grows a grander vision.

A large church in Indianapolis envisioned planting twenty churches in twenty years. Their tremendous goal was actually accomplished in seventeen years. Having watched their vision become reality, this church began imagining how many more churches could be planted if they strategically partnered with others. Their decision to bring associates together to invest in this work with them lifted the vision from planting twenty churches over two decades to sixty-five churches in the next ten years.

As this church pioneered new ways of partnering with other churches and organizations in church planting, other benefits of their partnerships began to emerge. Several other large churches in their fellowship caught the church planting vision. These congregations continue to contribute significant spiritual, financial, and human resources to new church projects across the country. The vision grew grander as these partners considered how much could be done if each new church they launched committed to planting a daughter church within three years. This commitment effectively built church planting into the core value system of each new church, therefore producing even more church planting partners for future years. One church's philosophical shift to forging strategic partnerships fueled a vision that would become the genesis of a church planting movement.

Greater Volume

The true value of partnership is seen not only in the grander vision it produces, but also in the greater volume that results. Solomon wrote, "Two are better than one, for they have a better return for their labor" (Eccl 4:9). When people work in partnership, the sum total of what they accomplish together is always greater than the sum of their individual efforts. The old story of a horse-pull at a county fair demonstrates this point. The winning horse pulled 8,000 pounds to the finish line while the runner-up managed to tow 7,000 pounds. When the officials hitched these two horses together they were expected to haul some 15,000 pounds. But because "two are better than one" these horses amazed onlookers by pulling over 22,000 pounds. This was the effect of a phenomenon known as "synergy."

The synergy of partnership creates "partnership math."

The synergy produced by partnership creates what I like to think of as "partnership math." This system is not based upon addition but multiplication, and ultimately becomes exponential in its results. The rate of production always increases when we harness the power of synergy through strategic partnerships. John Maxwell captures the powerful dynamics of synergistic relationships with this simple formula: 1 beside 1 = 11.

A church planting organization based in northern California experienced the tremendous growth that results from partnership. This organization decided to involve each of its new churches in church planting by asking each church to give back an average of 7.5% of offerings received over a twelve-year period. The exponential results of harnessing these new churches together in the "yoke" of church planting soon silenced the skeptics. The organization went from planting one church every two years to planting eleven churches annually. The charts below demonstrate how these partnerships produced a greater volume in both the number of churches planted, and in the donations given to that end.

Northern California Evangelistic Association (NCEA) Churches Planted

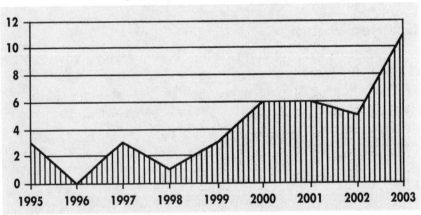

NCEA New Giving to Church Planting

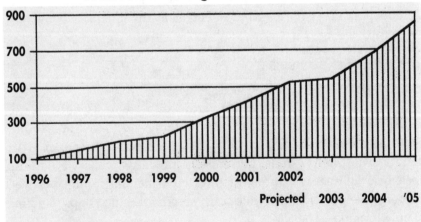

Greater production in the planting of new churches is inevitable as more partnerships like these are developed. This is true because it represents the genius of the "and" at work—you *and* me working together—as opposed to either/or. Mother Theresa brilliantly summed up the potential for greater volume through partnerships with her words, "You can do what I cannot do. I can do what you cannot do. Together, we can do great things."

God-Glorifying Victories

Partnering increases the opportunity to experience shared wins.

Ultimately, the true value of partnership is seen in the God-glorifying victories that it produces. Partnering increases the opportunity to experience shared wins. The very nature of a partnership ensures that no single individual takes all the glory for its victories. Rather than clamoring for the credit, partners are better able to focus on the ultimate power source for their successes. As Paul points out in Ephesians, it is God's power at work within us that produces our victories. That perspective keeps us humble. The fact is that anything Christians accomplish individually is actually the result of God's decision to partner with them by allowing His power to work through them. It is a sign of emotional and spiritual health when we give God the glory for the victories we enjoy.

An important manifestation of the humility created by partnership is openness to confronting outdated or ineffective paradigms and methods. According to the Glenmary Research Center, one of the fastest growing religious organizations in the United States over the past decade has been the Christian Churches/Churches of Christ.[1] This growth has been partly due to the spirit of humility that was cultivated through strategic partnerships in church planting. Involving more people in the birthing of new churches naturally generates more questions and input. Positively receiving tough questions like, "Are we being as effective as possible?" and "How can we do it better?" requires a certain degree of humility. The outcome of such sincere evaluations, however, is greater effectiveness and bigger victories.

Partnerships, by their very nature, facilitate better-laid plans. By involving a broader representation of minds and perspectives in our endeavors, we multiply our creative energies. The humility stimulated by partnerships has benefited the church planting movement with results ranging from better cost effectiveness to more accurate assessments of church planters. More churches are planted more successfully through partnerships because the nature of a joint venture keeps us humble and focused on God's glory, not our own. And when God receives glory for the victories we experience, His power flows more freely through our efforts.

> When God receives glory for the victories we experience, His power flows more freely through our efforts.

Overall, the true value of partnership is revealed through the grander vision, the greater volume, and the God-glorifying victories that it produces. But there remain significant obstacles to forging these strategic relationships in the work of church planting. Overcoming the enemies of partnership requires an awareness of what they are, as well as an ongoing commitment to defeating them.

Enemies to Successful Partnering

Making a Name for Ourselves

One enemy of strategic partnerships is the human aspiration to make a name for ourselves. This was the downfall of the leaders who rallied people together to build the Tower of Babel. Genesis 11:4 reveals their motive, "Then they said, 'Come, let us build ourselves a tower that reaches to the heavens, so that we may make a name for ourselves.'" This passage depicts the prideful pursuit of reputation that has rendered countless leaders ineffective. God put an abrupt stop to the Tower of Babel project. In doing so, He demonstrates His disdain for people primarily motivated by the desire to further their own name. The Bible consistently teaches that God opposes the proud. He frustrates the plans of those who seek to build their own "little kingdoms" on earth, as opposed to building up His eternal kingdom. Seeking to make a name for ourselves has often prohibited the kind of strategic partnerships that would greatly benefit church planting. Squarely admitting this reality and accepting responsibility when we have pursued reputation and recognition, therefore, are critical in defeating this enemy of partnership.

Keeping to Ourselves

Another enemy of strategic partnerships in church planting is the "Lone Ranger" mentality that pervaded new church work through the mid-twentieth century. While most people respect the individual strength represented by the Lone Ranger, the tendency for this mentality to develop into a spirit of isolationism must be avoided at all costs. Keeping the goal of church planting confined to our own associations can produce an undue sense of significance at least, and tragic consequences at worst.

During the 1920s and 1930s America was in isolation. She kept to herself and took little part in international relations. To protect American industry, stiff tariffs were put on foreign goods. Because European countries could no longer profitably sell their goods to America, they could not afford to buy agricultural goods from the United States. This turned out to be one of several unexpected causes of the Great Depression. This period of history also records America's rejection of the opportunity to influence world affairs by participating in the League of Nations, formed after World War I. This spirit of isolationism certainly contributed to the conditions that allowed the Third Reich to rise and thrive in Germany.

When we avoid strategic partnerships, the attitude of isolation that develops can have devastating effects. In keeping to ourselves the vision for what could be is stunted. By assuming that we can accomplish our goals and prosper without the help of others, we lose touch with the very culture we are trying to reach. Working in partnership, on the other hand, promotes the cooperative spirit that produces better solutions to the problems we encounter in church planting.

Working in partnership promotes the cooperative spirit that produces better solutions.

In 1997 a new church was formed in the Atlanta area and has grown steadily to over eight hundred in attendance. This congregation quickly developed a vision for planting what they called "Continental Impact Churches" on every inhabited continent. They envisioned establishing churches in the most influential cities in the most strategic countries on each continent. Each church would be resourced and equipped to function as an "epicenter" for a church planting movement that would sweep their respective continents. After three years of failing to mobilize toward this goal, key leaders began to realize that their vision was simply too large to accomplish on their own. They admitted their need for greater expertise, additional resources, and a broader perspective. The result was a concerted effort to build strategic partnerships to see their vision fulfilled. Within two years of diagnosing the problem as "keeping their vision to themselves," this congregation helped start two high impact churches through strategic partnerships and committed to its first Continental Impact Church.

Jesus never encouraged his followers to keep their work in the kingdom of God to themselves. Rather than isolate His followers as "Lone Rangers" in the task of sharing the good news, Jesus sent them out two-by-two. Christ even invited His disciples to partner together in prayer. Matthew 18:19-20 records this powerful affirmation of sharing the work of ministry, "When two of you agree together on anything at all on earth and make a prayer of it, my Father in heaven goes into action. And when two or three of you are together because of me, you can be sure that I'll be there" (*The Message*). Intentionally and consistently stretching our comfort zones to include working with partners will keep the enemy of isolationism at bay.

Doing It by Ourselves

How often have you caught yourself thinking, "I could get this task done much better if I just did it myself"? Doing it ourselves is sometimes easier, but "easier" does not always equal "more effective." Partnering with others to accomplish a goal takes real effort. Like most investments, partnership requires short-term pain to achieve long-term gain. And there is also a degree of risk involved. Those with whom we partner must prove trustworthy in doing their part or the entire partnership suffers. Effective partnerships presume that each partner joins the endeavor with full commitment to seeing it through. When commitment to the ultimate goal prevails, then partnerships will always prove better in their results compared to what can be accomplished without cooperation.

"Easier" does not always
equal "more effective."

Competition is a common adversary of strategic partnerships. The goal of competition in every sport is for one team to win and the other to lose. For every win there is a corresponding loss. When the competitive attitude of doing it on our own creeps into the work of church planting, logic tells us that someone wins and someone loses. Partnership, however, is about all the partners winning. It's always a win-win scenario. All the partners must benefit from their union or, by definition, it's not a partnership.

At a small resort nestled in the Rocky Mountains a number of church planting leaders gather each year for a working retreat. There executive directors representing church planting associations from across the country discuss innovative ways of working together to plant churches. It has not always been this way. Organizations often find themselves competing for the same limited supply of funds and church planting prospects. Such competition has hindered church planting efforts in the past, but gatherings like this retreat in the Rockies demonstrate how everyone can mutually benefit through greater cooperation.

Story after story from these leaders affirm how the power in "doing it together" trumps the advantages of "doing it by ourselves." One such story reflected the cooperation of three different church planting organizations joining forces to start a new church and church planting beachhead in Toronto, Canada. After two years this church averaged over 400 in attendance, was reaching people from 40 different nations, and registered among the largest and most effective churches in Canada. The vision for planting more churches in Toronto has been fully embraced by this new church and her leaders. All three organizations have benefited from their partnership in this venture. More significantly, so have hundreds of people in Toronto.

The key to more cooperation in church planting is keeping a clear focus on the true enemy. Our competition is not with those who are planting more churches, but with the myriad of distractions that cause people to look elsewhere for hope.

Robert Lewis points out how the enemies of partnership contributed to the tragic bridge collapses of the nineteenth and early twentieth centuries. He records,

> In 1845, Robert Stephenson's Dee Bridge, the longest metal truss built to date, buckled, claiming five lives. In 1879, Thomas Bouch's Tay

Bridge over Scotland's Firth of Tay went down in a gale killing seventy-five people. In 1907, the collapse of Quebec Bridge over the St. Lawrence in Canada caused the death of another seventy-five.[4]

Lewis notes that experts now believe these disasters would have been averted if bridge companies and their engineers had worked more closely together. He concludes, "Their failure to cooperate with others, to seek help and assistance, and, where appropriate, to work together became the tragic downfall of their bridge-building efforts."[5]

Triple L True Value Hardware closed its doors in the early 1990s. Though the partnership had sustained its strength through two generations, it failed to build a bridge that would reach the next. Our challenge is to build bridges through strategic church planting partnerships that will not only reach the next generation, but also every generation to come.

The apostle Paul expresses the true value of partnership through his words to the church in Philippi, "In all my prayers for all of you I always pray with joy because of your partnership in the gospel from the first day until now" (Phil 1:3-5). The Lusby family found their store's true value in its "Triple L"—Hubert, Delbert, and their dad. The Bible underscores the true value of partnership in Ecclesiastes 4:12, "Though one may be overpowered, two can defend themselves. A cord of three strands is not quickly broken."

There is incredible power in partnership. Because of their true value, we must purposefully forge strategic partnerships in church planting. Partnership is an endeavor worthy of our most dedicated efforts because it has consistently proven its true value, even from the very beginning of time.

For access to the downloadable Partnership Worksheet visit **www.collegepress.com/churchplanting**.

---

[1] All Scripture quotations are taken from the *New International Version*.

[2] John Maxwell. *The Power of Partnership*, Vol. 14, No. 7 (Atlanta, GA: Injoy Life Club, 1999).

[3] Laurie Goodstein, "Conservative Churches Grow Fastest in 1990's Report Says," *New York Times* (Sept. 18, 2002) final edition, A22.

[4] Robert Lewis, *The Church of Irresistible Influence* (Grand Rapids: Zondervan, 2001) 155-156.

[5] Ibid.

Paul Williams is the longtime President of the Orchard Group, a church planting non-profit organization in the Greater New York City area. The Orchard Group has been a pioneer in creating partnerships for church planting in the Northeastern United States. Paul is also Editor at Large for *The Standard*, a Christian periodical, and can be seen as a regular host of the Worship Network. Paul and his wife Kathy are the parents of three grown children.

The New Church Management Team

I'm really hurt you weren't at the meeting." Not the words you want to hear when you've missed a Management Team meeting at a new church. I feebly protested: "Well, I had two scheduled on the same evening, and a crisis came up in the other situation." It didn't change the young church planter's opinion. "I need you at the meetings," he said. "You bring the most experience and, frankly, some of the only encouragement I get." Those words stuck with me—"Some of the only encouragement I get."

The Management Team of a new church rarely gets any credit for getting the new church underway, even when it does its job extremely well. But poorly functioning Management Teams can hurt a new congregation.

Fifteen years ago there were no new church Management Teams. New churches were planted by a single entrepreneurial church planter who often was planting a church because he or she did not, in fact, want input from anyone besides God. And God would only be heard from when the church planter felt like it! But church planting has changed over the past twenty years as it hadn't changed in the previous eighty. And most of the changes have been for the better. One of those was the creation of new church Management Teams.

Church planting has changed over the past twenty years as it hadn't in the previous eighty.

First of all, the term "Management Team" is actually a misnomer. Most new multiple-staff congregations are managed by staff. "Oversight Team" would be a better term. Unfortunately, the "Management Team" term has stuck, and doesn't appear to be going out of use anytime soon. A well-functioning Management Team can create a healthy foundation for a vibrant new church.

Getting the Management Team Underway

The responsibilities of a Management Team begin almost immediately after a new church is envisioned. In the current environment most new churches are not started by a single congregation or church planting agency; they are planted by a team of supporters. To create a Management Team from those supporters is the first task of the new church project.

The Management Team will usually consist of at least one representative from each of the sponsoring churches or organizations, plus the senior minister, once this individual has been selected. Management Teams seem to work best with seven to eleven members. Fewer than seven fails to provide critical mass throughout the oversight period, while more than eleven dilutes the team to the point where creating a strong synergy is difficult.

Management Teams function best when there is a single church or church planting agency that serves as the final "organization of record" for the new church. At Orchard Group Church Planting (OG),[1] it has been our experience that the Management Team functions more smoothly if the Chairperson of the Team comes from the "organization of record." After the senior minister of the new church, the Chairperson of the Management Team may be the most important individual in the early life of the new church. He or she assures meetings are held in a timely fashion, financial reports are timely and accurate, and the senior minister is adequately communicating with his supporters.

From the time of project inception, the Chairperson of the Management Team will carry the "ownership" for the new project. While that responsibility transfers to the senior minister after the church gets underway, the Chairperson will still carry the major ownership for the functioning of the Management Team. The individual chairing a Management Team should have previous experience serving on one or more teams.

The first task of the Management Team is to determine its own responsibilities. Many teams now utilize variations of "The Basic Principles of Policy Governance" by John Carver and Miriam Mayhew Carver (Jossey-Bass Publishers). Under Policy Governance, the Management Team accepts four major responsibilities:

1. Determining the Ends of the New Church Project

The Management Team will determine the "ends" of the new church. What good will be accomplished for whom? Will it be a church that is expected to grow large, or will it be a neighborhood church? Will the church be urban or suburban? Will it be affiliated with a specific religious fellowship, or an independent congregation? Will the church have a multiple staff or a single church planter? All of these are "ends" issues to be discussed in the early life of the Management Team.

2. Executive Limitations

The Management Team determines the "ends" of the new church project, but the staff determines the "means" of the project, how the new church is to be planted. Through Executive Limitations, the Management Team sets the boundaries within which the senior minister and the church planting team must operate. For instance, the Management Team may determine that the senior minister can set the amount of funds that ultimately need to be raised for the project, but that outside funding must be completed within five years. The five-year limit would be an Executive Limitation.

3. Management Team-Staff Linkage

The Management Team determines how they will communicate with the new church staff. The normal channel is that communication with the staff will only occur through the senior minister of the new church. No "back channels" from staff to Management Team members should be tolerated.

4. Management Team Process

The Management Team will determine its own structure, including who will participate, how long the Team will operate, and when they will disengage from the project. Management Teams usually disengage when the project has received its last outside support, and an Internal Management Team has been chosen by the senior minister and approved by the Management Team.

Determining the Overall Budget

After setting up its basic governance model, the Management Team will proceed to the next important step. How much funding will be brought to the project? Who will provide it? And in what time frame?

Many Management Teams bring great grief to the church planting staff by not answering these questions before the senior minister is hired. Various funding methods and time lines are acceptable for a new church, from one month's salary for a single staff member, to hundreds of thousands of dollars over five years, including salaries, start-up costs, and state-of-the-art equipment. The issue is not how much is being spent, but is agreeing to the amount to spend, and then providing the funds in a timely manner. Many a senior minister has had to take valuable time from the ministry of the brand new church to travel the circuit in search of funds promised, but not delivered, by the supporting entities.

In most joint-venture church plants we have attempted to date, Orchard Group Church Planting has had to loan funds, interest free, because other partners in the project did not follow through with their commitments. In every joint venture but our first, it has not been a major problem, since we built that possibility into our operating plan. We want to encourage new entrants into the church planting field, and we don't want them to become discouraged if they bite off more than they can chew in their first venture. By anticipating problems and planning cash flow carefully, the Management Team can avoid an embarrassing meltdown early in the life of the new congregation.

By anticipating problems the Management Team can avoid an embarrassing meltdown.

Start-Up Costs and Salaries

After determining the overall budget and timelines, specific financial questions need to be answered before the senior minister is hired. How many staff will be allowed? Many new churches start with a Senior Minister, Worship Minister, Children's Minister, and one other professional staff position. Will additional staff be allowed? What is the ceiling for staff salaries? Will raises be offered in the years the church is on outside support? If so, will they be covered by the supporting entities or through funds raised by the staff members themselves?

What will be the time frame in which funds are to be received and forwarded to the new church? Will start-up costs, including equipment and advertising, be covered by the project? If so, how much? Will staff be expected to raise any portion of their financial support? Many think that some level of self-developed support is a critical indicator whether or not a potential staff member is qualified for the church planting task. If no one wants to support you, will new church members be likely to follow you?

Another question concerns "grace periods." After a team member is at a new church, how far behind will the Management Team allow them to fall in their support account before salaries are cut? If funds are left at the end of the project, who will determine the use of those funds?

Also, how long will outside support continue? Over the past ten years, new churches have often received 100% of outside support for six months before the new church starts, and for the twelve months immediately after it gets underway. Year two brings outside support down to 75% or 66⅔%. Year three drops to 50% or 33⅓%. Year four drops again to 25% outside support for some churches, complete self-support for others. Again, the question is not whether six months of outside support or five years of outside support is best. The question is whether all members of the Management Team have agreed on the length of outside support before the senior minister is brought on board.

Yet another important financial issue is whether or not the new church must tithe back to church planting. Which sponsoring partner will be the recipient of the ongoing church planting funds? Will they be divided between supporters and projects, or focused in a single direction? Will they give 10% of their offerings, or 5%? Again, there are no right answers. It is just as important for the Management Team to have an answer to each of these vital questions. It is equally essential that the Management Team instill the multiplication principle in the new church's DNA by giving a percentage of its income from day one.

Financial Reporting and Board Oversight

The reason an "organization of record" is critical for the new church is to be sure all legal regulations are followed and project reports can be expected monthly from one single location. In most church planting projects, the supporting entity opens an exclusive account for the salaries and start-up costs of the new church. Once staff members are hired and small groups begun, the church opens its own account from which it draws funds for its own internal operation. Both accounts should be open to the Management Team, with monthly reports from both to all Management Team members.

It is also important for the Board of Directors of the supporting entity to transfer all management issues related to the new project to the designated Management Team. At Orchard Group Church Planting, the only time the OG Board of Directors will intervene in a new church is when the Management Team has allowed the church to stray in the area of core essentials. Otherwise, oversight of that new church is fully vested in the hands of the Management Team.

Securing Staff

The single most important task of the Management Team, after deciding to start the new church, is selecting the senior minister. This process should be covered by prayer at every step along the way.

It is always best to begin with multiple candidates, hopefully individuals with church planting or senior ministry experience. The first step is to receive resumes and statements of faith. A good statement of faith gives a written record of where the candidate stands on all core issues. The second step is a good church planting questionnaire.[2]

At Orchard Group Church Planting, we follow the questionnaire with the Personal Profile System DISC test. We have used it on hundreds of church planters, and have found it to be a good tool in helping candidates know how best to utilize their strengths in the church planting environment.

After the DISC test, we check references and former employers. Assuming those conversations go well, it's off to an assessment center. We use the Church Planting Assessment Center (CPAC)[3] affiliated with Stadia Southeast and Orchard Group Church Planting that is held on a regular basis at Emmanuel School of Religion in Johnson City, Tennessee. The Center is a three-day evaluative and educational process that has proven to be quite helpful in focusing on the best candidates for church planting.

Though all of the above prove to be quite helpful, nothing beats a behaviorally based interview in selecting a final candidate. Questions should always be along the lines of "Tell me what you did when?" Those questions are always preferable to those that begin, "Tell me what you would do if?" Remember, the best indication of future behavior is past behavior. It is important to ask behaviorally based questions in each of the five "knockout" areas:

1. **Visionary:** Tell me about a time you had a crazy idea that you actually pulled off in a successful way.

2. **Intrinsically Motivated:** In your last job, what time did you get to work in the morning, and how many hours did you work each week?

3. **Relates Well to the Unchurched:** Tell us about a good friend of yours who is not a Christian. How did you meet the individual? What is the level of your friendship?

4. **A Leader People Will Follow:** Talk about one time you turned an obstacle into an opportunity? How long did it take before people started to believe in your solution?

5. **Cooperative Spouse:** How does your spouse feel about the church? Does your spouse enjoy doing new things?

After the interview has been completed, the Management Team should not shortcut the discussion process. Remember, after deciding to start the new church, selecting the senior minister is the single most important job you have. It is more important than funding. It is more important than specific church location. It is more important than any other single factor. Also, like the senior minister, other potential team members should undergo a quality assessment process.

Additional Staff and Church Location

Once hired, the senior minister chooses additional staff, with the approval of the Management Team. Staff should understand they work for the senior minister and the church. Only the senior minister reports to the Management Team.

The other major area the senior minister owns in the start-up phase is final church location. While it is fine for the Management Team to set broad geographical boundaries, the senior minister should be allowed to choose the specific community that best fits that individual's personality and style.

After the Start-Up

Management Teams will generally meet no less than quarterly in the months before a senior minister is hired and a new church gets underway. After the church starts, quarterly meetings are still the norm in the first year. After the first year, the Management Team may drop to three meetings in the second and third years, and two meetings in the fourth.

The Chairperson of the Management Team is critically important in making sure the team meets on a regular basis. It is best to choose a Chairperson who has the time and inclination to devote himself/herself to the specific project that is being overseen. Even a good Chairperson, stretched too thin, can hinder a Management Team's effectiveness.

After the church has started, the Management Team only has four basic jobs.

1. The Management Team monitors its own funding for the project.

Watching cash flow, raising adequate funds, and monitoring the expenditure of those funds is the responsibility of the Management Team until the church is self-supporting.

2. The Management Team evaluates the senior minister each year.

The Management Team should do an annual evaluation of the senior minister. They should be sure the senior minister is evaluating the church planting staff, and receiving 360-degree feedback from the staff. The Management Team should ask to receive written reports of those 360-degree evaluations, so they can see how staff members are performing, and how the staff report on their relationship with the senior minister.

3. The Management Team approves new members to the Internal Management Team.

By the end of the second year of the new church, the senior minister and the church planting team should choose church members for an Internal Management Team that will oversee the church after the external Management Team disengages, until elders can be chosen. The Management Team will approve the members chosen by the senior minister and staff, and will serve alongside those new members until the church becomes self-supporting.

4. Crisis Intervention.

The Management Team should always be available for crisis intervention. The most common area where the Team's intervention will be needed is in staff conflict situations. Even in those situations, however, the Management Team needs to work closely with the senior minister in resolving all conflicts.

Finishing Well

The final act of a Management Team is to pass the baton of leadership to the Internal Management Team of the church. Often this is done in an official "self-support" service. As a part of the close-out process, the Management Team should also assure that the senior minister and team members are preparing for the first daughter church, and for a strong focus on church planting to be an integral part of the culture of their congregation for a long time to come.

There is no more effective way to expand the Kingdom of God than by planting new churches. And while church planting Management Teams will never be recognized as the "founders" of a new church, if they do their job well, they can know they will be smiling well into eternity because of the great things done in the name of Christ through the new church they helped to start.

There is no more effective way to expand the Kingdom of God than by planting new churches.

---

[1] Orchard Group Church Planting is a nonprofit organization that starts churches in the Northeastern United States (www.orchardgroup.org).

[2] For the reader's convenience, a downloadable church planting questionnaire is available at www.collegepress.com/churchplanting.

[3] For more information about CPAC, see www.churchplanting4me.org.

A veteran church planter and pastor for over twenty years, **Dr. Tom Jones** is a widely sought after new church development coach, consultant, assessor, seminar leader and teacher, and mentor. He has a Doctor of Ministry Degree from United Theological Seminary in Dayton, Ohio, with an emphasis in church planting. Tom received his Master of Divinity Degree from Emmanuel School of Religion and his Bachelor of Arts Degree from Milligan College. Among other things, he now directs the Supervised Ministerial Experience (SME) Program, teaches in the Christian Ministries area at Emmanuel School of Religion in Johnson City, Tennessee, and is Director of Recruitment and Assessment for Southeast Stadia, a national church planting movement. Tom and his wife Debbie led the church planting teams at SouthBrook Christian Church in Dayton, Ohio, and Princeton Community Church in Princeton, New Jersey. They have two children, Melanie and Tom. Tom can be reached at **jonest@esr.edu**.

Creating a Church Planting Team

One of the most remarkable sports teams in the history of America came on the scene in the 1930s.

In 1938, near the end of a decade of monumental turmoil, the year's number-one newsmaker was not Franklin Delano Roosevelt, Hitler, or Mussolini. It wasn't Pope Pius XI, nor was it Lou Gehrig, Howard Hughes, or Clark Gable. The subject of the most newspaper column inches in 1938 wasn't even a person. It was an undersized, crooked-legged racehorse named Seabiscuit.[1]

The "Biscuit" mesmerized America. He broke track records, attendance records, and gave hope to a nation that was in need of a hero. How did this happen?

In 1936, on a sultry August Saturday in Detroit, Pollard, Smith, and Howard formed an unlikely alliance. Recognizing the "talent" dormant in the horse and in one another, they began a rehabilitation of Seabiscuit that would lift him, and them, from obscurity.[2]

Team Seabiscuit consisted of rather ordinary members. Seabiscuit, the horse, was tired and rundown. He was small with crooked legs. Tom Smith, the trainer, was an old eccentric loner who had a way with horses but not much horse racing reputation to speak about. Red Pollard, the jockey, was a tragic personality. Abandoned as a boy, he took to jockeying, but initially made his way through back-town prize fighting. He had little success as a jockey before his tenure with Seabiscuit. Charles Howard, the owner, became wealthy in the automotive business, but had rather a heart-breaking early family life that led to a divorce and the death of a beloved son.

Individually, each of these characters was worn out and broken. Together, however, they formed a team that stormed America. In the 2003 motion picture, *Seabiscuit*, Charles Howard said, "The horse is too small; the jockey is too big; the trainer is too old, and I'm too dumb to know the difference."[3] At the end of the movie, Red Pollard said, "Everybody thinks we found this broken down horse and fixed him. But we didn't. He fixed us, everyone of us; and I guess in a way, we kind of fixed each other, too."[4]

Teams have a way of doing that kind of thing. Whether it's horse racing teams, baseball teams, business teams, or church planting teams, we are far better together than we are apart.

Reasons for the Team Approach for Church Planting

The Team Approach Is Biblical.

Obviously, the greatest model of team ministry for kingdom expansion was our Lord Himself.[5] Jesus understood that the best way for His mission to be fulfilled and to have an eternal impact was to gather and send out a team.

The greatest model of team ministry for kingdom expansion was our Lord Himself.

"He called his twelve disciples to him . . ." (Matthew 10:1).

"Calling the twelve to him, he sent them out two by two . . ." (Mark 6:7).

"After this the Lord appointed seventy-two others and sent them two by two . . ." (Luke 10:1).[6]

In Acts, the early church follows the example of Jesus. On the day of Pentecost, when the church was born, Peter preached, but he was not alone. Acts 2:14 states, "Then Peter stood up with the Eleven. . . ." Later, in Acts 13, Barnabas and Paul were sent out as a team by the church in Antioch. From that point on, a team always surrounded Paul. Barnabas, John Mark, Timothy, Silas, Luke, Lydia, Priscilla, Aquila, and others were all a part of Paul's team at one time or another. Paul was the most successful church planter that the church has known. He understood well the importance of team church planting.

The Team Approach in Church Planting Encourages the Ministry of All Believers and the Use of Spiritual Gifts.

When used in church planting, the team principle allows the ministry of all believers to be experienced and modeled.

> It was he who gave some to be apostles, some to be prophets, some to be evangelists, and some to be pastors and teachers, to prepare God's people for works of service, so that the body of Christ may be built up (Eph 4:11-12).

Taken seriously, the team concept taught by Paul provides a way for many people to use their spiritual gifts in church planting. On the other hand, if a lone church planter directs a church, then usually that person tries to do everything. As a result, often ministry is ineffective because no one person has all the spiritual gifts necessary to lead a successful church plant. That person becomes frustrated because he or she is forced to do nongifted tasks, while others are stifled because they are not given an opportunity to use their gifts. Together, the misappropriation of spiritual gifts drastically affects both the spiritual and numerical growth of the church.

If a new church sees a *team* leading, however, then from the beginning the ministry of believers is modeled to the whole congregation. People are empowered and affirmed to use their gifts immediately. Within little time, the whole church can function as a team, each person being encouraged to fulfill his or her particular God-given ministry.

The Team Approach Models the Church.

The team, in a very real sense, serves as the church in the beginning. This being the case, the relationships formed between team members, their families, and others should illustrate how God has called His Body to relate to one another and to the unchurched. Shenk and Stutzman write:

. . . in the New Testament the missionary enterprise was almost always carried forward by teams. The missionary teams working together in love and harmony were a sign revealing what the nature of the gospel is, the story of reconciling love.[7]

If new Christians witness healthy, mature relationships between their leaders, then they are bound to follow with similar ones.

More People Can Be Recruited in the Team Approach for Team Church Planting.

Team church planting allows people to be involved who otherwise would not venture into new church work. There are only a limited number of people who have the giftedness, personality, commitment, and leadership abilities to succeed in church planting by themselves. These people do exist. However, the team concept encourages all kinds of people to get involved with new church starts, people who would not and could not do it by themselves. These people have a particular function on the team, and they do well as long as they serve on that team.

> The team concept encourages people who would and could not do it by themselves to get involved with new church starts.

Too many solo church planters have been sent out, and they simply cannot endure. In being a part of a team, they would survive and even thrive.

Team Church Planting Is Healthier for Families.

Unfortunately, countless families have not survived starting a new church. Many were sent to an unknown city full of excitement and faith, but left years later bitter and discouraged. What happened? The pressure of church planting, the lack of encouragement and friendship, the neglect of children, and other stresses finally became too much. It's a tragedy that has ruined many families over the years.

I believe team church planting provides a healthier environment for church planting families. In fact, my wife and children are one of the main reasons why I chose team church planting. With multiple families involved in the work of the church, then no one family bears all the pressure. As a result, time for family activities outside of the church plant exists.

In many ways, the whole family is informally part of the team. Relationships between families provide encouragement, support, and needed friendship. Children learn about the church. When a child helps set up for worship, passes out flyers, or participates in team prayer times, then that child gains understanding of the mission and nature of the church.

Team Church Plants Are Able to Accomplish More and Impact a Community Quicker.

All over the world, across all denominations, team church plants are experiencing great success. New churches are beginning with 200–500 unchurched people. Whenever a church begins with that many people, a noticeable impact on the community occurs immediately. I am not saying that smaller churches don't make impacts for the kingdom, but when large numbers of people are converted, others take notice. The excitement becomes contagious, and much can be accomplished when a team disciples, organizes, teaches, and ministers to their community. When a team is not in place to assimilate the newcomers, then many times the crowd dwindles quickly, leading to lost ministry opportunities.

A team produces synergy. The team that properly works together has greater power and impact than individual workers.[8] Why the difference? Synergy. Synergy is not only a scientific principle; it's a biblical one that should be claimed in church planting.

Synergy—The interaction of two or more agents or forces so that their combined effect is greater than the sum of their individual effects; cooperative interaction among groups, especially among the acquired subsidiaries or merged parts of a corporation, that creates an enhanced combined effect.

"synergy," *The American Heritage Dictionary of the English Language*, Fourth Edition (Boston: Houghton Mifflin, 2000).

Team Church Planting Can Provide Apprenticeships.

The apostle Paul had an apprenticeship relationship with Timothy. As his mentor, Paul wrote concerning what he taught Timothy:

"What you heard from me, keep as a pattern for sound teaching . . ." (2 Tim 1:13).

"And the things you have heard me say in the presence of many witnesses entrust to reliable men who will also be qualified to teach others" (2 Tim 2:2).

"But as for you, continue in what you have learned . . ." (2 Tim 3:14).

"To Timothy, my dear son . . ." (2 Tim 1:2).

Obviously, Paul and Timothy had a mentor-apprentice relationship that reveals itself in Scripture. Can you imagine what Timothy must have learned from the greatest church planter who ever lived?

I believe that successful church planters possess the awesome responsibility to recruit potential church planters as part of their team. The seasoned church planter should share all aspects of church planting with the apprentice. With two or three years of firsthand experience outside the pressure of being the team leader, the apprentice will be equipped to start another church along with an equally equipped team. This process should be repeated in every new church, guaranteeing significant numbers of new church planters ready to be commissioned.

Considering the magnitude of church planting apprenticeships, denominations and even local churches should provide the necessary finances to foster mentor-apprenticeship relationships. If the finances are not available, then the apprentice should consider bivocational work.

A Team Best Fulfills the Church Planter Profile That Is Required for Long-term Success and Continued Growth.

Charles Ridley, longtime expert in assessing church planters, says there are thirteen essential qualities for a successful new church leader.[9] They include:

- Has capacity to vision
- Is intrinsically motivated
- Creates ownership of ministry
- Relates to the unchurched
- Has cooperation of spouse

127

- Effectively builds relationships
- Is committed to church growth
- Is responsive to community
- Utilizes giftedness of others
- Possesses flexibility and adaptability
- Builds group cohesiveness
- Displays resilience
- Exercises faith

Without all of the above characteristics, a church probably will not reach its ministry potential. Knowing this, do you know one person anywhere in the world who fits this profile? Doubtfully. Thankfully, teams can meet this profile. In fact, ministry teams that possess all of the profile characteristics most likely breed success.

How to Build a Team

I have spent a great deal of time explaining the significance of team planting. Still, church planters may ask, "How do I build a team?" Here are several significant aspects when composing a church planting team:

Find a Called Team Leader.

As the most important factor in all of church planting, the topic deserves careful, thoughtful, and prayerful consideration.[10] The importance of leadership cannot be overemphasized. This is true in every area of life. An athletic team can be made up of great athletes, but without leadership the team will not be a winner. Corporations may have a great product to sell, but a lack of corporate leadership will doom the company. Families, schools, local governments, civic clubs, and other groups all need effective leadership to sustain success, growth, and health.

Without a doubt, the most important factor in the successful establishment of a new congregation is the selection of the church planter, the leader of the baby church. Additional staff, demographics, site location, worship, finances, and church growth principles are all quite important; however, if the wrong person is chosen to lead the new work, the likelihood of success is dim at best. The new church will struggle, leaving wounded Christians and a bitter pastor, until finally it dies.

Peter Wagner agrees when he writes, ". . . the leader is the principal key to a successful church plant endeavor."[11] Jesus understood this, and that's why He spent so much time preparing the future leaders of His church.[12] The importance of the lead church planter cannot be overstated.

Build a Team That Complements the Profile of the Team Leader.

Great care should be taken to put together a well-balanced team. Start with the team leader, and understand that teams should be built around this individual. With this in mind, you don't have to select a *perfect* team leader. More than anything, you need a leader with vision, faith, and who won't run roughshod over team members. Team leaders must also understand their weaknesses, strengths, and role as just one part of the entire team. From there, a team should be built accordingly. Peter Drucker writes:

> The leaders who work most effectively, it seems to me, never say "I." And that's not because they have trained themselves not to say "I." They don't think "I." They think "we"; they think "team." They understand their job to be to make the team function. They accept the responsibility and don't sidestep it, but "we" gets the credit.[13]

George Barna adds:

> In the end, the outreach of the church may have had the pastor as front man, but his influence was only as strong as the support team backing him. In successful churches, those teams were deep both in numbers and in capabilities.[14]

In my own case, I have the leadership ability, vision, faith, passion, and creativity necessary to lead a church planting team. However, sometimes I struggle with relational skills, often needing a team around me who can make up for that weakness. I also don't have worship leadership skills, nor do I relate well with youth. Although I have definite ministry abilities, I still need a team supporting me who doesn't duplicate my gifts, personality, and skills. Every church plant must consider the skills and talents of its members, beginning with the team leader. Then, as new members join the team, ask these questions: "What piece of the puzzle is still missing? What other kind of person(s) do we need to reach this particular community?"

Without seeking the installment of a
well-balanced team, trouble abounds.

Without seeking the installment of a well-balanced team, trouble abounds. Disharmony, bad relationships, and ineffective ministry eventually surface. The Lord's church is too worthy to make this costly error. Essentially, mistakes in choosing a well-balanced team translate into lost souls, making the next point one of the most crucial in the team-building process.

Adopt a Careful Selection Process.

A well-thought-out, careful selection process means eternal dividends. From a practical standpoint, it also means saving money. Charles Ridley has produced an extremely helpful manual entitled *How to Select Church Planters*. According to his manual, every selection process should include the following activities:

Taking a close look at the community where the church will be started

What are the demographics of the community where the church plant will occur? What will you do to reach these people? What kind of person(s) will help the team get the job done? Peter Drucker says, "To build a successful team . . . you ask: What are we trying to do? Then, what are the key activities?"[15] If the demographics show a large population of residents with children, then recruit a children's minister. If there are thousands of singles, then think seriously about a singles' ministry. I even suggest going a step further and taking the time to survey the community by phone. By the time 200 surveys are completed, you should have a good idea about what team members are needed to most effectively reach the immediate needs of the area.

Considering a number of candidates

In addition to neglecting the demographics of the community, Charles Ridley claims that one of the most common errors made in church planter selection is not considering enough applicants. According to Ridley, the best personnel decisions are made with a 4:1 or 5:1 selection ratio.[16] Team selection is no different; it requires patience and resources (people included).

Securing complete background materials on candidates

Begin by asking potential candidates to submit complete résumés. After résumés are received, make an informative decision about candidates outside of the running. Do not spend too much time with people you know are unqualified. However, be sure to treat all applicants with respect and fairness. Communicate with all candidates promptly when résumés have been received and when decisions have been made.

If a candidate's résumé is approved for further consideration, next check references thoroughly. With the candidate's permission, talk to former employers, asking questions on the candidate's work ethic, personality, and skills. Ridley provides a helpful telephone checklist in his manual that I recommend when talking with a candidate's former employers.[17] Finally, remember that when checking references, ask specific questions about behavior in the workplace. Past behavior most likely indicates future behavior.

For all qualified candidates at this point in the selection process, a thorough questionnaire should be completed by the potential team member. Although some of the information may be repeated from the résumé, in the end all of the candidate's important information should be housed in one document. The questionnaire should include personal information about the candidate and spouse (if married), as well as information concerning education, marital status, children, health, finances, personality, spirituality, and various opinions about church or doctrinal issues.

I also recommend having multiple telephone conversations with the candidate. Much can be learned about an individual over the course of several personal telephone calls, including responses to questions from the résumé, reference check, and questionnaire. Answering questions that might arise from these preinterview contacts over the telephone will allow the interview time to be used more wisely and efficiently.

Conducting thorough personal interviews

As mentioned, interviews are vital. Only interview those candidates whom you consider potential team members. Charles Ridley states two purposes for interviewing:

1. To obtain reliable and valid information to predict the future performances of candidates.

2. To lay a foundation for the relationship that may continue beyond the interview.[18]

Ridley also provides seven helpful principles for selection interviewing.

1. The best predictor of future behavior is past behavior.

2. Behavior performance within the behavior setting is significantly more important than work experience.

3. The focus is not on a single behavior, but a class of behaviors.

4. Selection interviewing is based upon the indirect observation of behavior.

5. Maintain decision uncertainty.

6. Selection is a mutual decision-making process.

7. Effectiveness in selection is a function of the match between the person and the job.[19]

Finally, Ridley suggests seven characteristics for effective interviewing that I have found most beneficial.

1. Remain in control.

2. Strive for completeness.

3. Work toward depth in responses.

4. Be flexible.

5. Create an interview environment of "low threat."

6. Develop a good system for adequate retention.[20]

7. Be informative.[21]

After the completion of all interviews, decisions need to be made about who has a high probability of being a successful part of the team. Those decisions should then be confirmed at a church planting assessment center.

Sending Candidates to a Professional Assessment Center

Ideally, all potential team members and their spouses (if married) should participate in a two- to four-day assessment center. These centers are gaining popularity and acceptance all over the country. Attendance at professional assessment centers includes the following activities: psychological testing, individual and couple interviews, problem solving, conflict management, team building, and a final summary interview. At this interview, participants hear about strengths, weaknesses, and recommendations concerning church planting.[22]

During the assessment period, seasoned church planters and trained psychologists observe all participants. The results of the assessment aid in final team selections as well as help team members understand each other. Although extremely valuable in the team selection process, assessment centers represent only a part of the entire process.

Requiring Team Members to Raise at Least Partial Financial Support

I am convinced that team members should be willing to raise at least partial financial support for the church plant and their position on the church planting team. This requirement will accomplish several things:

1. It will discourage those who really aren't committed to church planting.

2. It will increase church planting visibility when team members raise support and allow more of God's people to be involved in an indirect way.

3. It allows for more team members.

If a person makes it through a selection process, then there is a good chance the individual will be an asset to the team. There is no way to quickly run through this process; it takes time, commitment, and much prayer. Church planting leadership is too essential to the kingdom of God to be left to a shallow selection process.

Church planting leadership is too essential to the kingdom of God to be left to a shallow selection process.

Consider Students, Part-time Staff, and Bivocational Candidates for the Team.

Think outside the box when considering team members. Your team is available if you are willing to be creative enough to find them.

Conclusion

Although not the only way to start a church, I believe that team church planting presents the best means for effective church planting and development. Biblical evidence clearly supports this claim. Team church plants throughout the world have shown great success in all denominations, and have made an impact on their communities for the kingdom of God. If you are serious about starting a new church, then you should think first about building a well-balanced ministry team.

---

[1] Laura Hillenbrand, *Seabiscuit, An American Legend* (New York: Random House Ballantine Publishing Group, 2001) p. xvii.

[2] Ibid., p. xviii.

[3] Kathleen Kennedy, Frank Marshall, Gary Ross, and Jane Sindell, *Seabiscuit*, VHS, directed by Gary Ross (Universal City, CA: Universal Pictures, 2003).

[4] Ibid.

[5] David W. Shenk and Ervin R. Stutzman, *Creating Communities of the Kingdom* (Scottdale, PA: Herald Press, 1988) 51.

[6] All Scripture quotations are taken from the *New International Version*.

[7] Shenk and Stutzman, *Creating*, 43.

[8] Ibid., 49-50.

[9] Charles R. Ridley, *How to Select Church Planters* (Pasadena, CA: Fuller Evangelistic Association, 1988) 7-11.

[10] For additional information on finding a called team leader, see chapters on the call, management teams, and assessment.

[11] C. Peter Wagner, *Church Planting for a Greater Harvest* (Ventura, CA: Regal Books, 1990) 51.

[12] Rick Rusaw and Paul Williams, *Leadership and the Church Planter*, A Master's Thesis (Cincinnati: Cincinnati Bible College and Seminary, 1990) 14.

[13] Peter F. Drucker, *Managing the Non-Profit Organization* (New York: Harper Collins, 1990) 18-19.

[14] George Barna, *User Friendly Churches* (Ventura, CA: Regal Books, 1991) 154.

[15] Drucker, *Managing*, 152.

[16] Charles R. Ridley, *How to Select Church Planters* (Pasadena, CA: Fuller Evangelistic Association, 1988) 5.

[17] Ibid., 42.

[18] Ibid., 49.

[19] Ibid., 50.

[20] This refers to a god system of note-taking or perhaps a tape recorder to be sure you accurately remember what was said and your impressions.

[21] Ridley, *How to Select*, 52-54.

[22] Paige Mathews offers an excellent chapter in this book dedicated to assessment.

R. Paige Mathews is an experienced and sought-after church planting assessment veteran of fifteen years. He is one of three Directors of the Church Planting Assessment Center (CPAC—**www.churchplanting4me.org**) held at Emmanuel School of Religion in Johnson City, Tennessee, and sponsored by the Orchard Group. Paige is the Business Manager for LifeBridge Christian Church in Longmont, Colorado, a church of approximately 4,000, and serves as President of FIA Consulting which continues to serve Capital Stewardship Development needs across America. He held ministry positions in Tennessee, Florida, and Pennsylvania. He directed the Christian Evangelizing Association, a new church planting ministry, for sixteen years while living in Pennsylvania, and helped start a new church in Lancaster, Pennsylvania. Paige received a BS in Bible and Preaching from Johnson Bible College in 1979, and a MA in Communication Studies from Bloomsburg University in 1987. He is married to Lynne and they are the parents of two grown daughters.

Church Planter Assessment

I am old enough to remember the early days when television networks began broadcasting college and professional football games. One camera on the 50 yard line soon became three sideline cameras. Cameras were added in the end zones along with a blimp flying overhead. I remember the networks trumpeting the "reverse angle" camera. Now we have skycam, helmet-cam, slow motion, stop action, instant replay, and commentators writing all over the screen with electronic chalk. Virtually every perspective imaginable is used to analyze, review, second-guess, criticize, and praise each play, and each player. One moment in time viewed from every possible perspective with the purpose of understanding what happened, or might have happened, or may yet happen.

Welcome to church planter assessment.

The purpose of church planter assessment is to view a single individual or a couple from a wide variety of perspectives with the purpose of understanding their histories, experiences, and potentials, all in the context of starting a new congregation. Whether the individual or couple aspires to team leadership or team membership, assessment helps them understand their unique contribution to this ministry, and helps sponsoring organizations make wise employment decisions.

For church planter assessment to be effective, we first have to know what qualities make church planting leadership successful. Then, we need processes whereby the qualities are evaluated in such a way that appropriate decisions can be made. This is especially critical as the financial investment in the process increases.

What in the World Am I Looking For?

Dr. Charles Ridley led a research project sponsored by more than a dozen denominations to determine the characteristics of an effective church planter.[1] The results of the study revealed thirteen competencies that a successful planter should possess. The order of the characteristics stems from the results of the study. The first five characteristics are considered essential for the team leader while the remaining eight are desirable. The competencies, with Dr. Ridley's brief definition, include:

1. **Has a Capacity for Visionizing**
   ▶ Projects into the future beyond the present.
   ▶ Develops a theme that highlights the vision and philosophy of ministry.
   ▶ Persuasively sells the vision to the people.
   ▶ Approaches challenges as opportunities instead of obstacles.
   ▶ Copes effectively with nonvisionizing people.
   ▶ Does not erect artificial walls to limit capacities.
   ▶ Believes in God's capacity to accomplish great things.

2. **Is Intrinsically Motivated**
   ▶ Committed to excellence.
   ▶ Stick-to-itiveness and persistence.
   ▶ Aggressively, yet positively, takes the initiative.
   ▶ Self-starter, willing to build from nothing.
   ▶ Willing to work long and hard.

3. **Creates Ownership of Ministry**
   ▶ Helps others "buy in" and feel responsible for the growth and success of the ministry.
   ▶ Wins the commitment of the people to the vision.
   ▶ Establishes a congregational identity.
   ▶ Avoids imposing unrealistic goals on the congregation.

4. Demonstrates Spousal Cooperation (if the candidate is married)

▶ Has an explicit agreement regarding each partner's role and involvement in ministry.

▶ Has explicit rules regarding the use of the home as an office.

▶ Evaluates the consequences of ministry demands upon the children.

▶ Functions as a team through individual and corporate action.

▶ Models wholesome family life before church and community.

▶ Agrees upon and shares ministry vision with spouse.

▶ Deliberately plans and protects family life.

5. Reaches the Unchurched

▶ Communicates in a style easily understood by the unchurched.

▶ Understands the "psychology" or mentality of the unchurched.

▶ Moves and functions in the "personal space" of the unchurched without fear.

▶ Quickly gets to know the unchurched on a personal level.

▶ Breaks through the barriers erected by the unchurched.

▶ Handles crises faced by the unchurched.

6. Effectively Builds Relationships

▶ Responds with urgency to expressed needs and concerns of others.

▶ Displays godly love and compassion to others.

▶ Makes others feel secure and comfortable.

▶ Does not respond in a judgmental or prejudicial fashion to new people.

▶ Appreciates and accepts a variety of persons.

▶ Spends quality time with present members without overlooking them for the sake of newcomers.

7. Is Committed to Church Growth

▶ Appreciates steady and consistent growth without looking for "quick successes."

▶ Is committed to numerical growth within the context of spiritual and relational growth.

▶ Establishes the goal of becoming a financially self-supporting church within a specific period of time.

▶ Does not fall into a maintenance ministry.

▶ Sees the church project within the larger context of God's Kingdom.

8. Is Responsive to the Community

▶ Understands the culture of the community.

▶ Identifies and assesses community needs.

▶ Organizes internal and external church resources to respond to community needs.

▶ Efficiently utilizes resources on a basis of priority.

▶ Determines effectiveness of other organized attempts to respond to community needs.

▶ Does not confuse community needs with what the church wants to offer.

▶ Learns the character and pulse of the community.

▶ Adapts the philosophy of ministry to the character of the community.

9. Utilizes the Giftedness of Others

▶ Releases and equips people to do the tasks of ministry.

▶ Discerns the spiritual gifts of others.

▶ Matches people with ministry needs and opportunities according to giftedness.

▶ Delegates effectively in areas of personal limitation.

▶ Avoids assigning ministry responsibilities before others are adequately prepared.

▶ Does not place unwarranted restrictions on the spiritual giftedness of others.

10. Possesses Flexibility and Adaptability

▶ Copes effectively with ambiguity.

▶ Copes effectively with constant and abrupt change.

▶ Adapts the methods to the uniqueness of the respective church planting project.

▶ Readily shifts priorities and emphases during various stages of church growth.

▶ Does whatever is necessary, whenever necessary.

11. **Builds a Cohesive Church Body**
    ▶ Develops a nucleus group as a foundation.
    ▶ Quickly includes newcomers into a network of relationships and meaningful church activities.
    ▶ Monitors the morale of the people.
    ▶ Uses groups effectively.

12. **Demonstrates Resilience**
    ▶ Experiences setbacks without defeat.
    ▶ Rides the ups and downs.
    ▶ Expects the unexpected.
    ▶ Rebounds from loss, disappointments, and failure.

13. **Exercises Faith**
    ▶ Possesses a conviction regarding the call to church planting ministry.
    ▶ Believes in God's action.
    ▶ Is marked by expectation and hope.
    ▶ Is willing to wait for answers to specific prayer requests.[2]

The Church Planting Assessment Center (CPAC)[3] process is designed to discover the level of maturity and degree of competence the candidate exhibits with regard to each of these characteristics. These thirteen items are referred to as the "Core Competencies." Notice that very little attention is given to the actual nuts and bolts of doing the church planting work. Rather, the emphasis is on finding a leader who possesses the necessary core competencies and then trusting that the candidate will do what it takes to learn the basic tasks involved in planting a church. In fact, there are numerous resources available to help competent leaders excel in the work of church planting. This book is one of them.

The emphasis is on finding a leader who possesses the core competencies and then trusting that the candidate will do what it takes to learn the basic tasks involved.

How Will We Know What We're Looking For?

It is one thing to know the essential core competencies desired in church planting leadership. It is quite another to determine if a specific individual or couple possesses those qualities. The key to seeing the desired qualities is looking from a variety of perspectives. Church planter assessment utilizes a plethora of tools, people, resources, and methods to provide the needed perspective. Some of the following processes we may conduct ourselves; others require the use of trained professionals or a formal assessment center. Some of these processes are relatively simple and inexpensive; others require a significant commitment of time and resources. Regardless, the investment is minimal when compared with the cost of failure—lives hurt, resources wasted, and time lost!

Written Documents

The most fundamental and inexpensive part of the evaluation process is that of collecting the paperwork. Ask potential candidates to submit a narrative résumé and complete a questionnaire.[4] The candidates put what they want on the résumé. Those doing the assessing decide what goes on the questionnaire. Most of the time consumed is the candidates', and the cost is minimal. You glean real information that can be used during personal interview times. You learn how thoughtful and articulate the candidates are while pre-screening them for your initial key knockout factors.

A narrative résumé pushes candidates to tell their stories. We receive more than just bullet points; we get real information about past job experiences and educational opportunities. As they tell their story, we discover who they are, what they think is important, and what they value. We walk with them on their journey through life, noting the key events that marked real change in direction and purpose.

An assessment questionnaire allows us to develop our own agenda and to acquire information not generally asked in employment interviews. For instance, candidates can be asked to respond to key doctrinal points, discuss their opinions on the sacraments and ordinances of Scripture, and elaborate on their thinking with regard to a myriad of issues such as gender bias and polity in the church. Furthermore, one can begin the process of exploring the candidate's financial condition, level of marital satisfaction, and family origin issues. A well-designed questionnaire may ask a candidate to respond to thirty or forty different items of inquiry. We can learn things even from the comprehensive nature, or lack thereof, of their responses.

In and of themselves, written documents may help eliminate candidates, thus saving time. At the very least, written documents enable you to focus and maximize the use of time in evaluating candidates. Together, these written responses provide direction as you check references and move to the next stage of the process.

Standardized Testing

The second perspective is that of standardized testing and relying upon trained professionals to interpret and contextualize the results. Literally hundreds of testing instruments exist to evaluate all areas of the human condition. For the purposes of church planter assessment, it is helpful to look at three areas: psychological/temperament testing, behavior styles testing, and leadership style evaluations.

For the purposes of church planter assessment, it is helpful to look at three areas.

Psychological and temperament testing accomplishes two things. First, it looks for evidence of mental pathology. Is the candidate struggling with depression, schizophrenia, borderline personality disorder, bipolar disorder, or another of the many possible disorders or phobias so readily found in people? This testing may also reveal destructive patterns of behavior related to experiences with the family of origin. Historically, there has been such an aversion to psychological treatment, such a stigma attached to those who seek out counseling, that many disorders have gone undiagnosed. Fortunately, this is changing. You absolutely do not want to place an individual in church planting ministry if they are working through these types of challenges.

Second, short of identifying a specific pathology, the psychological and temperament testing can identify levels of marital satisfaction or difficulties in anger management, conflict resolution, anxiety, or assertiveness. Temperament testing also reveals degrees of introversion, extroversion, intuition, judgment, narcissism, histrionics, and many other factors. These issues rarely disqualify candidates; rather they enhance a coach or mentor's ability to give direction and help. Identifying these traits may result in a better church planter because you provide training and support in precise areas of need or weakness.

Among the most common Psychological and Temperament Tests are the Minnesota Multiphasic Personality Inventory (MMPI), Sixteen Personality Factor Questionnaire (16PF), California Personality Indicator (CPI), Millon Clinical Multiaxial Inventory iii (Millon iii), Taylor-Johnson Temperament Analysis (T-JTA), and the Myers-Briggs Type Indicator (MBTI). These tests should be administered, scored, and evaluated by trained clinicians who have the opportunity to interview the respondents in person. At times, more than one instrument may be administered to refine the clinician's opinion or conclusion. Obviously, moving to this step incurs additional expense and time, for the instrument, the expert, and the candidate.

Behavioral styles testing is most often accomplished through the Personal Profile System 2800 instrument available from Inscape Publishing Company.[5] More commonly referred to as the "DiSC" test, this tool identifies the preferred behavioral strategies for each candidate. This process reveals whether an individual is more interested in accomplishing tasks or spending time with people. It reveals whether individuals view themselves as more or less powerful than their environment; whether they work at a fast or slow pace, whether they are interested in the grand scheme of things or prefer the minutiae.

It should be noted that successful church planters may be found with all combinations of behavioral styles.

It should be noted that successful church planters may be found with all combinations of behavioral styles; however, certain combinations of behaviors lend themselves to new churches being established quicker, larger, and self-supporting sooner. Again, this instrument is most beneficial when administered, interpreted, and explained by someone trained in its permutations.

Finally, leadership is critical in new church planting. Does the person engender trust, delegate responsibility, empower and train other leaders? Inscape Publishing also features an instrument entitled "Dimensions in Leadership Profile" which may help identify strengths and weaknesses in various leadership styles. Other instruments of this type are also readily available. Regardless of the standardized testing utilized, the results should be confirmed through personal interviews and personal observations.

A Formal Church Planter Assessment Process

The most recommended course of action is to send candidates through a formal church planter assessment process. A structured assessment center includes the generation of written documents and the administration of standardized testing with professional evaluations and interviews. In addition, a formal assessment process adds the added information of evaluations by subject matter assessments, peer assessment, and self-assessment.

Generally, a professional church planter assessment process involves three to five days of intensive interaction and evaluation. Candidates should be required to experience the process with their spouses, if married. The assessors are selected from a variety of experts in church planting, psychology, marriage and family therapy, theology, and practical ministry. Multiple assessors utilizing multiple assessment tools provide the range of perspectives needed to make reasoned decisions regarding team leadership or team membership in church planting ministry.

During the assessment process, the candidates are asked to engage in a number of exercises. In some cases, the exercises reveal the candidates' subject matter awareness. In some cases, the exercises reveal more about the candidate's interaction with other people than their personal knowledge of some church planting factor. Other exercises reveal various talents or gifts. All of the exercises are observed by assessors who have the benefit of reviewing the written documents and obtaining some of the results of the standardized testing. Furthermore, the assessors have the added benefit of observing the candidates during leisure times, at meals, and other unstructured moments. These periods of observation often provide serendipitous insight into the character and personality of candidates.

Toward the end of the formal assessment period, the subject matter experts have an opportunity to engage the candidates in personal interviews. Utilizing behaviorally based questions and their own observations, the assessors refine their opinion of the degree to which various core competencies are present in the individual candidates. These interviews enable the assessors to recommend specific courses of action to candidates to further prepare them for church planting leadership.

Regularly in the assessment process, opportunity is granted to the candidates to evaluate each other. Peer assessment provides a critical perspective. The common questions are revealing and crucial. Was this person easy to work with? Was this candidate open to the ideas of others? Would you like to work with this individual again? Did this person make the most valuable contribution to the exercise? What comments would you make regarding your experience with this candidate? Church planters have to work with people. Working with their peers in the assessment process provides a unique perspective into this ability.

Perhaps the greatest benefit derived from formal assessment participation is self-evaluation. As the assessors engage the candidates in exercises and interviews, the candidates themselves begin to form conclusions about their own abilities, gifts, and competencies in the area of church planting. It is common for the candidates themselves to arrive at precisely the same conclusions as the assessor staff. For some, this self-assessment is empowering. They come away from the process believing in themselves and challenged to greater efforts. For some, this self-assessment results in a change of focus, career, or direction. A few even come away knowing that they face personal challenges and periods of preparation before they can engage the task of new church planting. No one leaves the process unchanged.

A formal church planter assessment process typically provides feedback to both the candidates and the sponsoring organizations. Clear and specific recommendations are offered regarding the candidate's core competencies and his or her suitability for church planting ministry. Generally, these recommendations are offered in the context of a two-year time frame, with no presumption as to what God may choose to do in the life of a candidate beyond that period. With the recommendations come a set of developmental suggestions to enhance the candidate's ministry, relationships, and personal effectiveness. Candidates and sponsoring organizations are then free to follow the recommendations and suggestions, or choose another course of action.

Over the years I have had to tell a team that one of its members had a problem with sexual orientation. I had to tell a husband that his wife was diagnosed as borderline personality disorder and watch his face as the realization of what they had been experiencing in their marriage crystallized. I have had to ask church planters and team members to resign because I did not do my homework in the hiring process. I have also had the opportunity to tell many candidates to go do the work of church planting with God's speed, and I have watched with joy as they have excelled. I can remember when church planters were called on the basis of two questions, do you like to evangelize and where do you want to go? Of course, I remember single camera football broadcasts as well. I much prefer instant replay, skycams, and the full church planting assessment process with all of its varied perspectives. I expect you will as well.

---

[1] "Back in the mid-1980's, 13 different denominations came together with the common problem of church planter misplacement. The problem in their past was that good and godly persons had been placed by them in church planting assignments for which these people were neither gifted nor suited. The result of those misplacements over the years had cost these denominations in the United States and Canada literally millions of dollars. In some places districts had bought land, built a building and fully supported the church planter financially. But the church planters themselves, the most important key in new church development, were not assessed correctly for this unique calling and role. Out of their discussions, these 13 different denominations hired a psychologist from Fuller Theological Seminary, Dr. Charles Ridley. He was charged with the responsibility of studying 100 church planters from these denominations to determine the common characteristics that effective church planting leaders have. Out of Dr. Ridley's work came the 13 characteristics that became "the standard" for what numerous denominations began looking for in church planters. After concluding his study, Dr. Ridley made the observation, 'The job you are asking these people to do, the job of a church planter, is awesome!'" New Church Specialties, *How Church Planter Assessment Was Developed* (updated 1 August 2003; cited 9 December 2003) available from **http://www.newchurchspecialties.org/8-01-202.shtml**.

[2] Charles R. Ridley, *How to Select Church Planters* (Pasadena, CA: Fuller Evangelistic Association, 1988) 7-11.

[3] The Church Planting Assessment Center (CPAC) is a professional assessment center event hosted by Emmanuel School of Religion in Johnson City, Tennessee, and sponsored by the Orchard Group, a church planting agency in the Greater New York area. CPAC is directed by Paige Mathews, Brent Foulke, and Tom Jones. It is open to all denominations. For more information, go to **www.churchplanting4me.org**.

[4] See Tom Jones's Potential Staff questionnaire, downloadable from **www.collegepress.com/churchplanting**.

[5] The Personal Profile System is available to you by contacting R. Paige Mathews at **pmathews@lbcc.org**.

Dave Smith first felt God's call to ministry in April 1983. Over the years, his experiences in ministry positions have pushed him toward church planting, an area of ministry he still serves today. After finishing his fourth year of obligation to the U.S. Army, Dave attended and then graduated from Trinity Evangelical Divinity School in Deerfield, Illinois. Dave has served as the Minister of Outreach at East 91ˢᵗ Street Christian Church in Indiana and the lead planter and Senior Minister of CrossWay Christian Church in New Hampshire. In late 2000, he returned to Indianapolis, Indiana, to take on two roles—Minister of Church Planting for East 91ˢᵗ Street Christian Church and Vice President of Development for Go Ye Chapel Mission (GYCM). In the spring of 2003, he joined the faculty at Ozark Christian College in developing a church planting program for the school. Dave has been married to wife, Nancy, for 21 years, and loves spending time with her and their three children, Katie, Joshua, and Amy.

Faith and Family

*T*ony Twist and I used to meet for dinner weekly at a local cafeteria in Indianapolis, Indiana. He was the youth minister at East 91ˢᵗ Street Christian Church, and I was a young Army officer and a new Christian. I had begun to sense God calling me into vocational ministry. When I shared this with Tony, he began to invest more time in me. He would call and say, "Let's go to dinner, so I can disciple you," and over a "Jack Benny" special, he would pour himself into me.

One day Tony said to me, "Going to seminary is a lot like going to chef's school. They teach you to prepare all kinds of fancy dishes: flaming pepper steak, pheasant under glass, chocolate mousse. If you don't eat, however, you will starve to death. When in school, you will spend all kinds of time in the Bible: studying passages, doing exegesis, writing papers. Still, if you don't eat, if you don't spend time with God, developing intimacy with Him, you'll starve to death."

I never forgot Tony's advice. His counsel led me to pray these words as I sat down at my desk each night: "Lord, help me not just to know about you. Help me not just to know how to serve you. Help me to know you personally." God honored Tony's insights and my prayers, and I emerged from seminary not only with greater knowledge, but also with a deeper devotion to God Himself.

Planting a church is as spiritually dangerous as going to seminary. The task is difficult, and we may be doing all kinds of things:

preaching weekly, leading a staff, and sharing our faith. If we don't nurture our own relationship with God though, we will dry up and be of no use to God or anyone else. You can't give away what you don't have.

The Foundational Relationship

Jesus defines eternal life this way: "Now this is eternal life, that they may know you, the only true God, and Jesus Christ, whom you have sent" (John 17:3).[1] God created us for fellowship with Him. "And our fellowship is with the Father and with His Son, Jesus Christ" (1 John 1:3). David, a man after God's own heart challenges us to "Taste and see that the Lord is good" (Ps 34:8), and to "Delight yourself in the Lord" (Ps 37:4). Regarding his intimacy with God David writes, "You will fill me with joy in your presence, with eternal pleasures at your right hand" (Ps 16:11).

The danger of church planting is that in the midst of establishing God's work, we may miss God.

The danger of church planting is that in the midst of establishing God's work, we may miss God. We overlook the reason we were created and Jesus died—fellowship with God. If we are not careful, we discover over time that we don't really know God. We don't experience intimacy with Him.

There is no greater calling than knowing God. If we fail to live out that conviction, we hurt our families, our new churches, and ourselves. So how do we know God? There are no magic answers, but this chapter is written with a desire for you and your families to know and experience God within a new church context. It is written hoping the people God brings to your new church will see Him in you and in your home.

Behind "The Greatest Commandment"

One day a teacher of the law asked Jesus which was the greatest commandment. Jesus replied, "Love the Lord your God with all your heart and with all your soul and with all your mind and with all your strength" (Mark 12:30). Many of us plant churches as an expression of love for God. God calls us. We love Him. We obey Him.

Behind the command to love Him is a greater truth however, a truth affecting *how* we plant churches and live life. "This is love: not that we loved God but that He loved us and sent His Son as an atoning sacrifice for our sins" (1 John 4:10). The greatest truth in the world is not that we love God, but that He loves us. God loves us. This truth should undergird everything we do in church planting. We plant churches resting in the truth that God not only loves lost people, but He also loves us, the church planters.

> We plant churches resting in the truth
> that God not only loves lost people, but
> He also loves us, the church planters.

Too many people do not live by the grace through which we have been saved. We don't grasp what Paul prays, "how wide and long and high and deep is the love of Christ" (Eph 3:18). We don't "know this love that surpasses knowledge" and we don't experience the "fullness of God" (Eph 3:19). Instead, we seek fulfillment by working constantly and seeking to please people, all within the pseudo premise that we're doing new church work. This hurts us, and those we love. God wants us to live as a called people: called to know Him, love our families, and let Him build healthy new communities of faith through us.

We need to recalibrate our lives to the reality of God's love. We need to live with an abiding sense of the love with which God loves us, even now. Like Jesus, we need to spend time with our Father, basking in His love and allowing Him to direct our days.

Experiencing God

Many of us who plant churches struggle with finding time for God. If we are honest, we often find it boring. This is especially true in the fast-moving pace of a new church. A first step in breaking away from this mentality is realizing it is not so much a duty, as an opportunity to delight in the God who loves us. But even with this knowledge, our prayer and Bible reading times may be unrewarding. We may not have any sense of experiencing the God who made us. How can we connect to the God who called us into church planting?

Back in August of 1999, I attended a Willow Creek Leadership Summit via satellite. At that conference, minister Bill Hybels introduced thousands to the idea of pathways to God. The basic idea is that we experience God in different ways. Some sense His reality while thinking on His great truths, others by serving or by interacting with other Christians. I most experience God through the pathways of nature and solitude.

As I reflected on those times I felt closest to God, it was usually when I was alone with Him in His creation. The challenge for you is to discover the context in which you most deeply experience God. Then work prayer and God's Word into that context. For me, it means regular time alone with God, and, when possible, doing that outside in His creation.

The challenge for you is to discover the context in which you most deeply experience God. Then work prayer and God's Word into that context.

Many have been helped not only by discovering how we best connect with God, but also by viewing time with God as a series of rhythms. For example, my best daily times with God occur in the morning. I like beginning my day in worship, prayer, and Bible reading. It is the time I delight in the God who loves me.

When I am sincerely seeking God, I also have a longer time with Him weekly. When I was planting the church in New Hampshire, God led me to a retreat house. It was associated with the Catholic church and the priests allowed me to go there as often as I desired. Every Monday afternoon I showed up. First, I would go to the chapel. It was so quiet, and I enjoyed the light through the stained glass windows. I would just sit there, exhausted from Sunday, and let God love me. After a while, I would wander down to the multipurpose room. It was warm, sunny, and smelled like wood smoke. It felt like home. I would look out at the sky and the tall evergreens. I let God remind me He was bigger than any church planting challenge I might be facing. Then when I felt it was time, I went outside and walked the trails through the woods. Sometimes, I meditated on the Stations of the Cross. Other times I sang and skipped through the pine needles. I felt like the kid that I am—a child of the God who loves me.

Every few months, as part of my walk with God, I would spend at least one overnight with Him. There are places all over this country that will give free lodging to ministers in search of sacred space. I have spent multiple days at the retreat house mentioned above. On one such occasion I read through the New Testament. I have danced with God in a lakeside cottage on the Vermont/New Hampshire border. I have felt His presence in the White Mountains and heard His majesty in the breaking of waves along the coast of Maine.

However you most experience God, make time to experience Him in that setting.

However you most experience God, make time to experience Him in that setting. Receive the love of Jesus and let it transform your life and ministry. John Piper, in his book, *Desiring God*, says our biggest challenge is to learn to desire God for Himself, not God and something else, but simply God.[2] Sometimes I imagine everything I value being stripped away. When everything is gone, one thing still remains: the love of God for me in Christ Jesus. Plant churches out of the depth of your spirituality and the reality that God loves you. "But God demonstrates His own love for us in this: While we were still sinners, Christ died for us" (Rom 5:8).

The Priority of Family

One time, early in my ministry, I was praying with a church leader. I had been sharing with this leader the challenges of doing my vocational ministry while being the husband and dad God called me to be. After listening to me, this leader prayed, "Dear Lord, help Dave with his family, but we know your work comes first." His prayer puzzled me. I remember thinking, "Lord, I thought my family was part of your work. You gave them to me." I still believe families are part of God's work, a work that often gets neglected in the planting of churches.

Before Jesus ascended to be with the Father, He gave this command to the disciples: "But you will receive power when the Holy Spirit comes on you; and you will be my witnesses in Jerusalem, and in all Judea and Samaria, and to the ends of the earth" (Acts 1:8). We use this verse to talk about the importance of reaching those near and far with the gospel of Jesus Christ. Yet we often fail to apply this verse to those geographically and culturally closest to us: our own families.

After watching many shipwreck their families in the name of church planting, I decided that if I was going to err, it would be on the side of investing too much, not too little, in those closest to me.

The Next Most Important Relationship

Though God created us for fellowship with Him, it was also God who said, "It is not good for the man to be alone. I will make a helper suitable for him" (Gen 2:18). So God gave man the gift of woman. Jesus would later challenge the religious leaders,

> Haven't you read, that at the beginning the Creator made them male and female, and said, "For this reason a man will leave his father and mother and be united to his wife, and the two will become one flesh"? So they are no longer two, but one. Therefore, what God has joined together, let man not separate (Matt 19:4-6).

I recognize God calls many women to lead and be a part of church planting teams. He called one to be a member of our team. Much of what I will say is applicable to wives and moms, as well as husbands and dads. However, I am directing my remarks primarily to men, many who will find themselves in the role of lead planter.

Most of you will not legally separate from your wives in the name of church planting, but in reality, you will be gone: physically, emotionally, mentally, and spiritually. I remember a conversation with Rick Stedman, church planter and senior minister of Adventure Christian Church in Roseville, California. Rick told me of a young church planter who came to him and said, "I told my wife not to expect to see me for the next three years, since I will be planting this church. What do you think?" Rick responded, "Well, that depends on who is planting the church, you or God."

The bottom line is that Jesus Christ is the church planter. He does His work through us. The same God who calls us to plant churches commands us, "Husbands love your wives as Christ loved the church and gave Himself up for her" (Eph 5:25). How did Jesus love the church? How did He give Himself up for her? He died for her. And in the same way, we are to love our wives and give ourselves up for them.

The bottom line is that Jesus Christ is the church planter.

There is no biblical justification for neglecting our wives in the name of working for God. God goes on to call us to love our wives as our own bodies, to love our wives as we love ourselves (Eph 5:28,33). So how do we do it?

In Mark 10:45, Jesus said He came not to be served, but to serve. A place to start is for husbands to see themselves as servants of their wives. Living this out can take many practical expressions; from domestic tasks, to helping with the children, to being supportive of their God-given profession. I have also been helped by Gary Chapman's book, *The Five Love Languages*.[3] Just as there are different pathways in which we experience God more fully, there are different ways people experience love from their mate. Chapman identifies five love languages: words of affirmation, quality time, receiving gifts, acts of service, and physical touch.

Each of us needs to talk with our wife and discover in what ways we make her feel most loved. We may have been devoted to giving flowers, when what she really wanted was for us to do the dishes. We may have been affectionate but failed to build in regular blocks of time alone with her. We tend to love most naturally in our own love language. This may not be hers. Take the time to find out. Talk it over. Also realize it may change over time. Historically, my wife has been fairly balanced in all of them. But with the progression of her Multiple Sclerosis, acts of service have taken on renewed meaning for her.

> ## We may have been devoted to giving flowers, when what she really wanted was for us to do the dishes.

For the twenty-one years we have been married, we have also had regular date nights. Some years, it has been once a week, other years, every other week. Take time to get away and talk about your lives together. Listen to her needs, hopes, and dreams. Build in rhythms where every few months you get away, just the two of you. Our best conversations about faith and life and love take place when we get away.

We have never been too successful going through the standard couple's devotional books. It never worked well for us to study the Bible together. What has worked is for each to have our own time with God. Then we live life together, and talk about what God is teaching us. We do pray together every night before bed. Like the pathways or love languages, you may live out your marriage covenant differently. But the point is, live it out! Become in experience what you are in position: one. There are no shortcuts to a healthy marriage. It takes deliberate, intentional work. Your marriage, family, and new church deserve the best effort you have. In fact, one of the most important things you bring to church planting (if married) is your marriage. Don't neglect it.

The Gift of Children

We had a difficult time having children. When God answered our prayers and gave us three healthy kids, we were thrilled. Over time however, it is easy in church planting to see our children as just one more task that needs to be done. Remember this—children are a gift from God. Psalm 127:3 says, "Sons are a heritage from the Lord, children a reward from Him."

Much of what has been said about investing in your wife also can be said about your children. Find out how they best experience love. Speak their language. Spend time with them. Take them on regular dates. Get away for an extended period, with each of them, at least once a year.

A foundational passage for raising children to love God is Deuteronomy 6:4-9. Essentially, these verses challenge us to present God to our children by example and teaching, informally and formally. We begin with our own love for God. If we don't love God, we can't expect that of our children. Children are far more perceptive in spiritual matters than we realize. They do not merely respond to our words. They need to sense our own faith and love for God. They experience this as we live out our faith by asking for forgiveness when we blow it and granting forgiveness when they mess up. They see our love for God when we continue to live for God, despite adverse circumstances. My children have learned much about the Christian life through my apologies, in the midst of my sinfulness, and my wife's faithfulness, despite her Multiple Sclerosis. They know that God is real and that we love Him. They are learning to love Him too.

Despite the power of example, we still must teach them God's Word. They need to know the reason for the hope that is within us. They need to know of God's love for them and His purposes for their lives. Like couple's devotionals, our family devotionals have rarely worked well. They often ended in arguments. What has worked well, however, is for Nancy and I to rotate each night what child we put to bed. It is during that one-on-one time that we read the Bible, talk about it, and pray together. Those have been incredibly rewarding times. I have answered many an apologetic question from my son, Josh, who at an early age asked things like, "How do we know God is real? How can we trust the Bible? Why did God make man if He knew man was going to sin?"

As rewarding as those times have been, I must tell you that I have had equally deep conversations about Jesus at McDonald's or Dairy Queen. Take time to be with your children. I can't remember where I read or heard it, but as Zig Ziglar says, "Kids need quality time, lots of it." Realize the importance of routine, family traditions, regular dates, and how children are put to bed each night. I believe the time before bed is one of the most important times of our children's lives. Don't miss it. If you spend time with your children, the church planting experience can be incredible for them. They will learn from a young age what the church is all about. Allow them to be a part of your experiences.

> If you spend time with your children, the church planting experience can be incredible for them.

Final Thoughts

In church planting, you set the culture. So make it as family friendly as possible. For example, I did not make evening appointments until after 8:00 p.m. I told people, "Having dinner with my family and putting my children to bed is very important to me. Therefore, I can meet you after 8:00 p.m." I also did not schedule evening meetings. We met early in the morning. Take responsibility for your family and do what needs to be done. Your family and new church will both benefit.

As important as bedtimes are to children, dinner times are to families. Don't sacrifice family intimacy on the altar of traveling soccer teams. Limit the amount of extracurricular activities in your children's lives. We have found time around the table to be essential in loving one another. We listen to one another's days, laugh together, and enjoy the gift of family. Biblically, we see the importance of table fellowship. It was important to Jesus, despite the criticism of the religious leaders. It was important to the early church. Don't relegate it to a holiday activity. Sit down together regularly and be the family church God desires.

Sit down together regularly and be the family church God desires.

Besides the regular dinnertime together, build in times to get away as a family. Some of our best memories are adventures we have had all over the country. Like our relationships with God, our spouse, and each child, our families will benefit as we leave the routine and get away.

There is more to family ministry than ministry to family. There is ministry with your family. Church planting presents ideal opportunities for your family to serve together. But don't miss your primary callings. Love God. He has created us for relationship with Him. Love your wife. She is your helpmate. Next to Jesus Christ, there is no greater gift you can give your children than a godly marriage. Love your children. They are gifts from God and teach us so much about Him. From that healthy church in your home, allow God to build His church in your community, a church against which the powers of darkness will not prevail.

Church planting presents ideal opportunities for your family to serve together.

[1] All Scripture quotations are taken from the *New International Version* unless otherwise noted.

[2] John Piper, *Desiring God* (Sisters, OR: Multnomah Books, 1996).

[3] Gary Chapman, The *Five Love Languages* (Chicago: Northfield Publishing, 1995).

A veteran church planter and pastor for over twenty years, **Dr. Tom Jones** is a widely sought after new church development coach, consultant, assessor, seminar leader and teacher, and mentor. He has a Doctor of Ministry Degree from United Theological Seminary in Dayton, Ohio, with an emphasis in church planting. Tom received his Master of Divinity Degree from Emmanuel School of Religion and his Bachelor of Arts Degree from Milligan College. Among other things, he now directs the Supervised Ministerial Experience (SME) Program, teaches in the Christian Ministries area at Emmanuel School of Religion in Johnson City, Tennessee, and is Director of Recruitment and Assessment for Southeast Stadia, a national church planting movement. Tom and his wife Debbie led the church planting teams at SouthBrook Christian Church in Dayton, Ohio, and Princeton Community Church in Princeton, New Jersey. They have two children, Melanie and Tom. Tom can be reached at **jonest@esr.edu**.

Show Me the Money!
Financing a New Church

I received a call from John late one night saying he was in the hospital in Princeton, New Jersey. He was suffering from a painful and fast-growing illness known as *Flesh Eating Disease*. John scratched his elbow during a pickup basketball game at the local YMCA, and a few days later he found himself in the emergency room with the dreaded disease. At one point the infection was growing at the rate of one inch per hour, and John was in danger of losing his arm and maybe even his life. John asked if I could come and pray for him. I rushed to the hospital and prayed. John, his wife, and I spent many hours together that night. The next day John was scheduled to have surgery to cut away the infected tissue. When the doctors examined him further, they were surprised to find that the infection had stopped growing and John was stable. When the doctor gave John the good news, he said, "We don't know why this happened." John responded by saying, "What do you mean you don't know what happened? I'll tell you what happened. It was a . . . miracle! That's what happened." It wasn't long before I baptized John into Christ in a friend's outdoor hot tub. He became a leader in our drama ministry and his family was involved in almost every aspect of our new church.

Why do I share this story about John in a chapter about finances? Because Princeton Community Church would not have been in existence to minister to John and his family if it had not been for the generous financial gifts of God's people. When I think of John and others like John who are being reached in the name of Christ through new churches, I become passionate. I want to share John's story with Christians everywhere, and shout that famous phrase from the movie *Jerry McGuire*, "SHOW ME THE MONEY!"

New churches require money. It's plain and simple. The first few years are particularly important because they set the tone for years to come. If a new church does not implement a strategy to raise resources, failure is almost certain. For the most part, in our society it takes money to start, maintain, and grow healthy churches. Don't apologize for resource-raising. It's not a dirty thought; rather, it's a biblical concept.

If a new church does not implement a strategy to raise resources, failure is almost certain.

Building a Healthy Financial Base

How are churches initially financed?

1. In the **Mother Church** concept, one church fully finances a new church start. The mother church gives birth to the baby church, and just like a parent, it is responsible for the new baby (and its finances) until it can survive on its own.

2. The **Association** method of starting churches involves a group of churches and individuals cooperating to start new churches. Each participant in the association is interested in church planting, but may not be strong enough financially to support a new church alone. When these churches band together, however, they create a strong financial base, enabling them to start new congregations.

3. Although accomplished in various ways unique to each denomination, the key for **Denominational** church planting rests in the particular denomination's understanding that funds must be set aside for new church development. This can be accomplished through districts, states, or on a national level. Thankfully, growing denominations have come to understand the urgency of church planting.

4. The **Partnership** concept is perhaps the newest solution in financing church planting. This idea is expressed when two or more groups join for a particular project. The idea is becoming increas-

ingly popular as well-churched areas look to start new congregations outside their area or state.

The team concept of church planting complements the partnership concept. For example, each partner would be responsible to finance one team member and would share start-up costs. Perhaps a denomination and a Mother Church could become partners or two associations could join hands. The partnership idea creates exciting possibilities and promotes a Kingdom mentality.

5. **Self-support** church planting is probably the toughest financially. In this model, a church planter personally raises full support. It can happen a number of ways. One avenue is to be bivocational. This is where church planters support themselves and the church with employment outside the church. Bivocational church planters are increasing in number, particularly in ethnic churches. In comparison, some independent church planters raise support the same as independent foreign missionaries. They seek financial support from friends, relatives, and churches but are independent of any formal organization's oversight.

The list above is by no means comprehensive. In fact, for church planting multiplication movements to evangelize the world, even more creative methods of funding must be put into practice.

Resource-Raising Suggestions for New Churches

1. Make sure you are clear about your call and vision.

It is incredibly difficult to raise resources for any project you are not passionate about. Many church planters fear raising funds. When they express that fear to me, I always ask them, "Has God called you to start this new church? If He has, then what's the problem?" Called planters lie awake at night dreaming about how the Lord will make His vision for their new church a reality. That includes dreaming about ways to finance the project. However, the opposite is also true. If you simply look at this ministry as a job, don't attempt to raise funds. Your vision will not be compelling and God's people will not finance it. Get another job, but don't plant a church. Questions that help to clarify your call and vision include:

▶ What do I feel called to do?
▶ Where am I called to do it?

❱ Why there?

❱ Why me?

❱ When are we going to do it?

❱ How will we do this?

❱ Who is partnering with us?

❱ How much money will it take?

❱ How can others partner with us?

❱ What are we going to ask of partners?

2. Start with a team, and then require every member of the team to raise funds.

If at all possible, a new church should start with a team. Each member of the team should be required to raise resources with no exceptions. Why? The network of support is expanded, more money can be raised, and it shows the team member is not just looking for a job but has been called by God to be a part of your church planting team. Team members can include bivocational workers, students, volunteers and part-time team members. I believe team church planting leads to financial independence sooner than solo church plants.

Team church planting leads to financial
independence sooner than solo church plants.

---

3. Create a quality communication piece that clearly states who you are, what you want to do, and what you want the giver to do.

It is essential that you take the time, effort, and expense to create a brochure that paints a vision for your project. Donors need something tangible in their hands that gives them a reason to make a donation, and explains the giving process. I suggest you make tangible suggestions to the giver in the brochure by asking them to give for __one year __two years __three years and asking them to commit monthly to give __$500 __$200 __$100 __$50 __$25 _____ other amount. It should be clear where to send the gift. There also should be a process explained that makes the giver feel confident their donation will be well received, receipted, and dispersed for God's work.

4. Make an exhaustive list of individuals (e.g., friends, relatives, classmates, acquaintances), churches, and organizations that might support you.

This step might be the most important one. This list includes the future financial and prayer partners for your new work. Make the

159

list as long as possible. The key word is *network*. Who have you, your spouse, team members, family members, good friends and others interested in the work known that might be willing to support the church plant? Be creative. You will be surprised by the number of people, churches, Sunday School classes, and other groups who will support your work simply because they were asked.

5. Once you create the list, work the list!

It's all about relationships. Develop relationships with the people and groups on your list so they know they are integral partners in this God-ordained project. Help people understand this is an opportunity for them to be involved in a God-thing. You do this through letters, telephone calls, breakfast or lunch meetings, small group meetings, church presentations, videos, e-mails, and other forms of communication.

> ### Help people understand this is an opportunity for them to be involved in a God-thing.

6. Ask for continued support (monthly) and one-time gifts.

Ideally, you'd like to have as many monthly donors as possible. This gives your new work a broad base of financial support that can be counted on. However, one-time gifts are also needed. Many wealthy people give large one-time gifts each year. Every gift, large or small, is essential to your financial success.

7. Have in mind what you want churches or individuals to give. Ask for a specific amount, and always ask for more than you think you will get.

Givers will appreciate a specific request. It gives them a definite amount to discuss and pray about. You will always get more money by being specific. The individual or church will always fall back to a lesser amount if you make no suggestions.

8. Don't give up if someone says, "no." Ask again and keep asking.

When raising funds for the two churches I started, I never took "no" as a final "no." It was just "no" for right now, and I would begin to think about how I could turn the "no" into a "yes." I couldn't comprehend how anyone would say "no." Therefore, I was just not communicating it in a way that would allow them to say "yes." Persistence pays huge dividends.

9. When someone says, "yes," overcommunicate your thanks.

One of the greatest criticisms of mission organizations all over the world is they fail to say "thanks." Shame on us if we make the same mistake. Every person or organization that gives a gift has the right to feel his or her gift is valued and appreciated. If you take this step seriously, most individuals and churches will give to your new church well beyond what they committed.

10. Send updates about what's going on. Communication is everything.

Supporters should know how their dollars are being invested. Send updates through mail, e-mail, web sites, and other means of communication. Tell stories of real people who are being won to Christ because the donor has partnered with your new church. Communicate needs, prayer praises, and concerns. I promise your financial partners will respond positively.

Tell stories of real people who are being won to Christ because the donor has partnered with your new church.

---

11. Always ask supporters to come visit. Always ask them to pray. Communicate that you don't just want their money.

Remember, you are building relationships and partnerships. It's not just about money. A criticism of mission organizations and churches is, "They just want my money." Overcoming that criticism requires you to show you covet partnership and want prayer and other input from supporters. This is really a three-way relationship between God, the giver, and you. Ask individuals, families, and church groups to visit. They will rarely come, but if they do, they will support you with greater passion and commitment. When they see and experience a new church's set-up and teardown process they move to another level of support and commitment.

12. People have different pockets for different things. Be creative in trying to get people to open their pockets.

Christians will give out of various giving pockets. These pockets include regular support for salaries and operational expenses, children's ministries, teen programs, land or building needs (including renovation of a leased or purchased space), worship ministry needs, and others. Money not received from certain pockets will be lost. Therefore, be creative when you ask. For example, every new church should have a baby church shower. This is where the new church leadership creates a list of needed items (large and small), and asks individuals, groups and churches to send a donation to cover the cost of items listed. This kind of creative fundraising always gets people to open different pockets.

13. Make a goal to be self-supporting within 2-5 years, and communicate that to supporters.

It is healthy for every new church to create a strategy for becoming self-supporting. It is important for the new church to take responsibility for its finances as soon as possible. This accomplishment is a spiritual mark for the church plant. Additionally, outside supporters appreciate the notion that they don't have to give to this project until the Lord returns, and they also feel good knowing this particular mission has a plan to be financially independent.

14. Have a good system of receiving and receipting gifts. Communicate that system to supporters.

As mentioned earlier, donors want to know their gifts are in good hands. It is essential that the church planting team or organization have a credible system of receiving and receipting. This plan should be overcommunicated to potential and current supporters. The church planter should never be responsible for the physical receiving and receipting of money. The lead planter is responsible to make sure a system is in place, but should stay away from handling finances. For example, gifts should never be received at a planter's home address. There should be a post office box or, better yet, an organization responsible for this task. When financial systems are all done aboveboard and are communicated well to financial partners, all the potential risk is taken out of the financial picture.

Ten Principles That Lead to Financial Independence

Two important questions in church planting are, "How do we become financially self-supporting? And how does our church build a solid financial base?" Let me share with you ten principles that help new churches answer these questions.

1. Balanced, biblical stewardship training creates a spiritually mature church.

If a church plant wants to start a church that will become spiritually mature, they first need to produce spiritual people. Teaching biblical stewardship does just that. Stewardship entails "the proper management of my whole life in order to enhance the kingdom of God." New churches must teach this concept from the onset. Usually, if this concept is practiced from birth, there will not be long periods of financial trouble in the church. Practicing stewardship encourages people to be not only fiscally responsible, but also to be good managers in all areas of their lives. It helps them discover their spiritual gifts (1 Corinthians 12), increases their faith, and encourages them to be active participants in the Lord's church. Proper stewardship teaching challenges people to discover where they fit within the local church family. People who are active and involved in ministry are almost always sacrificial givers. In doing so, they become partners in the gospel.

If a church plant wants to start a church that will become spiritually mature, they first need to produce spiritual people.

The main emphasis in stewardship training should always be the person and not the purse. For instance, don't only focus on how the local church will benefit, but also give attention to what stewardship will do for the person and his or her family. Concentrate on changing the person.

When teaching stewardship, it is important to stress three biblical truths. Together, these three principles create spiritual people and spiritual churches.[1]

- God is the owner while I am a manager.
- Stewardship begins with loving rather than giving. I can give without loving, but I can't love without giving. Love asks how much can I give? Legalism, on the other hand, looks for how little I can give. There must be a base of love before grateful giving can occur.
- Stewardship starts with present resources.

2. Communicate the vision of the church over and over again.

Money is never the problem in stewardship! Instead, a lack of

God-sized dreams is the problem. Proverbs 29:18 states, "Where there is no vision, the people perish" (KJV). The people aren't the only thing that perishes with no vision—so do the bucks! Church planters must have a God-directed vision for where the new church is going. They must dare to dream, and then share the dream in an exciting way with everyone who will listen. Big dreams attract big dollars. There are many ways to communicate a vision. Internet-based communication, newsletters, bulletins, a statement of purpose, and informal lunches are just a sampling of how dreams can be shared with others.[2] Dare to dream big, not because of what you can do, but because of what God can do through His people.

> Dare to dream big, not because of
> what you can do, but because of
> what God can do through His people.

3. Develop leaders who are models in giving.

Leadership is influence. "People do what people see."[3] If leaders model sacrificial giving, others will follow. A church cannot rise higher than its leaders. A person should never be a part of an official leadership team if not committed financially to the church.

The leader-model principle begins with the church planter. In I Chronicles 29, King David publicly announces how much he will give. He provides the model. The church planter cannot expect people in the new church to give sacrificially if their guide is not personally willing to do it. If leaders do not model sacrificial giving, they should not expect their church to be blessed financially.

> If leaders do not model sacrificial giving, they should
> not expect their church to be blessed financially.

So, how can a new church leader model sacrificial giving? Testimonies are a great way for leaders to express personal experience in giving. Effective testimonies should follow the outline below:

- ❯ An expression of love and gratitude to God
- ❯ An expression of love for the local church
- ❯ An expression of excitement about the church's future
- ❯ The personal process used to make the stewardship decision
- ❯ For maximum effectiveness, it is good to share specific amounts

Challenge the congregation to give serious consideration to what God would have them give.[4]

4. Be a generous-minded, giving church from the very beginning.

God will not bless a stingy mind-set. He blesses us so that we can pass it on to others. John Maxwell states, "The greatness of the church is not judged by what comes in the offering plate on Sunday. The greatness of a church (in terms of money and people) is based on what goes out."[5] The Lord blesses a church that is a channel for money and ministry. Begin by establishing a well-balanced mission program. Many church planting organizations require their church plants from day one to give a percentage of their offerings back to church planting. This principle finances church planting multiplication movements.

The Lord blesses a church that is a channel for money and ministry.

5. Teach committed, sacrificial giving at membership.

There has to be a time when people make a commitment to faithful stewardship. Membership is the time when commitment has to begin.[6] It can begin sooner, particularly in a new church; however, it should begin no later than membership. Consider teaching biblical stewardship in a new members' class, emphasizing that stewardship involves more than money. It involves a way of life.

Churches should ask for concrete commitments. If you don't ask, you won't receive. By asking people to give, you are actually doing them a favor. The Bible is clear about blessings received through giving (Luke 6:38). "Your church will be hurt more by those who would have said 'yes,' but weren't asked, than those who were asked and said 'no.'"[7]

6. John Maxwell stresses that if you want more money or more talents, find more pockets.[8]

Creatively survey your environment, looking for more pockets such as:

> ▶ **People who attend church, but are not good stewards**—In most congregations, a large percentage of the people are not reaching their potential in giving.

▶ **People outside the church**—Attract more people. After all, more people means more pockets. A good evangelism program is one of the best assets a healthy stewardship program has. New people bring new money and new talents!

▶ **Present givers**—Challenge and educate present givers to raise their giving. Encourage people who have never tithed to begin. Challenge others to go beyond the tithe and give according to grace.

Some churches have more defined pockets. Most church members will give differently to various pockets. These pockets include daily operation expenses, new church work, international missions, social concerns, higher education, and others. All of the above areas are important and should be utilized. However, money in one pocket usually won't be given to another. Money not received from these pockets will be lost; therefore, you have to ask. Once a pocket is opened, it will open again, and again, and again!

7. Keep congregational morale high.

Without a positive spirit, it is very difficult to remain healthy financially. From a financial standpoint, how stewardship is taught will influence morale considerably. Giving should be taught as a response to grace and not from a legalistic perspective. Christians should come to view stewardship as an act of worship that benefits them. The goal is to lead people to discover the joy of giving by showing that abundant living begins with abundant giving.

> From a financial standpoint, how stewardship is taught will influence morale considerably.

Decreased offerings are indicators of low morale. If someone plans to leave a church, they stop giving first. The higher the morale is, the higher the giving will be.[9]

8. Keep the congregation tuned in.

All churches, particularly new churches, need to work overtime to keep communication flowing. This principle relates to congregational morale in that people seem to be down on what they're not up on. With this in mind, financial communication is essential. When reporting on finances, three things should be emphasized.

▶ Facts—where do we stand?

❭ Focus—where are we going with this money?

❭ Faces—who benefits? Always put faces with money.[10]

In addition, go overboard when thanking people for gifts. Be creative and thank them in many different ways. They like to know their gifts are appreciated.

9. After the first year, schedule an annual stewardship emphasis month.

A new church should plan its first stewardship emphasis month sometime after the first year. This important step will help the church become self-supporting within a few years.

This principle works. It has been proven successful in many new church contexts, and if planned in the right way, it can work almost anywhere. Scheduling an annual stewardship month makes a constant plea for finances unnecessary. Consider the following essentials to a successful stewardship month:

❭ Prayerful planning times

❭ Challenging theme

❭ Right time of the year

❭ Motivating sermon series

❭ Testimonies

❭ Handouts that communicate well

❭ Follow-up letters[11]

11. Be creative when raising funds.

Think outside the box. We were so sold out to fulfilling our mission in Princeton, New Jersey, we raised funds through a number of creative ways. We held an annual Talent and Gifts Auction where we underwrote the Children's Ministry budget. People in the church gave talents (chef, electrical work, carpentry, and others) or gifts (timeshares, purebred puppies, airline tickets, golf outings, and others). We also solicited items from the local business community. Then we had a great meal one Sunday after church along with the auction. Every year we raised over $15,000. It was also an awesome fellowship time. I remember one guy bidding $100 against me for an elderly lady's pie! Another idea is a golf or tennis marathon. We raised over $20,000 in our annual golf marathon. Also, every church should have a year-end giving campaign for special projects. Gifts in kind are also important. For example, each congregation should be able to receive stock gifts. Giving appreciated stock gifts is a double benefit to the giver because they get the tax deduction of the stock's value, but do not have to pay tax on the appreciation. A word of caution, don't do anything that goes against your particular congregation's theological beliefs. Given that caution, the bottom line is—BE CREATIVE!

Conclusion

Creating a healthy financial base is absolutely essential to the success of a new church and to the future multiplication movement the church is committed to being a part of. Obviously, rising costs in the United States and around the world make this goal increasingly difficult. Creativity, planning, sensitivity, good biblical teaching on stewardship, and reliance on God's Spirit will help make this seemingly impossible task a reality. Finances should never be a stumbling block when multiplying the Lord's church. He will provide the means if we have the faith. I wrote about my friend John at the beginning of this chapter. Raising resources is all about people like John. He and others like him deserve our very best efforts. Don't you agree?

Finances should never be a stumbling block when multiplying the Lord's church.

---

[1] John Maxwell, *Increase Your Church's Giving in 1990* (Pasadena, CA: Pastor's Update, 1989) sound cassette.

[2] Ibid.

[3] Ibid.

[4] Rick Warren, *How to Raise Money for Ministry and Property* (Mission Viejo, CA: The Encouraging Word, no date), sound cassette.

[5] Maxwell, *Increase.*

[6] Ibid.

[7] Warren, *Raise Money.*

[8] Maxwell, *Increase.*

[9] Ibid.

[10] Ibid.

[11] Ibid.

John E. Wasem is married and the father of three. Included in his 30 years of ministry leadership is serving as the founding/lead pastor of Suncrest Christian Church in St. John, Indiana (southeast of Chicago), since 1994. He has directed the Master of Arts in Ministry degree for church planting at Lincoln Christian College and Seminary in Lincoln, Illinois, since 1994. In 1998 he developed the New Church Leadership Certificate Program dedicated to providing affordable, high-quality training for church planters as well as emerging new church leaders. John's contact information: **john.wasem@suncrest.org** or **www.churchleader.net** or **www.suncrest.org**.

Coaching: Getting beyond New Church Mediocrity

*T*he Chicago Bulls of the 1990s were legendary. The team had two of the 50 greatest players of all time. However, it was clearly the transition to Phil Jackson as the head coach in 1992 that transformed this sleepy NBA franchise into a dynasty. Coach Jackson was able to blend superstars and role-players into a united, focused team that accomplished history-making results.

The Chicago Cubs have not won a World Series title since 1908. Before 2003, they had not won a postseason series since 1948. The excuses range from the "curse of the billy goat" to a lack of true passion under pressure. However, with the acquisition of a proven coach and leader of players, Dusty Baker, the 2003 Cubs fell just one late-inning questionable call short of a trip to the World Series. Everyone, from players to fans, media to management, agreed that the major difference for the Cubs in 2003 was coaching.

All leaders greatly benefit from intentional, consistent and regular coaching. However, in the specialized environment of the new church, coaching should not be viewed as a luxury or an optional "add-on" as funding and time permits. Rather, it should be viewed as a nonnegotiable essential to enabling a new project to launch, get into proper orbit, and have a productive, fruitful mission. Sports championships and, even more importantly, the eternal impact of new church ministry, depends more on the coaches than the players.

> **Both sports championships and success in church ministry depend more on the coaches than the players.**

The classic biblical relationship of Saul of Tarsus and Barnabas recorded in the early chapters of Acts is marvelously instructive. Joseph of Cypress (nicknamed Barnabas) was a model influencer of people. He was a mentor and coach of the highest order. He saw great potential in Saul (the Apostle Paul) when other church leaders kept their distance. Even after his Damascus Road conversion (Acts 9:1-31) and his transformation into a zealous apologist for Christianity, he was still feared and shunned by Jews and Christian leaders alike. "But Barnabas took him and brought him to the apostles" (Acts 9:27).

Unintimidated by this brash convert, Barnabas invested in, vouched for, consistently gave guidance to, and patiently taught the gifted young "ecclesiastical entrepreneur" who would later be considered the greatest church planter ever. Most appropriately, Barnabas literally means "Son of Encouragement" (Acts 4:36). This name refers to "one called alongside to help." Barnabas was with Paul in the good times (Acts 13:2) and the tough times (Acts 13:50). He was confident and secure enough to disagree with his "rising star" protégé (Acts 15:36). He put the kingdom impact of the mission and team above himself as evidenced by the shift of leadership (Acts 11:26 and 13:50).

Mentoring is not a new phenomenon. It is as old as the legend of Odysseus, one of the Greek leaders in the Trojan War (1287 B.C.), who put his son in the trust of a mentor for his education and life development. However, a welcomed recognition of the value of mentoring in leadership development and productivity has occurred in the last two decades.

> **A welcomed recognition of the value of mentoring in leadership development and productivity has occurred in the last two decades.**

Coaching is just one of many specialized expressions of mentoring. On the mentoring spectrum that ranges from highly intentional, active mentoring to more unintentional, passive mentoring, coaching certainly leans strongly toward the active end of the scale. Coaches develop skills and motivate people to use their giftedness well. A quality coach knows every nuance of his or her "sport" inside and out. They are veterans. They know the agonies and ecstasies of "playing" that "sport" from firsthand experience. However, most of all, they have a burning desire to help new "players" understand, embrace, and enjoy the very essence of the "game." They want to see the "sport" propagated after they are gone. They know that the best way to accomplish this is to reproduce themselves in emerging leaders.

As somewhat of a veteran of church planting with 20 years of involvement, I enthusiastically testify that my levels of fulfillment, excitement, anticipation, and sheer joy are just as high, if not higher, when I witness the ministries of my coaching protégés as it was nearly a decade ago when I was privileged to plant Suncrest Christian Church in suburban Chicago. My hope is that the majority of the church planters I have coached will, in the near future, be coaches themselves. This will be a "win-win-win" for the new church project, the planter, and the "player-coach," my protégé.

Working Definitions

> "Mentoring is a relational experience through which one person empowers another by sharing God-given resources."

In the current generation, few people have contributed more significantly to the church's understanding of mentoring than Dr. Robert Clinton of Fuller Theological Seminary in Pasadena, California. His books and articles in this field are prolific. Consider his fundamental definition: "Mentoring is a relational experience through which one person empowers another by sharing God-given resources."[1] Mentors tend to have certain important characteristics in common:

- An innate ability to see potential in others

- The freedom of heart and mind to be flexible in dealing with diversity in people and circumstances
- The wisdom and patience to permit a leader to develop
- The perspective and vision to help the protégé see "down the road"
- The temperament and ability to encourage and empower without sacrificing truth and reality
- An uncanny sense of timing and sensitivity to the Spirit's leading
- Awareness of resource networks to which the protégé can be directed

A coach is a specialized form of mentor. Coaching is a form of apprenticeship that demands practice and feedback. The coaching process includes four dimensions.

1. **Demonstrating.** It is important for a coach to demonstrate a skill or model a particular leadership trait in such a clear and compelling way that the protégé will both learn and be motivated to act. In some cases, the coach and the planter might observe an example of the desired result in another new church ministry.

2. **Debriefing.** The bulk of learning and inspiring will take place when the coach and planter discuss the focus of the demonstration. Insights regarding application should surface in abundance during debriefing times.

3. **Doing.** When the planter puts a strategic process or vision emphasis into practice, evaluation of that action, the planter's skill, and the timing will prove invaluable. It is generally advised that such action be in a nonthreatening or low-risk context whenever possible. This type of "test piloting" is very prudent and advisable.

People generally have a tendency to attempt to live up to the expectations of those whom they greatly admire and respect.

4. **Releasing.** After additional debriefing that provides clarification, correction, enhancement, encouragement, and seeking God in prayer together, it is appropriate for the coach to affirm

and release the planter to use the skill or ministry tool. Coaches must remember that people generally have a tendency to attempt to live up to the expectations of those whom they greatly admire and respect.

Also, there are five predictable dynamics that should be present in a coaching relationship.

1. **Attraction.** In order for the coaching effort to be fruitful, there must be a mutually recognizable attraction affecting the coach and the planter. A coach will be strongly motivated if he or she is matched with a protégé who has significant potential, a strong hunger to develop, and a passion to succeed. On the other hand, a church planter will naturally learn more and develop more completely if matched with a coach that has a great deal of expertise to offer and ability to impart it.

2. **Relationship.** Effective coaching is an individualized matter. Therefore, the relational aspect of coaching is highly significant. As with any relationship, trust is the key. If a coach wants a protégé to develop and excel, it will require far more than simply teaching skills and applying strict discipline. This is the reason that I recommend the coach to planter ratio be kept low. Rarely should it exceed 1:3. Adequate time and energy cannot be realistically invested in more than a few protégés at a time. The bond of a coach and "player" is a major link in an effective coaching "chain."

3. **Accountability.** Although typically the church planting coach is not expected to ensure daily project accountability (that is the role of the project management team or evangelizing association), a coach must hold the planter accountable regarding assignments given by the coach. Failure to do so can destroy credibility.

4. **Empowerment.** A coach must have standards to judge the progress of a planter and the planter's project. Once a protégé has sufficiently mastered a particular aspect of leadership, a wise coach will be certain that empowerment has been experienced. One way to accomplish this is for the coach to utilize the planter in assisting other planters who need help in the aspect of ministry the protégé has mastered.

5. **Responsiveness.** Unresponsiveness is a protégé trait that cannot be tolerated. Chronic tardiness for coaching appointments, lack of engagement with the coach during appointments, absence of proactivity by the planter in suggesting topics for coaching focus, lack of follow-through on assignments and lack of planter-initiated communication between appointments are behaviors that warn of a waning level of protégé responsiveness. To tolerate any of these may appear to be an expression of compassion and mercy, but inevitably adds to the ineffectiveness of the planter and the new church project.

The values of good coaches include excellence, teamwork, discipline, and fundamentals.

In the coaching paradigm, Steven L. Ogne and Thomas P. Nebel identify several distinct values and behaviors that quality coaches will embrace and demonstrate.[2] The values shared by good coaches include: excellence, teamwork, discipline, and fundamentals. The behaviors that should be evident in the lives of coaches include: objectivity, challenging, caring, encouraging, motivating, listening, strategizing, and celebrating. Ogne and Nebel also identify seven steps to effective coaching.

1. **Listen actively.** A coach who does more than 35% of the talking in a coaching session is most likely minimizing effectiveness. A good coach prepares well for a given coaching appointment (see Coaching Log Form at **www.collegepress.com/ churchplanting**). The maintenance of a thorough record of coaching interactions, correspondence, and project reports is essential. By reviewing the last report, the coach should be able to identify the issues that ought to be addressed in the next coaching appointment. The planter should submit in advance the agenda of topics needing to be addressed. The coach's job is to know the crucial matters needing focused attention at any given juncture as well as to ask the necessary questions that lead to the discovery of solutions, new strategies, and fresh outlooks. Overall, the coach must be more of a listener than a talker. He or she must listen to the feelings and attitudes of the protégé with special attentiveness.

The coach must be more of a listener than a talker.

The impact of your coaching with a given planter will depend more on your relationship with the protégé than it does on your level of expertise or the planter's level of proficiency. When a church planter is confident that respect and value are being extended, the coaching payoff is significant. The receptivity of the protégé is increased. A coach can accomplish this best by being an unselfish, careful listener. Avoid overtalking by "storytelling" with your planter. Coach by being fully "in the moment." Listen with great care and focus so that you can ask pertinent questions. A common mistaken management practice results in listening to a protégé for a brief time (normally under 30 seconds), and then immediately attempting to fix the problem. Following this model will greatly undermine the coaching process.

Another important aspect to being an effective and caring coach is to listen empathetically to your church planter. Make it your top priority to understand your planter rather than making sure that your protégé understands and obeys you. The key is diagnosing before prescribing. Too easily, veterans impulsively thrust solutions on a planter due to impatience, laziness, or arrogance. This is counterproductive as well as potentially harmful to the planter and the new church.

To demonstrate true caring and interest, a coach would be well served to consider these additional suggestions:

➤ **Be accessible.** As necessary, clearly define the boundaries for your coaching relationship. It will greatly enhance your credibility with your planter to provide faster access to you than others may normally have. I usually designate a certain day of the week for coaching to balance my multiple roles as a church leader, professor, and coach. However, I am more than willing to connect with my protégé on other days and even more than once per week if needed. If the boundaries were to ever be violated for unimportant or unhealthy reasons, then I would immediately discuss the matter with the planter and seek to restore balance.

➤ **Stay in touch.** Make an effort to keep current with your protégé's family as well as project personnel. An occasional "surprise" phone call, card, handwritten letter, or gift demonstrates that the planter is not "out of sight and out of mind" except on appointment days. If you are coaching a planter over a long period of time, then be certain to make field visits on at least a quarterly basis in the early stages of the new church project. After the first year, this frequency could be decreased by 25% and then by 50% beyond the second year.

> **Phone calls, cards, letters, and the like demonstrate that the planter is not "out of sight and out of mind."**

Coaching should be maintained for at least the first two years of new church public operation as well as during the prelaunch phase, which can be as long as one year itself. Not all church planters are "wired" to think beyond the catalytic start of a new church venture. These planters could be very effective coaches for the start-up segment of projects, but make undesirable choices for long-term project coaches. A quality, long-term coach is a planter who has successfully navigated the leadership shifts necessary to go from prelaunch to launch to ministry development to leadership development to the strategic development necessary to sustain new church vitality and momentum into the fifth year and beyond.

2. **Celebrate wins.** In the midst of delays, transitions, and "closed doors," there will always be successes, even though they appear to be small and seemingly insignificant. A wise coach will be alert for those "wins." He or she should be quick and thoughtful in celebrating them with the protégé. The progress may be related to staff, funding, facilities, marketing, evangelism, attendance, or leadership procurement. On the other hand, it may be progress on a personal level involving spouse, children, health, housing, professional recognition, or relational breakthrough.

One of the ways to sustain new church vitality is to maintain a church culture of celebration. Church planters can miss this dynamic due to tunnel vision and the pressure of constant attention to details. Coaches must model for planters the value of regular, appropriate, refreshing celebration. Both the new church and the church planter will greatly benefit.

One of the ways to sustain new church vitality is to maintain a church culture of celebration.

3. **Care Personally.** It is best to begin a coaching appointment by asking questions that help the coach assess the state of the planter's personal life. Listen for the unspoken cues that come from tone of voice, posture, word choice, and energy level. The freedom to delve into the personal realm of the planter should be secured in the planter/coach covenant that is established at the outset of the relationship. This freedom will be enhanced by a consistent embodiment of true caring demonstrated first by the coach and then reciprocated by the planter. Make note of specific needs. Pray faithfully for the planter. The new church leader will definitely know if you are doing so without your even having to communicate your thoughts. Note crucial dates related to needs and take the initiative to check in with the planter to demonstrate your concern. This includes reoccurring significant dates such as their birthday, wedding anniversary, and church birth anniversary.

   The coach should not feel the pressure to meet every need of the protégé. Discretion must be exercised to avoid unhealthy dependencies. However, a caring coach will gladly help the planter network into resources. A coach is not charged with the responsibility of solving the planter's problems, but rather with strengthening the protégé's ability to develop plans and solutions.

4. **Strategize Plans.** An unwise coach will propose strategies to deal with specific challenges or opportunities faced by a planter. Often the recommendations come from the coach's personal experience in new church leadership. The suggested solutions may be culturally out-of-sync with the protégé's context. In this case, it is far better to ask questions and inject creative alternatives for the purpose of helping the planter

devise an independent plan. Utilizing experience, the coach should help the planter eliminate roadblocks, maximize resources, and focus priorities.

5. **Develop Skills.** It is always better if the coach and protégé can observe, learn, and practice ministry or leadership skills together. This is not always possible. However, for a coach and planter to attend training events, seminars, and conferences together is a tremendous relationship builder and will increase the insight of the coach. A conference call involving the coach, protégé, and an outside expert recruited by the coach is a tremendous way to benefit from a wide range of quality resource people. Interactive web chats can be used in this way as well. The coaching site—**www.churchleader.net**— offers monthly web chats for church planting leaders and team members focused on various topics. This is a tremendous way to inexpensively and conveniently link up with peers and experts on topics of mutual concern and interest.

6. **Develop Character.** Character deficiencies or attitude issues, not skill-related weaknesses, are often at the heart of leadership ineffectiveness. Good coaches help the planter identify those deficiencies and issues.

Church planter assessment should be completed in advance of the new church project. The debriefing of that assessment by both coach and protégé early in the relationship will prove extremely valuable. Not all coaches are "on site" and therefore cannot provide mentoring and face-to-face coaching for character and leadership development. However, the trusted coach may be in the optimal position to encourage personal coaching and even professional counseling to release blessing into the life of the planter. A wise coach will seek to balance personal growth and ministry contribution. The latter will suffer if the former is neglected.

A wise coach will seek to balance personal growth and ministry contribution.

7. **Challenge Specifically.** The coach must be committed to gaining a thorough knowledge of the history and progress of a protégé's new church planting project. This perspective is

needed to challenge the planter in specific ways. A coach cannot ensure an honest adherence to the vision and values of the project unless he or she knows what those are. A good coach will not leave the coaching appointment with the "lion's share" of the assignments. Keep the ball in the protégé's court. Do not foster dependence. Rather, confirm specific "next steps" at the end of each appointment. With the next appointment, updates on each of those assignments should be given in response to the coach's questions. Do not permit a protégé to seize control of a coaching appointment and spend the majority of the time giving reports. This tactic is often a conscious or unconscious "control" move by the planter to avoid being asked the hard, important, and strategic questions by the coach. As an appointment concludes, always set the date, time, and place (in many cases it will be a "telephone number" in lieu of a "place") of the next appointment. If this is not possible, make it the protégé's responsibility to set the appointment.

The Future

The future of church planting will in part depend on the work and reproduction of new church leadership coaches. This challenge is intensified by errors in recruitment, accountability, and quality control. Recruiting and training church planters who are expected to evolve into church planting coaches can best address recruitment difficulties. If successful, this approach results in protégés who understand the importance and function of coaching, thus making them more receptive to the process. Planters who had positive, helpful coaching experiences will naturally be effective coaches themselves. Therefore, in any church planting system, the first wave of coaches must be well resourced and trained. These coaches must meet high standards in terms of the following:

⋄ Spiritual health
⋄ Personal and relational maturity
⋄ Passion for new church multiplication
⋄ Positive attitude and demeanor
⋄ Loyalty to and interest in the church planting group

 ✧ Respecter of unity and harmony
 ✧ Humble, servant-oriented spirit
 ✧ Reputation above reproach
 ✧ Demonstration of continuing learning in the field of new church leadership
 ✧ Availability and approachability
 ✧ Support from his/her current ministry leadership for this role
 ✧ Above average time manager

It is strongly recommended that coaches be compensated for their services. These funds may initially come from the sponsoring body, but should eventually come from the operational budget of the new church project. When a new church and church planter have a financial investment in the coaching service, the consistent use of the service is far more likely.

An efficient way to maximize the energies of the "coaches of the coaches" would be to have regular coaching clusters. There are many benefits to the coaching cluster approach:

 ✧ Development of peer network and accountability
 ✧ Cost-effective means of delivering skill training
 ✧ Guarantee of regular interaction for coaches
 ✧ Maximization of the coaches' time investment
 ✧ Synergy of idea and resource sharing
 ✧ Encouragement of prayer partnerships
 ✧ Improvement in quality control

Conclusion

"No man is an island, entire of itself; every man is a piece of the continent."
— **John Donne** (English poet, 1573–1631)

If a church planter feels like, desires to be, and by default is "an island," then that church planter is doomed to excessive stress, disappointment, and a lack of fruitfulness. May the future of church planting be characterized by leaders who desire, applaud, welcome, fund, and engage in high quality new church leadership coaching for the sake of the harvest.

To access the downloadable Coaching Log Form and Coaching Test, visit **www.collegepress.com/churchplanting**.

[1] J. Robert Clinton, *Connecting: The Mentoring Relationships You Need to Succeed in Life* (Colorado Springs, CO: NavPress, 1992) 12.

[2] Steven L. Ogne and Thomas P. Nebel, "Empowering Leaders through Coaching," audiocassette (Carol Stream, IL: Church Smart Publishing, 1995).

Phil Claycomb is a passionate advocate of church planting. Phil's father was a church planter, and Phil's earliest memories are of that new church. Phil and his wife Barb planted two churches in the suburbs of Chicago, and each church gave birth to a daughter church. Phil is currently the National Director of Planter Care for *Stadia: New Church Strategies*. Phil's current tasks involve the design and implementation of Stadia's training, mentoring, and coaching systems. Stadia's Planter Care system seeks to provide church planting couples the best care possible. Phil and Barb are the parents of two children.

The Hard Work of Contextualization

Oops! I Planted the Wrong Church.

The biggest challenge facing many church planters is not planting the church right, but planting the right church. It is possible to plant the wrong church. Some churches are a wrong fit for their community. Still others grow into something very different from what the church planter expected. While these churches fit the community, they are a wrong fit for the church planter. The bottom line is that church planters can find themselves saying, "Oops! I planted the wrong church."

How does this happen? Unfortunately, it is a simple thing to do. It happens when we forget or ignore one of our earliest childhood lessons. Most of us were taught how to safely cross the street: "Stop, look, and listen before you step off the curb." Church planters need to exercise the same cautious behavior before starting their churches. Missiologists refer to this as *contextualization*. The purpose of this chapter is to help you contextualize your ministry. It involves stopping, looking, and listening to the community context as well as God's particular calling on your life.

Church planters start the wrong church when they ignore contextualization and implement models of ministry that do not encourage them to stop, look, and listen.

Church planters start the wrong church
when they ignore contextualization.

Models of Ministry
The "Just Do It" Model

A "Just Do It" model of ministry does not encourage contextualization. As soon as a church planter makes the decision to start a new church, the adrenaline and vision motor start running overtime. The planter soon becomes overwhelmed by a wave of visions, dreams, hopes, and aspirations. The clamor for decisions-made and actions-taken becomes overwhelming. In the process, the church planter may not afford the time to slow down and contextualize.

Church planting is like trying to
drink from a fire hose or hopping
aboard a full-speed bullet train.

Church planting is a fast-paced affair. One planter said it was like trying to drink from a fire hose. Another said it was like hopping aboard a bullet train without it slowing down. During the launch phase of my most recent church plant I saw a bumper sticker that summarized exactly what I was feeling. It read, "Get in, sit down, shut up, and hang on!" I felt a tremendous pressure to get things done, to produce something—anything! It is hard to stop, look, and listen when you are running too fast.

As the pressure to "Just Do It" builds, the church planter must do the most counterintuitive thing imaginable. The new church leader must slow down and act deliberately. Every part of the planter's being may call for a rapid succession of decisions and actions, but the strong leader demonstrates leadership savvy by resisting this urge. Strong leaders discipline themselves to become students of their surroundings. Thomas Oden challenges us to study our context by saying, "Since the gospel addresses us in a particular here-and-now situation, rather than as a timeless abstraction, it is impossible properly to conceive of ministry apart from studied awareness of its current context."[1]

Our fast-changing context requires that we dismiss our assumed understanding of our here-and-now situation. Church planters need the attitude John Stott is said to have demonstrated when asked to address a conference on the topic, "What should the church say to the world?" Stott insisted that a prior question should be asked, "How can we listen to the world before we speak?"

A "Just Do It" rush to hasty action leaves leaders running blind. They do not stop, look, or listen to anything or anyone, and they often end up starting the wrong church.

The "Production" Model

A second approach to ministry is the "Production" model.[2] In this approach to ministry the church planter indiscriminately reproduces a familiar church model. This church planter does not ask, "What does this community need?" or, "What is my particular sense of calling?" Normally the planter simply reproduces familiar church behaviors and structures. Production-oriented leaders listen only to their past experience. These leaders should heed Leonard Sweet's warning that "to lead by traditional maps is to set a whole train of losses in motion."[3]

> "To lead by traditional maps is to set a whole train of losses in motion."

Francis Schaeffer, the noted lecturer and author, was credited with saying that if he had only one hour to share the gospel with a person, he would spend the first forty-five minutes finding out what the person believed about God and the last fifteen minutes presenting Christ from that basis.[4] This process of listening first and reacting second is starkly different from a production model of ministry. Production-oriented leaders assume that yesterday's solutions are today's answers.

The primary problem with the production model of ministry is not that the methods are old, but that the attitude is disrespectful. Church planters who do not listen are disrespectful of the people around them. "The one who witnesses, therefore, is to be a learner, a respectful inquirer of the culture. This is not something that can be done in a mechanical way. It is an attitude, an actual mode of living and interacting."[5] How can we expect strangers to listen to us if we are not willing to first listen to them?

It is vital that we perfect the art of listening. If we believe that lost people matter to God, we must assume that God will not have completely abandoned them prior to our arrival on the scene.

Because God has cared for them, He will have already been at work among them. His prior activity in preparing the community for the gospel opens further opportunities for the church planting ministry. God will have already placed latent growth opportunities in the immediate context. God's calling for the leader's ministry can be discerned by noticing where He has already been at work.

God's calling for the leader's ministry can be discerned by noticing where He has already been at work.

Church planters can earn a lot of good will by simply listening. I believe that evangelical church planters must go out of their way to listen. My experience with the unchurched has convinced me that many of them view evangelicals as pompous know-it-alls. In my most recent church plant, we jokingly adopted the following church motto: "We're evangelicals who try not to act like it." The churched people in my audience did not care for the motto; however, our seekers loved it! Before starting our church we conducted a series of focus groups with unchurched people. At each focus group meeting we hung a banner which read, "How do you spell respect?—L I S T E N!" We found that they were willing to tell us how to design a ministry to reach them. We also discovered that many of them were willing to jump in and help us get started. A little respect can go a long way!

The result of a production-oriented mind-set is that leaders deafen themselves to their constituents. These leaders often reproduce the mistakes of the past. Many church planters have discovered too late that they have reproduced the very church they thought they were leaving behind.

The "Sales" Model

The "Sales" model is a third way of doing ministry. The emphasis here is on simply gaining more customers for the new church. As one author put it, "Whereas the production approach will produce a product and attempt to defend it against any change, the sales approach will pick and choose a form of ministry it thinks it can sell."[6] The danger of a sales-orientation is that the leader is tempted to water down the message in order to attract more participants.

Sales-oriented church planters are often excellent listeners. They carefully assess the needs of the community and are very responsive to their constituents; however, their focus on the customer can leave them deaf to God's particular call for their ministry. Leaders who are overly sales-oriented risk being diverted from their calling.

> The danger of a sales-orientation is that the leader is tempted to water down the message in order to attract more participants.

We should remember that Jesus was an excellent salesman. He masterfully packaged His message in forms that fit His listeners. He went out of His way to be seeker-sensitive; however, Jesus' agenda was not to simply complete a sale. His agenda was to communicate as accurately as possible. While He would adapt His language and approach to each new situation, He never compromised His message. Jesus was sales-oriented but not sales-focused.

Millard Erickson identifies the right balance between sales orientation and faithfulness to the mission.

> What we are calling for here is not to make the message acceptable to all, particularly to those who are rooted in the secular assumptions of the time. There is an element of the message of Jesus Christ which will always be what Paul called a "scandal" or an offense (1 Corinthians 1:23). The gospel, for example, requires a surrender of the autonomy to which we tend to cling so tenaciously, no matter what age we live in. The aim, then, is not to make the message acceptable, but to make sure, as far as possible, that the message is at least understood.[7]

The "Copycat" Model

A fourth model of ministry is the "Copycat" approach. This approach almost always results in the church planter starting the wrong church. "Copycat" leaders turn a deaf ear to both the community and their own vision. Their focus is on listening to the vision of another leader. They are wholesale borrowers. Their vision, values, methodology, and even terminology are pilfered from someone else's God-given calling.

While all of us can legitimately learn from other leaders, copycats push borrowing too far. They shirk their responsibility to plant the church God has placed inside them, and willingly choose to pursue the vision God has given someone else. Copycats fail to appreciate the vast difference between planting the unique church God wants them to plant, one that is right for both the community and themselves as the leader, and planting some other leader's church. These leaders might successfully start a church, but not their church. It is someone else's church, and it is the wrong church for them.

The "Contextualization" Model

Fortunately, there is another model of ministry that results in the "right" church. This is the "Contextualization" model of ministry. It involves stopping, looking, and listening to both the community and God's particular call. Contextualization helps the church planter develop a balanced emphasis on marketing insights (responding to the community) and missional convictions (responding to God's call).

God modeled contextualization as He communicated with individuals throughout Scripture. As the author of Hebrews notes, God spoke to the forefathers through prophets; however, when He wished to communicate with the alien cultures of Egypt and Babylon, He communicated through dreams. Both the Egyptian and Babylonian cultures had a strong belief in the importance of dreams. God's means of communicating with Pharaoh was to send him a dream as well as a Hebrew interpreter, Joseph. God's means of communicating with Nebuchadnezzar was also through a dream and a Hebrew interpreter, Daniel. Both instances are examples of God communicating His message in a receptor-oriented fashion. The means by which God conveyed His message was selected so as to best fit the receiver.

Jesus also modeled the practice of stopping, looking, and listening. The incarnation is itself an example of contextualization. James Engel notes that Jesus and His followers "always began with a keen understanding of the audience and then adapted the message to the other person without compromising God's Word."[8] Jesus became one of us, knew us, and understood us. If Jesus spent thirty years stopping, looking, and listening before He started preaching, surely church planters can invest several months in careful study of their context.

If Jesus spent thirty years before He started preaching, surely church planters can invest several months in careful study of their context.

Most discussions of contextualization focus primarily on the community and responding to felt needs. This is good, but we cannot forget that contextualization also involves listening to God's specific calling for the leader.

A dual focus on the community and God's calling is implicit in the definition of contextualization in the *New Dictionary of Theology*. "Contextualization is a dynamic process of the church's reflection, in obedience to Christ and his mission in the world, on the interaction of the text as the word of God and the context as a specific human situation."[9] A tandem focus on community and calling is parallel to the comparison John Stott made between being contemporary and faithful. Stott noted, "it is comparatively easy to be faithful if we do not care about being contemporary, and easy also to be contemporary if we do not bother to be faithful. It is the search for a combination of truth and relevance which is exacting."[10]

The contextualization model of ministry is equally interested in the community and God's call, in being contemporary and faithful, in both truth and relevance, in marketing the gospel and being missionally faithful to God's purposes. Church planters who wish to start the right kind of church are committed to becoming "marketing-oriented and missionally focused" leaders. This is not an either/or choice. Church planters must understand and respond to community needs *and* God's missional call.

An Example of Marketing-Oriented, Mission-Focused Leadership

An excellent example of contextualization is found in the earliest history of the church. The unnamed church planters who planted the church in Antioch (Acts 11:19-21) did so after stopping, looking, and listening. It is hard for us to imagine how challenging it must have been to start a church in this ancient setting.

Rodney Stark gives an excellent description of the situation facing the church planters in Antioch, and how they responded to their context.[11] The city of Antioch was relatively small, measuring only two square miles. Yet nearly 150,000 people were packed within the two square miles. This breaks down to 117 people per acre. Compare Antioch with modern day Chicago (21 people per acre) and New York City (37 people per acre). The church planters were dealing with a congested and multiethnic context.

Several additional factors made the ministry environment of

Antioch even more challenging. Ancient buildings were not as tall as those we build today. The populace squeezed into short, compact buildings. In addition, much of the space in ancient cities was devoted to public buildings and parks. If Antioch was similar to other ancient cities up to 40% of the scarce space was devoted to public use. The populace had little actual living space. As a result, the functional density of Antioch was close to 195 persons per acre. A modern comparison would be Bombay (at 183 persons) and Calcutta (at 122).

This population density contributed to other factors that impacted the ministry context of Antioch. To put it bluntly, the city was filthy and unhealthy. Inhabitants shared their living space with livestock. Sewage systems were nonexistent. As Rodney Stark puts it, "Tenement cubicles were smoky, dark, often damp, and always dirty. The smell of sweat, urine, feces, and decay permeated everything; 'dust, rubbish, and filth accumulated; and finally bugs ran riot.'"[12] Sickness and plague were common. The death rate in ancient cities was so high that a steady and substantial inflow of population from rural areas was required to maintain the urban population.

Stark points out that "any accurate portrait of Antioch in New Testament times must depict a city filled with misery, danger, fear, despair, and hatred."[13] And yet it was in this dark situation that the church presented viable alternatives to the religions of the time. How? By contextualizing!

The early church planters stopped, looked, and listened to the community as well as their God-given calling. As a result of contextualizing, the early church planters offered the gospel as a solution to the felt needs of the populace while remaining true to their mission. They acted in marketing-oriented and missionally-focused ways.

First-century churches in urban centers like Antioch dealt with people who were often poor, unsettled, recently bereaved, and facing sickness and disease. The early churches developed reputations for providing charity to the many poor people who populated the cities. In the crowded settings of urban life, the churches created a new sense of community, so lacking among the many newly displaced residents. In a context full of sickness and death the church excelled in providing care for the sick and bereaved.

These three dominant characteristics of early Christianity—charity, community, and caring—grew out of a commitment to meeting the needs of the community and remaining faithful to God's mission. New churches faced the ministry challenges before them and created a ministry style marked by charity, community, and care. The residents of Antioch quickly discovered that Christian solutions to their felt-needs were better than those offered by pagan religions.

> **New churches faced the ministry challenges before them and created a ministry style marked by charity, community, and care.**

The very factors that made Antioch a difficult context were the conditions that "gave Christianity the opportunity to exploit fully its immense competitive advantage vis-à-vis paganism and other religious movements of the day as a solution to these problems."[14] The church planters who first arrived in Antioch started the right kind of churches using the right model of ministry. By stopping, looking, and listening to both the community and their calling, they devised "marketing-oriented and missionally-focused" churches.

Starting the Right Church

As you prepare to start your church, make certain that it is the right church. Stop, look, and listen to the community. The needs and dynamics you discover will reveal a vision of the church God wants you to start. Also stop, look, and listen carefully to God's calling on your life. God has been hard at work building a ministry plan and vision within you. When you bring together the uniqueness of your community and your own individual calling, you start the right church. It will be the church you always dreamed of. It will be the church Jesus dreamed of when He called you to be a church planter.

To access the downloadable Focus Group Questions and Nuts and Bolts of Contextualization, visit **www.collegepress.com/churchplanting**.

---

[1] Thomas C. Oden, *Pastoral Theology* (New York: Harper & Row, 1983) 12.

[2] Norman Shawchuck, Philip Kotler, Bruce Wrenn, and Gustave Rath, *Marketing for Congregations: Choosing to Serve People More Effectively* (Nashville: Abingdon, 1992) 57-66. Shawchuck outlines three basic approaches to ministry: the production, sales, and marketing approaches.

[3] Leonard Sweet, *AquaChurch: Essential Leadership Arts for Piloting Your Church in Today's Fluid Culture* (Loveland, CO: Group, 1999) 18.

[4] Michael Depew, *Paul and the Contextualization of the Gospel*, http://pages.preferred.com/~mdepew/mis1.html.

[5] Dean Gilliland, ed., *The Word among Us: Contextualizing Theology for Mission Today* (Eugene, OR: Wipf and Stock, 2002) 25.

[6] Shawchuck et al., *Marketing*, 59.

[7] Millard Erickson, *Christian Theology* (Grand Rapids: Baker, 1985) 75.

[8] James Engel and Wilbert Norton, *What's Gone Wrong with the Harvest? A Communication Strategy for the Church and World Evangelism* (Grand Rapids: Zondervan 1975) 35.

[9] B.J. Nicholls, "Contextualization," *New Dictionary of Theology*, ed. by Sinclair Ferguson and David Wright (Downers Grove, IL: InterVarsity, 1988) 164.

[10] Bruce Shelley and Marshall Shelley, *The Consumer Church: Can Evangelicals Win the World without Losing Their Souls?* (Downers Grove, IL: InterVarsity, 1992) 199.

[11] Rodney Stark, *The Rise of Christianity: How the Obscure, Marginal Jesus Movement Became the Dominant Religious Force in the Western World in a Few Centuries* (Princeton, NJ: Princeton University Press, 1997) 147-162.

[12] Ibid., 154.

[13] Ibid., 160.

[14] Ibid., 149.

Brian Jones is the founding and senior pastor of Christ's Church of the Valley, a new church in the suburbs of Philadelphia. Brian and his wife Lisa also started a new church outside of Dayton, Ohio. Brian has a B.A. from Cincinnati Bible College and a M.Div. from Princeton Theological Seminary. Brian and Lisa have three daughters.

Thinking Strategically

Anyone who has ever started a new church will chuckle at seeing the word "strategic" placed next to the phrase "new church." Of all kingdom workers they know there are very few strategic things that ever happen in a new church. Usually, if we church planters dare to tell the truth, the new churches we start succeed in spite of our well-crafted strategies, not because of them.

> The new churches we start succeed in spite of our well-crafted strategies, not because of them.

Besides, who would claim to be *strategic* about any activity that involves moving to a community in which you've never lived to organize a church that doesn't exist with people who aren't yet Christians led by a God you can't see? To make matters worse, we attempt this with limited knowledge of our target community, minimal oversight, an uprooted family, unresolved sins, unrealistic time constraints, staggering expectations, declining finances—not to mention our own lack of experience and confidence! If a new church succeeds, it truly is a modern day miracle.

This is why, after being a part of a few new ventures, I've now come to the conclusion that there are only two truly strategic decisions a church planter has any control over. First, immediately after unloading your moving truck, buy burial plots. Next, after you've committed yourself to being there for the long haul, drop to your knees and don't get up.

That's it. Buy burial plots and stay on your knees. That's about all I can share with any measure of certainty.

Yet I'm betting that, since you parted with a few dollars for this book, you expect a little more than that. You may be contemplating whether or not to start a church. You may be a leader charged with overseeing this strange breed of spiritual entrepreneurs. You may be part-way into a church plant and are seeking a little refinement or encouragement or both. Or, you may be where I was in 1986—a freshman in college with maps taped all over your dorm walls dreaming of where God might send you to make a difference for His kingdom. Wherever you are and whatever your reason for thumbing through this chapter, I feel obligated to give you a front row seat and let you learn from my fumbling attempts to lead and think strategically.

What Is Strategic Planning?

If God has called you to move to a new community and start a new church, then coupled with that call is an invitation to become the primary ear to which God will whisper His desires for that new church. As the Lead Planter, this will be your primary role. It will be more important than preaching, vision casting, evangelism, and team building put together. Why? When all the elaborate definitions, flowcharts, arrows, and terms are stripped away, *strategic planning in the new church is nothing more than finding out what God wants your church to do next and doing it*. That's strategic planning in a nutshell, and that's your primary task as the point person.

Take an informal survey with me of new churches across the country. Tally up the ones you are aware of that have launched, are growing, and continue to be fruitful for the kingdom. Now, make a list of all the church plants that have burst out of the gates with tremendous fanfare only to fizzle after a few years. What's the difference? Money isn't the difference. I can point you to dozens of rapidly growing and effective churches across the country that started on a shoestring. Location isn't the difference. I can think of dozens of churches that have failed in booming metropolitan areas. Neither the size of the staff nor the sponsoring organization is the deciding factor. In my mind there is one key difference between new churches that flourish and ones that don't: the Lead Planter always seems to know what to do next.

Fortunately, like most other leadership skills, I believe strategic thinking is something you can learn and develop with time and practice. So in the following pages let me share five suggestions for becoming a strategic leader in the new church context. All five of these suggestions are things I've learned and applied while serving in three separate church plants.

Gain Altitude

A while ago I was going through one of the most difficult times I've ever experienced in church planting. I was dealing with a difficult staff relationship, an emerging land deal, financial stresses, vision clarification, and a dozen or so other issues that never seem to leave a church planter's desk. I felt like a deer caught in the headlights. I had major decisions to make and couldn't find the direction I felt I needed from God. In the midst of it all, I decided to hop on a plane to California to attend a church conference. As it turned out, the plane ride itself was a divine appointment. While jetting somewhere over Oklahoma, I felt God impress on my heart, "Brian, the problems you are facing are too close to you. Look out the window and notice how you can see to the horizon. When you spend time with me, I'll help you gain altitude and clarity."

You wouldn't think you would have to suggest to church planters that they need to spend time with God. Quite the contrary! Spiritual entrepreneurs are doers by nature. I hear planters complain all the time about working too much. But honestly, I can't remember a single time I heard a planter say they pray too much. You would think it would be the other way around. As planters we need to remember that our primary role, first and foremost, is to be a divine listener. How can we expect to know what to do next if we don't take long, leisurely walks with the Father?

> I can't remember a single time I heard
> a planter say they pray too much.

This is why, no matter how grueling my schedule becomes, I always try to make time for three things. First, I try to keep a daily time with God for 30 minutes of Bible study and 30 minutes of prayer—apart from sermon prep. Second, I try to take three to four hours a week to get out of the office with nothing but a Bible and a blank pad of paper to simply reflect. Third, I try to keep an all-day prayer retreat once a month at a local monastery or a state park. I find that these times are more essential to knowing what to do next than everything else I do combined. In fact, sometimes someone will ask me where I'm going as I'm walking out the door and I'll quip, "Going to gain altitude."

How can we expect to know what to do next if we don't take long, leisurely walks with the Father?

Make Decisions with Great Deliberation

The perception most people have of church planters is that they are risk-taking nuts that throw caution to the wind and forge ahead. While that may be true of some, that's not necessarily the case for the really good ones. To the contrary, the truly great church planters are not great because of their personality or intelligence but because they are great decision makers. After mulling over every aspect of a decision, thinking through every possible scenario and outcome, and beating a decision to death, they'll table it and approach it again another day just to be sure. Why? They know that the margin for error is much smaller in a new church than in an established church. For the most part, in an established church the organization is strong enough to handle bad leadership decisions. And, quite honestly, most nongrowing established churches are used to bad decisions on the part of their leaders anyway. In a new church, a wrong decision can be lethal. What makes matters worse is that sometimes you don't find out how bad a decision is until it's too late.

One new church I started was going gangbusters until we received word we were getting kicked out of the school we were renting. We quickly scanned potential sites and found a storefront that we could renovate. Churches were doing this across the country with success, so I assumed we would follow suit. Two years of slumped attendance and low morale just about killed our church, and me. It was the right decision for the wrong church. I learned then and there that if I had spent just a little more time thinking through that decision, we could have avoided a near-fatal leadership collision. The same will be true for you. Church planters charged with discerning the direction of a new church must approach critical leadership decisions with great trepidation and deliberation.

Resist the Desire to Fill in All the Blanks

I'll never forget sitting down with a seasoned church planter from another denomination who received my direct mail and offered to take me out to lunch for extra encouragement. I proudly laid before him my mission, vision, values, strategy, and a host of other things people told me I needed at church planting conferences. Midway through lunch he smiled and said, "Please don't be offended, but you remind me a lot of my four-year-old when she plays 'dress up' with my wife's clothing." I wasn't too thrilled with that statement at the time, but now I recognize the wisdom in what he was saying.

Most church planting books and tapes recommend you craft a well-defined philosophy of ministry *before* you launch. This may sound counterintuitive, but my suggestion is that you don't do this. Filling in all the blanks before you launch ought to sound as strange to us as an expectant mother saying, "It's going to be a boy and he'll be six feet five, love soccer, enjoy horseback riding, marry a girl from Texas, and work in a bank." Who would presume to know anything about a baby that hasn't been born yet? Why would a new church be any different?

Who would presume to know anything about a baby that hasn't been born yet? Why would a new church be any different?

The issue is contextualization. Too often we assume we know what God wants this church to become before it is even launched. Don't make that mistake. You don't want to create the right church for the wrong area. My suggestion is that all you start with is a very simple mission statement. That's it. Then as you observe what really works in your context, you identify and give vocabulary to what God is doing as it emerges. Yes, you are called to be the person who finds out what God wants the team to do next. However, in my experience, it has been helpful to discover that God only shares one leg of the journey with you at a time.

Get a Financial Crash Course

Early in my church planting calling I came to the startling realization that I couldn't tell the difference between a balance sheet and a bed sheet. Potential donors, office landlords, loan officers, and others began requesting things I had never worked with—quarterly projections, income statements, and other things they forgot to include in my M.Div. program. I knew then and there that if I didn't get a refresher course in basic accounting and business planning I was dead in the water. So over the next two years I gathered around me a few sharp business guys to teach me the ropes. By the end of my self-arranged M.B.A. program, I still wasn't ready to become CEO at GE or Microsoft, but I knew enough to keep our church from getting into trouble. More importantly, when I conversed with sharp business people whom I was trying to lead to Christ, I didn't embarrass myself or our church.

It's my conviction that the Lead Planter must have an accurate and comprehensive understanding of where the church is at all times—spiritually, numerically, and financially. Without that data, and a basic understanding of the processes for analyzing that data, strategic planning is impossible. You can't be strategic if you don't have a handle on current reality. In my current church plant, I always have on my desk, first thing Monday, a complete "Stat Sheet" which outlines weekly, monthly, quarterly, and annual statistics for offering, attendance, and baptisms. On top of that I receive a weekly Budget Report, Balance Sheet, and Income Statement. We review all four of those documents in staff meeting every single week without fail. Based on that data and a ton of prayer, we strategically create goals and projections for where we will be next quarter, next year, and beyond.

A wise church planter told me one time, "Brian, there are three things that never leave the plate of a Senior Pastor—money, facilities, and staff. Whether you are 100 or 100,000 you will always deal with the presence or absence of those three things." He wasn't lying. Whatever you do, learn from my mistakes and get a financial crash course *before* you launch.

Visit Churches at Your Next Stage of Growth

One key thing I've learned in new church work is *be wary of advice givers*. You can learn something from anyone, but you want to pay attention to planters who have recently led their churches *through* the growth barrier you are currently facing. Why? If someone hasn't actually led a new church through that barrier, their advice is theoretical at best. It may sound good, but how do you know if it will work?

This also applies to the advice of leaders *too far past* your current growth barrier. In my mind we church planters spend time and money visiting the wrong churches. Going to your favorite conference hosted by a megachurch is all well and good for inspiration but teaches very little in terms of the actual steps you need to take next. Seeking advice from a pastor leading a church 5,000 to 10,000 more in attendance than you is like asking potty-training advice from the parents of a thirty-seven-year-old. You need to learn lessons from leaders while those lessons are still fresh. In my mind, taking a red-eye flight three to four times a year to churches at your next stage of growth might be the most important investments you make as a leader. Every time I've visited such a church, I walked away with an important clue to our church's future direction.

People often think that some church planters have some sort of sixth sense—they always intuitively seem to know what to do next. While that may be true for some, the vast majority of times good church planters appear that way it's because they have taken the time to research what needs to happen to move to the next stage of growth. Ninety-nine percent of the time solid planters know what to do next because they have worked hard to gather, think through, and apply the facts—facts gained from research in the field and their own mental elbow grease.

Solid planters know what to do next because they have worked hard to gather, think through, and apply the facts.

Are You Willing to Pay the Price to Lead Strategically?

Finally, you might be disappointed that I didn't try to outline a detailed process whereby a planter could discern their mission, identify stakeholder needs, outline key objectives, and compose systems, methods, and procedures. Those things are very important, but I felt the most helpful thing I could do is share with you a few suggestions you could actually use as a church planter, right away, regardless of your context.

Before I quit, however, I have a question to ask.

As a church planter it is hard to exaggerate how difficult your task will be. The problem is, the more successful you are, the harder your job will become. Ask any church planter who has done it before, and they will tell you that leading a growing new church is exhausting and emotionally dangerous.

Let me explain what I mean. If you commit to becoming the kind of leader that walks close to God, continually pleading with God for the next steps He wants your church to take, you're in for a long, painful, joy-filled journey. Just meander through 2 Corinthians or Galatians again if you doubt that. You must ask yourself up front if that is the kind of tour of duty you want.

Earlier this year I felt a crystal clear call from God to lead our congregation through three difficult changes. I knew going into it that the changes would be immensely difficult on our church, our staff, and ultimately me. However, I was convinced these were the steps God wanted us to take to strategically move to the next stage of growth in our church. Three months after leading our church through those changes, we added 100 new people almost overnight. To me, the changes were clearly inspired and executed by the power of the Holy Spirit.

Nevertheless, I have to say that it would have been a whole lot easier to just keep things the way they were. After services one day, while we were in the middle of those changes, I was blindsided by one critical person after another who didn't understand the need for the changes. I could sympathize with them; I hardly understood myself. The only thing I knew was I was being led by God to make

Thinking Strategically Brian Jones

199

them. With tears in my eyes I walked off and hid in a room and took out a pad of paper and a pen and wrote the following words:

> The reason the vast majority of churches never reach their full redemptive potential is because at every stage of growth, the point person, the person charged with rallying the troops, figures out that the price is too high. Every leader, at some point, clearly sees the price that must be paid to achieve his or her vision. At that point a decision must be made: "Am I willing to pay that price?"

How would you answer that question?

Todd Wilson is the Executive Minister of New Life Christian Church in Centreville, Virginia, and the Director of Passion for Planting. Todd is passionate about church planting and helping church planters to stay focused on people. Passion for Planting (www.church-planting.net) is a nonprofit church planting support organization that exists to help church planters with the seemingly endless details associated with starting new churches. Todd may be reached at todd@church-planting.net.

Planning and Administration

Good planning and hard work lead to prosperity, but hasty shortcuts lead to poverty (Proverbs 21:5).[1]

Dave responded to God's call to plant a church because he was passionate about preaching and reaching lost people. Several months before launch day, Dave was asked, "What is your biggest challenge?" Without hesitation he said, "So many things, so little time. The to-do list seems endless. I need to spend more time meeting people, building my launch team, and communicating vision. I keep hoping the administrative crush will ease, but every day it seems to get worse."

Dave's experience is not unique. Why do so many church planters struggle with planning, and is it even possible to focus on people while still planning for launch day? Absolutely! Our challenge is to break the paradigm of always doing things the way they've been done in the past. This chapter addresses the basics of planning and its biblical mandate, including what it is, why it's important, and a simple yet disciplined approach to developing a launch plan.

What Is Planning?

Nehemiah took just 52 days to rebuild the wall of Jerusalem (Neh 6:15). Imagine turning over 1.5 miles of rubble into massive walls in 52 days—a work that is unimaginable even today. God provided the vision, and Nehemiah managed the plan. Armed with a strong sense of calling and God's blessing, Nehemiah organized and planned the project, motivated the people to join the work, and managed the details. Sounds much like the challenge church planters face!

Nehemiah 3 outlines the plan. Instead of treating the project as one large overwhelming task, Nehemiah divided the wall into smaller manageable tasks. Families were given the lead to complete smaller segments of the wall. In this way, large parts of the wall were constructed simultaneously. By dividing the project into smaller discrete tasks, each family dealt with a challenging, yet manageable opportunity in rebuilding the wall.

Solid planning is a key element of completing any major, complex task. *Planning is the process of developing a road map for turning a vision or preferable picture of the future into reality.* Through planning, we define what needs to be done, when it needs to be done, how it will be done, who will do it, and how much it will cost.

Consider the construction of a new house. The average house takes about 120 days to complete with hundreds of interrelated tasks. These tasks are completed by numerous people at a cost of thousands of dollars. Similarly, a new church takes months to plan, involves many interrelated tasks, and costs thousands of dollars.

In turning the vision for a new house into reality, specific actions must be completed before others can start. For example, the lot must be cleared before the foundation can be poured. The foundation must be in place before the framing can be done, framing before electrical and plumbing, electrical and plumbing before insulation, and so on. Typically, an experienced general contractor, armed with a plan (i.e., blueprints, a budget, and an estimated completion date) manages the tasks to completion. Imagine a house construction project without a plan or a general contractor—confusion, inefficiency, frustration, and turmoil would abound.

While the church planter is expected to manage a project that is at least as complex as building a new house, the average planter lacks experience in planning and management. But there is hope! God builds His church, and we are asked to cooperate.

God builds His church, and we are asked to cooperate.

Throughout the Bible we see examples of God calling men and women to turn vision into reality. For example, Noah was called to build a boat, Abram to become the father of nations, Moses to lead a people from bondage, Joshua to conquer the Promised Land, and Solomon to build a great temple. In each case, God provided the picture of the preferable future and relied on faithful individuals to solidify the vision. Each of these leaders used planning as a tool to cooperate with God.

Fear Not: Planning Is a Spiritual Thing

When Dave first responded to God's calling to plant a church, he was uncomfortable with the concept of planning. After all, it's all about God and not about us and our agenda. "Does God really care about planning? Doesn't planning just constrain God?" These are common questions asked by church planters.

In Proverbs we read, "Commit your work to the LORD, and then your plans will succeed" (Prov 16:3). "You can make many plans, but the LORD's purpose will prevail" (Prov 19:21). "Human plans, no matter how wise or well advised, cannot stand against the LORD" (Prov 21:30). These verses should challenge us to be cautious as we make plans. We see that there is only one plan that will succeed— that which is rooted in God's purposes. In our desire to move forward, we must continually check our hearts for the following:

✘ **Improper Motives**—God clearly states that His plans, not ours, matter. In fact, He cares more about our motives than our plans. Whatever we do, we should place God's glory above our own.

✘ **Getting Ahead of God**—Sometimes in our fervor to achieve what we want, we rationalize that we know what God wants. We try to help Him to help us. God promised to make Abraham's offspring like the dust of the earth (Gen 13:14-16). Imagine Abraham's excitement. Sometime later when no children had been born to Sarah, however, Abraham became restless. He said to God, "You have given me no children; so one of my servant's will have to be my heir" (Gen 15:3-4). Knowing that God intended for him to be a father, Abraham took matters into his own hands. Sarah's Egyptian maidservant bore Abraham a child. In going before God's plans, Abraham experienced tragic consequences that are still felt today.

Nehemiah got it right. He prayed, fasted, and confessed as he sought God's clarity regarding the rebuilding of the wall of Jerusalem

(Nehemiah 1). God answered Nehemiah's prayer with a clear vision and a passion to accomplish the vision. God was glorified. We read that the surrounding nations were terrified when they realized that this work had been done with the help of God. Nehemiah stepped out on faith to accomplish something so big for God's honor that the only way it could be successful was through God's provision. Through it all, Nehemiah's plan was simply a tool for cooperating with God.

> Nehemiah stepped out on faith to accomplish something so big for God's honor that the only way it could be successful was through God's provision.

God's Role, Our Role

In Matthew 16:18, Jesus said, "I will build my church." Ultimately, we are the workers who cooperate with God to fulfill His vision for the church. What is God's role in the process, however? To answer this question, let's consider the building of the ark by Noah and the building of the temple by Solomon. Both stories illustrate God's use of faithful servants to accomplish His plans, while also revealing His involvement in the process.

Noah and the Ark

Genesis 6:14-16 details God's plan for Noah and the ark:

Make a boat from resinous wood and seal it with tar, inside and out. Then construct decks and stalls throughout its interior. Make it 450 feet long, 75 feet wide, and 45 feet high. Construct an opening all the way around the boat, 18 inches below the roof. Then put three decks inside the boat—bottom, middle, and upper—and put a door in the side.

God provided specific details of what the finished boat should look like but not a specific road map for building it. Why? Most of us (including Noah) would have no clue how large the ark needs to be to accommodate two of every kind of animal. We could make estimates, but in the end only God knew exactly what was needed for accomplishing His purposes. Through His plans, the ark matched God's vision, not the limited visions we often submit to.

Today, skilled craftsmen spend years building small boats. Noah spent nearly a century building the ark, which was one-and-a-half football fields in length. In modern days, a boat of this size and complexity would take vaults full of blueprints and an army of highly trained craftsmen to complete. Amazingly, we were not told of any specific plans that God provided Noah for how to actually build the ark. In this case, God provided the vision for the finished product, but delivered Noah with the knowledge to accomplish the vision.

Solomon and the Temple

David said, "My son Solomon is still young and inexperienced, and the Temple of the LORD must be a magnificent structure, famous and glorious throughout the world. So I will begin making preparations for it now" (1 Chr 22:5). So David collected vast amounts of building materials before his death. "Then David gave Solomon the plans for the Temple. . . . David gave instructions regarding how much gold and silver should be used to make the necessary items. . . . 'Every part of this plan,' David told Solomon, 'was given to me in writing from the hand of the LORD'" (1 Chr 28:11,14,19).

Once again, God had a specific purpose and vision for the temple. In this case, we are told that God provided very specific detailed plans for every part of the Temple. David essentially handed the blueprints to Solomon. Whether because of his youth or inexperience, we are not sure, but God knew the degree of detail Solomon needed to complete His vision for the temple.

In both stories, God provided a vision for the finished product, along with varying levels of detail on how plans should be implemented. In some cases, God provides very little detail. In others, He literally provides the blueprints. Overall, by submitting to God and choosing to follow His plan, He then reviews our abilities and needs before providing the degree of detail needed to accomplish His work.

Starting with the End in Mind

Dave's first question as a new church planter was, "Where do I start, and how do I do this?" Earlier we discussed the task of building a new house. What is the first question that a general contractor will ask when talking with a potential home buyer? "What kind of house do you want?" The potential buyer does not hesitate to describe the completed house. "I want a two-story colonial with four bedrooms, three bathrooms, a side-entry garage on at least one acre." Armed with a clear picture of the product, the contractor can begin the planning process.

In every example in this chapter, planning starts with defining a preferable picture or vision for the future. God painted a color picture of the ark in the specifications He gave Noah. He provided a vivid picture of the Temple in the detailed blueprints He gave David. To Abraham, He promised offspring as numerous as the sands of the earth.

In church planting, we must start with a clear picture of what the new church should look like on opening day. Does it have one service or two, meet in a school or permanent facility, play contemporary music or hymns, have a full children's program or only a nursery? Start by making an initial list of at least fifty characteristics (similar to the list above) that define what opening day looks like. This picture will serve only as a guide and may change with time as the plan is refined.

Right to Left: The Key to Planning

We are conditioned to think from left to right. Imagine trying to read from right to left. For those of us brought up reading Germanic and Romance languages, it's just not natural.

When it comes to planning, most Americans naturally think from left to right. We look at where we are today, where we would like to be in the future, and we diligently work to get as much done as possible in the time available. This is the classic planning approach for most church planters. Unfortunately, if you try to fit 50 pounds into a 10 pound bag something will suffer; typically relationship building and the quality of what is being done.

We desperately need to change our paradigm and instead think from right to left. The basic principle of this approach is to start with the end in mind (i.e., first identify the preferable picture of the future), and then determine the steps to accomplish your vision.

In his best selling book, *The Seven Habits of Highly Effective People*, Stephen Covey says:

> To begin with the end in mind means to start with a clear understanding of your destination. It means to know where you're going so that you better understand where you are now and so that the steps you take are always in the right direction.[2]

For church planters, the practical implementation of this is to begin by defining what opening day looks like and then developing a road map for getting there. If I launch on October 12, preview services need to be on October 5. With preview services on the fifth, we need sound equipment ordered by September 5, and so on. The schedule is built from the future to the present rather than the present to the future. This forces the planter to stay purpose driven with a constant eye toward a healthy opening day.

Begin by defining what opening day looks like and then develop a road map for getting there.

In many cases, the planter will conclude at the beginning of the planning process that everything simply can't get done by launch day. The planter then proactively decides to change the date, eliminate specific actions/tasks, or to apply extra resources to get more accomplished in the same period of time. The alternative is to simply get as much done as possible knowing that many things will suffer.

To aid church planters in healthy pre-launch planning, Church Planting Solutions[3] maintains a template launch plan that includes nearly 300 actions.[4] The plan was developed using a "right to left" approach. Even for a relatively small launch, a church planter will work full-time for six solid months to complete all the actions. Of course this would leave virtually no time for more important intangible priorities such as communications, community networking, and core group development—items that most church planters desperately need to spend more time on during the months leading up to launch.

The "right to left" approach to planning is summarized as follows:

○ **Start with the end in mind.** Where are you headed and what will it look like when you arrive?

○ **Identify critical nonnegotiable areas that must be done well.** Failure to do well in any of these areas could jeopardize opening day. In church planting, the nonnegotiable areas include at least the following: prayer team, vision casting and communications, core group development, small groups, marketing, facilities, equipment, staffing, finance/fundraising, outreach/community networking, ministries, teams/leadership, and processes.

○ **Develop a written plan for each of these critical areas.** Start with a written purpose statement (one to three sentences) for each area. If possible, link the purpose to the broader church purpose. For example, the purpose of the marketing plan is to "break down barriers with the unchurched in our target demographic and to build positive name recognition in the community so that people will respond to an invitation to church—an invitation that may change their life for eternity because of a new relationship with Jesus Christ."

After defining a clear purpose, identify three to five key priorities (objectives) that need to happen for the purpose to be fulfilled. For example, in marketing one objective may be to ensure that each household within a three-mile radius receives at least six positive touches from the church before launch day.

After defining three to five key objectives, identify specific actions for each objective. One action may be to generate an exhaustive list of potential marketing tools (flyers, direct mail cards, radio advertising, or other such ideas). Another action may be to prioritize the list of marketing ideas. Most objectives will have at least three actions, with many having five or more. The resulting plan will have from ten to thirty actions on average (one purpose, three to five objectives that support the purpose, and three or more actions per objective).

○ **Compile the actions from the written plans into an integrated checklist.**[5] Include space to identify the cost and lead person for each action. Fill in this additional information for each action.

○ **Review checklists from other church planters looking for additional actions you may have missed, adding actions where necessary.**

○ **Identify the relationships between actions.** Go through the checklist action by action and identify which actions need to be finished before or after others. If necessary, draw the relationships on a large poster board or wall chart so the dependencies are easy to see. For example, church name is selected before incorporating, incorporation before obtaining a Federal Identification Number, a Federal Identification Number before filing for nonprofit status.

○ To simplify the management of the list, look for logical groupings of actions to designate as milestones. For example, the six to eight actions required to obtain 501(c)(3) status may be linked to a milestone called "Organizational Establishment." If possible, the milestones are strategically selected so that they are evenly spread throughout the launch phase rather than being due at the same time. Milestones are used on an ongoing basis to help prioritize a church planters work. By planning a milestone every one to two weeks, the planter will always know what the upcoming priorities are. Add the milestones onto the checklist.

○ Identify durations for each action (how long will it reasonably take to complete the action once it is started?). For example, obtaining 501(c)(3) nonprofit status will take approximately 90 days from the time the application is submitted. The application takes the average planter several weeks to complete before submission.

○ Once the interdependencies and durations for each action are identified, scheduled completion dates can be determined and added to the checklist.

○ To develop a budget, simply add up the total costs of actions as a function of completion dates.

What Is a Launch Plan?

A launch plan is the written product of the "right to left" planning process. It defines what will be done, how the tasks interrelate, who will do the tasks, when they will be done, and how much they will cost.[6] Regardless of whether you are building an ark or starting a new church, a good plan includes at least the following: a list of actions, interdependencies between the actions, scheduled dates, assignment of responsibilities, and financial requirements.[7]

Regardless of whether you are building an ark or starting a new church, a good plan includes several important elements.

A good launch plan:

○ Causes a church planter to be disciplined in thinking and

understanding before acting—Proverbs 13:16, 14:8, and 19:2, respectively say, "Wise people think before they act"; "The wise look ahead to see what is coming"; "Zeal without knowledge is not good; a person who moves too quickly may go the wrong way."

○ **Keeps the planter focused on people**—Many church planters become consumed by administrative details and don't spend adequate time networking in the community, communicating vision, and developing a core group. Good intentions often fall victim to the reality of administrative details. A good plan helps the planter set priorities early and serves as a tool for delegating responsibilities to others.

○ **Helps the planter to discern God's purpose and vision for the new church and to turn that vision into reality**—The launch plan is a tool for understanding God's vision and then cooperating with God to join Him in the work.

○ **Helps the planter establish a solid foundation that lasts beyond the plan**—The culture and foundation that are laid during the prelaunch phase largely determine the health of the church after launch. Most church planters fail to spend adequate time during prelaunch establishing healthy teams and processes. They pay a heavy price later as these same weaknesses become growth barriers.

○ **Is a flexible guide that embraces change**—Discerning God's will is an ongoing process that should not be constrained by a rigid plan.

○ **Starts with a clear picture or vision for the future**—Throughout the Bible we see God working to define a picture of a preferable future for His people. All plans should start with an understanding of God's vision for this preferable future.

○ **Does not require a detailed organizer**—Planning is a process, not a science. Church planters should not be afraid of planning. Instead, they should seek the counsel of experienced organizers for assistance.

○ **Helps the planter to clarify expectations and to gain an understanding of what needs to be done**—It's been said that if you can't articulate it in writing, you probably don't understand it. A written plan helps solidify your thoughts.

○ **Is a great communication tool for getting others onboard**—
The plan helps communicate the vision for the new church
and the plan for getting there. As people read your plan and
discuss it with you, the people God is leading your way will
get excited and want to join you.

○ **Helps church planters to accomplish more with their limited resources**—A plan serves to focus your resources and
helps you complete more than you otherwise could.

○ **Integrates wise counsel from other experienced people**—In
Proverbs 20:18 and 15:22 we read, "Plans succeed through
good counsel; don't go to war without the advice of others."
and "Plans go wrong for lack of advice; many counselors bring
success."

○ **Helps church planters to focus/quantify their priorities**—
Some things are more important than others. Without a clear
set of priorities, we tend to work on whatever is most urgent.
Often in church planting, the most urgent is not the most
important. A good plan helps the planter make wise choices
in deciding what to work on, including identifying when specific tasks should be accomplished.

Often in church planting, the most urgent is not the most important.

○ **Clearly defines responsibilities**—In addition to defining what
needs to be done, a good plan identifies who is responsible for
each action. A wise planter delegates tasks. The plan identifies who (the planter, spouse, friend, core group members,
contractor, or other person) is responsible for each specific
task.

○ **Clearly defines the sequence of tasks**—A good plan identifies
interdependencies between tasks, so as to promote the proper order of completing them.

○ **Clearly defines financial requirements**—With this information, a solid budget can be developed. If necessary, individual
tasks can be revised to increase or decrease the budget.

Where Do I Start?

If you are a church planter wondering where to start, try the following:

○ **Prayer, Fasting, and Confession**—Nehemiah gave us a solid example of how to submit to God and join His plans. Before putting pen to paper or jumping into action, spend whatever time is necessary with God to ensure your motives are right, and that you are fully submitted to Him in the new work.

○ **Vision and Philosophy of Ministry**—Before developing a detailed plan or moving forward with too many actions, answer these questions: (1) Who is God calling me to reach based on my unique gifts and calling? (2) What is the vision God is calling me to respond to? (3) What values are vitally important to me? and (4) What does opening day of the church look like?

○ **"Right to Left" Planning**—Work through the "right to left" planning process outlined in this chapter.

○ **In Everything, Remember It's God's Church**—Jeremiah 29:11 (NIV) reads, "'For I know the plans I have for you' says the LORD. 'They are plans for good and not for disaster, to give you a future and a hope.'" Church planting is an integral part of God's strategy for reaching a lost world. You are God's hero if you remain faithful in this cause and seek to cooperate with Him in everything. Against all odds, He will bless you. Keep the faith.

> You are God's hero if you remain faithful in this cause and seek to cooperate with Him in everything.

---

[1] All Scripture quotations are taken from the *New Living Translation* of the *Holy Bible*.

[2] Stephen R. Covey, *Seven Habits of Highly Effective People* (New York: Simon and Schuster, First Fireside Edition, 1990) 98.

[3] "Church Planting Solutions functions as a nonprofit support organization that exists to help church planters and church planting organizations to be more effective. We whole heartedly believe that the local church is the hope of the world and that church planting is the most effective way to reach the world with the Good

News of Jesus Christ! We offer project management services for church planters. With a template launch plan of nearly 300 actions, we help manage the details and we complete many of the actions for the church planter. The result: church planters stay focused on people!" (**www.church-planting-solutions.com**).

⁴ Go to **www.collegepress.com/churchplanting** for Church Planting Solution's template launch plan.

⁵ Go to **www.collegepress.com/churchplanting** for an example of an integrated checklist.

⁶ A more comprehensive launch plan includes documentation of all the steps in the "right to left" approach and is more useful in communicating vision and explaining how the list of actions was developed. Contact Church Planting Solutions (**www.church-planting-solutions.com**) for more information on comprehensive launch plans.

⁷ This simple plan may take the form of a checklist of actions. Such an example can be found at **www.collegepress.com/churchplanting**.

Brett Andrews is the Founding and Senior Minister of New Life Christian Church in Centreville, Virginia. Brett is passionate about helping plant new churches and is a Director at Church Marketing Solutions, a nonprofit marketing organization that exists to help churches reach their communities (**www.church-marketing.com**). He is a graduate of Cincinnati Bible College. Brett, his wife Laura, and their four children live in Centreville, Virginia. Brett may be e-mailed at **brett@newlife4me.com**.

Tim Stephens caught the church planting bug from a Church Planting Primer Class he took at Cincinnati Bible Seminary. He worked in West Palm Beach, Florida, on a church planting staff before going to Tampa to help start Journey Christian Church in 1999. The church started with a launch team of 40, but through prayer and marketing had over 500 people show up for their first service. Tim currently serves in Atlanta, Georgia, as Vice President of the Church Development Fund for the Southeast United States. Tim and his wife Amy have a one-year old daughter, Grace.

Marketing

How would Jesus market the church? Does it work? Is it necessary? Is it biblical, or is it fighting the battle with weapons of the world? Is it worth my time? Is it worth the expense? Is it too high risk? What if we spend $10,000 and no one responds? What kind of person comes to church because of a card in the mail?

Marketing the church demands time, thought, planning, and coordination. It's expensive and risky. Wouldn't it be more spiritual, and easier, to pray three hours a day and accept the people God sends?

Journey Christian Church (located in Tampa, Florida) had been meeting for several weeks when we held our first "Discover Journey" class in the fall of 1999. Thirty adults showed up for our first class. They were asked, "How did you hear about Journey?" Over twenty of the thirty people indicated they had received a card in the mail. Of those thirty people, twenty-six had not been to church for at least two years, over twenty had not been to church regularly for at least ten years, and many had never attended church.

> Could a series of four mass mailings of cards really spark hundreds of people with no church affiliation to show up one Sunday?

Could a series of four mass mailings of cards really have sparked hundreds of people with no church affiliation to show up

214

one Sunday? In the first three months of Journey Christian Church's existence, over forty people were baptized. Almost all of them came to Journey because they received a card in the mail.

What Is Marketing?

Mention marketing of the church to a group of Christians and you're likely to stir up a lively, if not heated, debate. Read the following e-mail received by Church Marketing Solutions:

> I'm a Christian, and I'm offended by your business. First, can you see Jesus "marketing the church"? Second, you do it to make yourself money. You are the Hophni and Phineas of the 21st century. Shame on you.[1]

For some, marketing the church is associated with shady practices involving selling, exchanging money, and making profits. Consider the following definition:

> Marketing *n*. The exchange of goods for an agreed sum of money. The commercial functions involved in transferring goods from producer to consumer.[2]

To add fuel to the fire, consider John 2:14-15 where we see Jesus' response to businessmen who turned the temple courts into a profit-making market (business):

> In the temple courts he found men selling cattle, sheep and doves, and others sitting at tables exchanging money. So he made a whip out of cords, and drove all from the temple area, both sheep and cattle; he scattered the coins of the money changers and overturned their tables. To those who sold doves he said, "Get these out of here! How dare you turn my Father's house into a market!"[3]

What is at the heart of Jesus' strong response? Is it the fact these men were opportunistic? Being opportunistic is not the problem; their motivation behind the opportunity is the problem. Unfortunately, their motive was making money and had little to do with God's agenda.

Church marketing is all about building bridges to lost people so they can hear the gospel message. This is why, among the Christian community, church planters and new churches have been the most willing to accept church marketing. Without a doubt, marketing is one of the most important steps a new church plant can take in communicating the Good News of Jesus Christ to the culture in which it lives.

Church Marketing Sets the Stage

According to research by Thom Rainer, "most Americans have never been invited to church—never. Yet, 82% indicate they would be at least 'somewhat likely' to attend if invited."[4]

Most experts on reaching people for Christ agree the most effective form of evangelism is friendship evangelism. The purpose of new church marketing isn't to stick a card in someone's hand and expect they will want a relationship with Christ and be baptized a week later. Effective marketing opens the door to a possible relationship. It does not take the place of authentic relationships, but it can set the stage for potential meaningful relationships. It can potentially connect a church with people who need to be pastored before they realize they need pastoring.

Everyone is spiritually restless until they connect with God. When crisis or life-transition exposes the restlessness, where will the unchurched person turn? They might reach out to the new church that's been pastoring them from a safe distance.

If the most effective means of reaching lost people is through personal invitation, how do marketing techniques such as mass mailings continue to make such an impact? Simply this: one of the purposes of every marketing touch is to make it easier for Christians who are part of the launch team to start a spiritual conversation with their neighbors. Church events that address children, marriage, or finances, for example, attract individuals to church who might otherwise not attend a Sunday service. When postcards go out, ask your launch team to pray as well as to ask their friends or coworkers if they saw the cards in the mail. Often, people with no other connection with the church will receive a series of cards, and later will begin a conversation with someone connected to the church. The bridge for a spiritual conversation has already been constructed, making it less intimidating for the newcomer to take the next step.

A new church marketing philosophy that simply focuses on getting people in the door on Sunday morning is doomed from the start. An additional goal is to help people cooperate with the Great Commission—make it easier for your launch team to share their faith. Effective marketing allows believers more opportunities to start conversations with spiritual seekers.

A new church marketing philosophy that simply focuses on getting people in the door on Sunday morning is doomed from the start.

Marketing Is Not Optional

Every church markets. In his letter to Titus, Paul instructs Christians to conduct themselves "so that in every way they will make the teaching about God our Savior attractive" (Titus 2:10). Everything the church does makes the teachings of Jesus either more or less attractive. Some market intentionally, while others market unwittingly. Some market a message they want people to hear. Some market a message that pushes people away. Do you have a church sign? If yes, then you are marketing. What about a logo, newsletter, meeting space, or even a worship service? Each is a marketing tool. Marketing may not be the primary motivation or objective of all you do, but everything you do markets the church.

Everything the church does makes the teachings of Jesus either more or less attractive.

For instance, what images do these church names conjure—Adventure Church, Journey, The Meeting Place, The Well, ForeFront? Or maybe Boring Christian Church, Holy Spirit Church, Apostolic Church, Covenant Church, The Chosen Church? Get the point? At New Life Christian Church (located in Centreville, Virginia), people sometimes say, "I saw your name, and that's what I need—new life." From the moment the church selects a name, everything the church does either helps people take a step closer to Jesus or creates a barrier for the gospel.

For most church planters lying awake nights thinking of ways to reach their community, pragmatism trumps theoretical hair-splitting. When planting a new church, the pressing question almost always is, "How can we reach more people as fast and as effectively as possible?"

How Does Marketing Work?

When we asked the question, "How did you first hear about Journey," we expected a slew of different responses. People admitted they had heard about Journey multiple times over the previous few months through various and multiple mediums.

Charlie and Edie Gonzalez, for example, were two individuals at our first Discover Journey class. Charlie was a manager at a local bread distributor, while Edie helped run a daycare. Their two children were in high school, and each had children from previous marriages. Charlie was a Cuban American and rode motorcycles on weekends. Edie liked to spend time with the kids and rode with Charlie on occasions. They were both raised Catholic, but had not been to church since getting married.

When asked how they heard about Journey, each credited the cards they received in the mail. But as we asked further questions, they quickly admitted they had heard about Journey many times over the last few months. Their daughter danced at the high school where we had sponsored a show. Their son played football, and we had bought an advertisement on the back page of his program. They had each seen several of our television ads in the weeks prior to the launch of the church. In addition, they had received at least one flier and had seen our slides in a local movie theater. Overall, we had "touched" the Gonzalez family ten times.

> Overall, we had "touched" the
> Gonzalez family ten times.

Many marketing experts propose it takes, "Six to stick." A consumer needs to be touched at least six times before he or she considers buying a product. At Journey, we believed it took even more "touches" for unchurched and irreligious people to consider giving church a chance.

The strategy included a several-month detailed plan as we tried to establish identity in north Tampa. We researched our context intensely to understand our target group's felt-needs, thinking patterns, and shopping habits. Before you spend money on advertising or brainstorming, hire a graphic artist, or start designing logos on napkins, please do the hard, but rewarding work of developing a new church marketing plan.

Jay Conrad Levinson, the author of the Guerrilla Marketing series of books, suggests beginning with a simple marketing plan. "The plan has only seven sentences. It should be that brief because you'll be forced to focus on your objectives and tactics and because brief marketing plans should be easy to understand when read by your employees or partners."[5] We believe new church marketing plans can be written with even fewer sentences.

The first sentence of a new church marketing plan should state the "why" behind the promotion of your new church. Secondly, you must define your target audience. This single objective is the most critical from a marketing perspective for church planters. You simply cannot be all things to all people. The third sentence is the longest. List what marketing techniques you're going to use. You will not be able to finalize this sentence until you have followed the four-step process we propose later in this chapter. The next step defines your new church's identity—what are your core values? The last sentence states how much money the church will spend each year on marketing.

It's important to remember church marketing isn't business marketing. If a margarine maker overpromises and underdelivers, your trust in that company won't be significantly impacted. You may even buy their product if it's on sale next week. However, if a church makes promises and then doesn't deliver, its integrity is at stake in the eye of the newcomer, and he or she may never return. Obviously, integrity expectations for those selling butter and toasters differ dramatically from expectations for churches—and justifiably so.

If a church makes promises and then doesn't deliver, its integrity is at stake in the eye of the newcomer.

Integrity in church marketing means honestly representing who you are. If your children's ministry stinks, don't quote parents saying it's the nation's best. If your worship team is just this side of senior citizenship, then don't produce radio spots proclaiming Britney Spears-style worship. When who you proclaim to be matches who you really are, it builds credibility and honors God. Misleading expectations, however, leave the first-timer disappointed, with little chance of a return visit.

Who has God called and gifted you to be? No church reaches everybody. No other church can reach the people you are created to reach as effectively as you. Each church has a unique personality. Some churches are great at creative communication. Some have more than their share of rock musicians. Some set the pace with children or student ministries. Others model fine arts ministry. No church does everything great. In fact, great churches discover what they do well and celebrate these strengths in the way they market their church, trusting God will connect them with His people.

No church does everything great.

As a church discovers who God has called and equipped them to be, three basic marketing questions emerge:
1. Who are we?
2. Who are we best at reaching?
3. How do we connect who we are with the felt needs of those we are reaching?

Four Marketing Steps

1. **Make an exhaustive list of methods you think can "touch" your target group over the three months prior to the launch of the new church.** Our list for Journey Church included:
> Adopting a litter-free road and getting our name on a street sign.
> Sponsoring a parenting seminar at the local high school.
> Hiring a graphic artist to design a logo and stationary.
> Buying pre- and postmovie slides at the two local theaters.
> Buying an ad in the high school football program.
> Inviting the community to a local park special event sponsored by our church.
> Sponsoring a Habitat home.
> Partnering with local media in donating time and supplies to the needy.
> Having a user-friendly, informational web site.
> Buying banners to hang at our office and other available sites.
> Sponsoring a high school drama presentation.
> Getting Chick-fil-A to hand out Journey fliers to all customers.
> Giving away thousands of Journey pens.

➤ Providing t-shirts to friends and acquaintances that work at Borders, Starbucks, and other public places.

➤ Paying teens to put "Discover Journey Church" bumper stickers on their cars.

➤ Sending a mass mailing to everyone in our 5-mile radius.

➤ Passing out business cards at bars, restaurants, and other public places.

➤ Placing small ads in homeowners association newsletters.

➤ Giving out water and squirt bottles at parades, parties, and other public events.

➤ Renting a billboard for three months.

➤ Having Papa John's give out fliers to all customers.

➤ Advertising via cable television.

➤ Putting door hangers on every home and car in our target area.

➤ Setting out A-frame signs each weekend at key intersections.

➤ Passing out fliers at Home Depot, Target, Wal-Mart, and other frequented retail stores.

➤ Writing personal letters to all homes within a one-mile radius of our meeting place.

➤ Placing classified ads in nontraditional newspapers.

➤ Securing newspaper ads in traditional papers.

➤ Renting exhibit or booth space at fairs or carnivals.

➤ Handing out fliers at Tampa Bay Bucs games.

This list is not exhaustive, but it was a starting point for us.

2. Contextualize your ideas. Not every idea at Journey Christian Church was valid for our demographic and target group. And some great ideas will not work in your context. We cut our list from hundreds of ideas to fifty we thought would be effective in our area.

3. Prioritize your ideas. Most church planters today do a mass mailing. In recent years, it has proven to be the most efficient method to repeatedly touch your target group. In our experience a four-card mailing to 30,000 homes will likely result in at least 150 first-time guests to a new church. So, for most church planters, mass mailing is the most important idea. After that, the effectiveness of other marketing techniques varies greatly depending on your context, style, purpose, and budget.

Don't just try some ideas. Try lots of ideas. Church planting veteran John Wasem says, "Don't put all your marketing eggs in one basket." Remember, the marketing rule of thumb: "It takes six to stick." A consumer needs at least six touches before he or she considers a product. For irreligious people, it may demand more than that. So, give it time. Years may pass before the new church fully realizes the harvest of its first outreach events and cards. But, with God's involvement, the harvest is sure. God is the Hound of Heaven, pursuing people on the run. He is a sending God, and He wants to be reconciled with lost people. When God prepares a heart, and the church's marketing touches reach that person repeatedly over a period of time, it creates an opening for a potential relationship. One attendee later commented on his decision to attend Journey, "I kept hearing about this church in all these different ways, and I knew I just had to check it out."

> **"I kept hearing about this church in all these different ways, and I knew I just had to check it out."**

4. Weigh the financial costs. Until this point, every idea should be valid without regard to cost. At some point however, you must do a cost-benefit analysis. It is important to know your budget. Contact a financial specialist for guidance. We recommend Church Marketing Solutions.[7] You can spend dozens of hours getting quotes and trying to contract all the vendors yourself, or you can let a specialist do the work and deliver a great product at an unbelievable cost.

Church planters quickly realize advertising can be very expensive. Hopefully, they also realize effective and efficient marketing can be done using few traditional means of advertising. With literally billions of dollars being spent each year by American industries, customers have become desensitized to most advertising. For example, although Budweiser is rewarded prestigious awards year after year by advertising agencies, their market share is decreasing annually. Comical advertising does not always correlate to effective marketing. Even memorable advertising does not often yield increased profits. Interestingly enough, one of America's fastest growing and most recognizable companies, Krispy Kreme, does not advertise.

The best form of marketing is saturation marketing. "Six to stick" is not just a catchy slogan. Touching people as many times as possible in as many ways as possible eventually brings people to church, many for the first time. Saturation marketing is an inexpensive way to reach people.

A front-page article in a major newspaper costs nothing. On the other hand, a back page ad on a weekend in that same major newspaper costs thousands of dollars. Spending time creating press releases, cold calling media outlets, and handing out flyers at concerts and sporting events will cost your new or established church little or nothing, but if you are able to create a buzz among influential people, your marketing plan has produced its desired results with little cost.

Your marketing plan will probably include some traditional advertising. Those ads may fit well into your plan and might help create the synergy you desire when starting a new church. Your ads may have a primary purpose of drawing attention among influential people. When we started the church in Tampa, we used cable television advertising. We thought the ads were great. They brought a few folks to the church, but more importantly, the local newspapers, including the *Tampa Tribune*, noticed the ads. They were looking for a human-interest story, and they called us. Because of networking like this, more people came to Journey Church because of newspaper articles than directly from our advertising.

More people came to Journey Church because of newspaper articles than directly from our advertising.

Most church planters we know budget between $15,000 and $50,000 on marketing. These numbers seem outrageous to some. Those who have worked in the corporate world may find these numbers ridiculously low. Regardless of your perspective, most church planters in America spend approximately 10%–20% of their first-year budgets on marketing. The percentage will almost certainly decline after the first year, but should not be drastically reduced.

A word of caution: the more money you budget for a new church marketing plan, the more research will be required to spend it efficiently. For example, in Tampa, radio advertising on two popular radio stations seemed to be the most effective means of reaching our target group. Yet the average spot on a radio station costs $80 per thirty second commercial if you buy a bundle of slots. Running a similar spot on VH1, MTV, CNBC, Lifetime, Discovery, and other channels often costs less than $10 per spot when buying in volume. Therefore, we had to determine if the radio ads were worth at least eight times as much as the cable television ads. If you are going to spend thousands of dollars on radio advertising, first see if you can achieve better saturation of your context for fewer dollars in a different medium.

Some Final Marketing Essentials

✔ Do a contextualization study using demographics and surveys to fully understand the people you are trying to reach. Based on this study, develop a new church marketing plan that will serve as a guide to all outreach activities.

✔ Establish a fully functional web site as soon as possible. List it on all advertising materials. An initial web presence can be established quickly and inexpensively. Your web site will help people feel comfortable visiting your church.

✔ Design a logo that communicates an image of who you seek to be.

✔ Design a high quality, "first touch" color brochure that communicates who you are to the unchurched people in your community.

✔ Design high-quality, color business cards for the primary purpose of drawing people to your web site. Give them to everyone you meet.

✔ Seek to have name recognition within your target area before sending out your final direct marketing campaign. (The effectiveness of your start-up mailing campaign will be better if you already have a positive image in the community.)

✔ Proactively determine what image you are seeking to establish in the community, and use outreach events and marketing to build this identity and image.

✔ Use multiple touches. The "Six to Stick" philosophy is solid and not as difficult to achieve as it first appears.

✔ Brainstorm a list of at least 50 possible marketing touches (see above list for ideas).

✔ Determine which types of marketing touches are already being used effectively in your target area.

✔ Grab the low-hanging fruit (cheap and easy touches—there are more than you think).

✔ Prioritize the list of possible marketing touches in light of your budget and your understanding of effectiveness.

✔ Maintain consistency of message by using the same branding on different touches.

✔ Get a nonprofit, bulk mail permit early. If you wait too long, it will cost you additional money.

✔ Find people in your church (or in your launch group) with marketing experience, and get their help.

✔ Negotiate the lowest possible prices, remembering there is considerable margin in areas such as yellow page ads.

✔ Candidly evaluate your readiness to deliver what you promise.

✔ Your marketing and outreach strategies are inseparable. Use every outreach event as an opportunity to get multiple marketing touches into the community.

✔ Stick with it. The harvest takes time. Marketing is a long-term investment. Repetition is essential. Be persistent.

Conclusion

Steve and Laura were living life to the fullest. Each had a great job that paid well. They had a four-thousand-square-foot house, a dog, and two happy children. They were members of various country clubs and fitness centers and vacationed regularly at ski resorts throughout the country. Life was unfolding nicely, but Steve and Laura had little use for church. Then during one doctor's appointment Steve was diagnosed, after a series of tests, with a brain tumor. God got Steve and Laura's attention. They became interested in spiritual things and remembered receiving postcards from a new church. Laura remembered seeing banners outside a school on Sunday morning identifying the church's location. Steve and Laura showed up for church one Sunday morning, found Jesus, were baptized into Christ, and experienced love from the community of faith. Six months later Steve died. His funeral was a celebration of Steve's graduation into a Christ-filled eternity. Where would Steve and Laura have been without the marketing of one new church that cared enough to reach their community through a marketing plan? Marketing is all about reaching people like Steve and Laura. There are millions of individuals and families in all walks of life still out there waiting to hear the Good News of Jesus Christ. Don't they deserve to be reached through a well-organized, creative marketing plan or whatever else it takes to communicate Christ? We believe they do.

Marketing is all about reaching people.

[1] For more information on Church Marketing Solutions and a closer look at what people are saying about church marketing, visit Church Marketing Solution's web site at **www.church-marketing.com**.

[2] Definition found at **www.dictionary.com**, 2002.

[3] All Scripture quotations are taken from the *New International Version* unless otherwise noted.

[4] Thom Rainer quote available in an article by Albert Mohler, *The Unchurched Next Door: A New Look at the Challenge*, found on **crosswalk.com**, 2003.

[5] Jay Conrad Levinson, *Guerilla Marketing for Free* (Boston: Houghton Mifflin, 2003) 12-13.

[6] Church Marketing Solutions is easily the best source for information today from trends to demographics to cost analyses available to all churches. Church Marketing Solutions helps churches deliver high quality marketing at the lowest possible costs. So before you spend a penny on marketing, contact them at **www.church-marketing.com**. For example, with their help, you can produce a series of postcards designed, printed, delivered, and mailed for a very low price. They use only the best printers in the country and have relationships with some of the best mail houses. Also, Church Marketing Solutions was started by church planters to help other church planters be more effective. Let them help you.

Troy McMahon is Executive Pastor of Administration where he oversees Facilities, Finances, and Serving Teams, and serves as Campus Pastor for the South Campus of Community Christian Church. He has led various Facility Task Forces in acquiring property, leading stewardship campaigns, and designing and constructing facilities. Troy left his corporate job in 1996 to do vocational ministry and is living out his dream. Troy lives with his wife, Janet, and three children, Jacob, Mitchell, and Judiann, in Naperville, Illinois.

Church in a Barn: Facilities

On Saturday afternoon the day before launch, a setup team was putting signs along the road to direct newcomers to the chosen location. As the fourteenth sign went up, the lead pastor began to doubt the selection of location. An easy to find location was considered crucial to the success of a new church launch, but this elementary school didn't fit any of the experts' criteria for a successful new church location. However, it did seem the place God had given to these church planters. Despite the belief in God's guidance, nagging questions remained. Would people be able to find this place? Once here, would they stay or even return for other weekly services? One way or another, the next morning would reveal answers to the questions and doubts.

Early Sunday morning the band arrived and started to jam, the ministry teams eagerly prepared for a large crowd, and the children's ministry leaders transformed the elementary school space into an environment that screamed, "WOW!" With the first celebration service scheduled to begin at 10:00 a.m., about 150 total people were in the building just five minutes prior. The launch team had prayed for 500, but promised to celebrate however many people God sent.

Across the country another church plant was preparing for its first Sunday. Its location was a well-known theater complex with great visibility, an abundance of parking, and little need for signage. The launch team was there early with the band jamming, the ministry teams preparing for a crowd, and the children's ministry space being transformed. The launch team had prayed for 400 people to show up. But would they come?

Back at the elementary school, 10:00 a.m. came with around 250 people gathered and ready for services to begin. As the lead pastor stood at the doorway greeting people, he saw people coming in droves. Many people were walking out the front doors of their homes and coming to this school in their neighborhood. During the next ten minutes, over 300 more people would join the others for a grand total of 552 worshipers. What a God Thing! Not bad for a location that took fourteen signs to locate off the major thoroughfare.

Across the country at the theater, the service also began with just over 100 people in attendance. Although numbers didn't match expectations, the team delivered their best.

Let's fast-forward five years. The church in the elementary school has moved to a new location and now has over 800 people in weekly attendance. The church in the theater, on the other hand, no longer exists.

So does location and choice of facility matter? Yes, definitely! Will the location of your launch and the specific facility you choose be the defining factor for the success or failure of your church plant? Not necessarily. So why discuss the matter at all? Because how you maximize the impact of where you choose to meet can increase the momentum of the launch.

> ### How you maximize the impact of where you choose to meet can increase the momentum of the launch.

A movement started long ago in a cave. A better location would have been a hospital or even an inn. Somehow, however, God decided to use this facility to change the world. If God could start His Son's life in a cave, we should be able to do church in a barn.

No matter what type of church you desire to plant, you will need a place to meet. If your plan is to launch a house church, then your facility needs will be met by available homes, apartments, lofts, or other spaces that your congregation owns, rents, or lives in. If your plan is to launch some type of cell/celebration model, you need to find a meeting space where your church can gather weekly. How do you choose your initial church plant location? Look closely at your options, and choose wisely.

Let's first assume that you have identified a target area where God is calling you to plant. Also, you have a basic understanding of the culture and/or subcultures in the target area. What are some of your options? Almost every urban, suburban, or rural area is consistent regarding available options. Schools/universities, theaters, community centers, hotels/banquet halls, office buildings, restaurants/bars, storefronts/warehouses, existing church buildings, and a variety of other choices dot the American landscape, and many are available for use on Sunday morning.

When deciding where God might be leading you to plant a church, first ask the most obvious question, "Where *is* God leading our church plant?" The answer to this question can be supernatural, extremely pragmatic, or both. Numerous church planters have chosen locations and facilities that were divine inspirations. During prayer, a vision came of a place never seen. A phone call from a stranger was received, asking if a given facility would be a good location for a church. A conversation occurred asking if a church would like to be planted in a community center not yet built. Each of these examples may be perceived as revelations from God. However, just as real and God-inspired is the situation where the church planter searches diligently for months and finds only one available location that doesn't meet the ideal, but is clearly in the place the Lord has chosen.

What if God gives you a choice? And for most church planters, this is a real situation or dilemma. The key to choosing comes from the church planter's understanding of the culture/subculture in the target area and the development of relationships with landlords, building owners, school principals, and other potential key facility people.

As the Apostle Paul demonstrated throughout his missionary journeys, an understanding of cultures present in an area can define the meeting place for the church.[1] Paul frequently met in the synagogue to teach, but he also used the marketplace (Acts 17:17), a lecture hall/amphitheater (Acts 19:9), a pagan temple (Acts 14:15; 17:23), and even a riverbank (Acts 16:13) as temporary locations for starting or growing churches. As you understand the subcultures in the target area, the choice between a school, theater, or nightclub will become apparent. Here are some questions to ask both yourself and others you are attempting to reach when considering a potential church location:

1. Will unchurched people come to this location/facility?

2. Is it good stewardship (can we afford) to rent/purchase this facility?

3. Can the type/style of church planned and the spaces needed be accomplished in this facility?

4. Can this location accommodate growth for 12–24 months?

Along with the cultural relativity of a given location or facility, consider relationships. A new church plant can save money, both short-term and long-term, by renting their initial facility. Purchasing a facility, even if it is "free," has many hidden costs that can financially strangle a new church plant and severely limit its outreach potential. Renting puts the new church plant in a landlord/tenant relationship. The key here is "relationship." Investing time and energy into developing a positive relationship personally with the landlord of choice will pay off many times over. When choosing the specific location, look closely at this landlord/tenant relationship. As the tenant, determine how a church plant in that facility can benefit the landlord. For example, a church meeting in a school may provide backpacks and/or school supplies for underresourced students at the beginning of school. A church plant meeting in a theater or restaurant can increase patronage to that establishment. Be creative. Each of these benefits are above and beyond the income generated by facility rental and can solidify the relationship between the church plant and the owner/manager of the specific location. This solid relationship will eliminate many hassles once the church is launched.

> Investing time and energy into developing a positive relationship personally with the landlord of choice will pay off many times over.

Surveying Some Viable Options

There are pros and cons to meeting in a given location or facility. Let's take a more detailed look at some of the options.

Schools

Schools are probably the most frequently used locations for new church plants. They are located in proximity to urban, suburban, and rural locations. Schools are almost always available on Sunday mornings. Schools also offer extensive space, which will allow the new church plant room to grow. School locations are usually centrally positioned and well known within a given community. High schools and universities typically have abundant parking available, while middle and elementary schools have limited parking. Schools can be very cost effective, but some school districts have rent and personnel requirements that increase costs, making some school rentals financially challenging.

Usage of schools varies depending on local or state school board rules and regulations. The U.S. Supreme Court has ruled churches cannot be discriminated against when it comes to school usage,[2] but a given district can develop specific guidelines for use. Some school districts will not allow any group to use a space "weekly" or "consistently." Other school districts have time limitations for weekly use (e.g., six months to a year maximum). Storage is also a consideration at schools. Few schools allow storage of equipment on site; so portable equipment and transportation will be required.[3]

Generally, church in a school has a positive, welcoming, family feel. Church in school forces the church to be a vital, contributing part of the local community. Church staff members have the opportunity to work alongside school staff; many have influence and visibility in the community.

A look at Evergreen Community Church (in Minneapolis/St. Paul) reminds us God uses school buildings as the place where He shows up to touch and transform lives. Evergreen Community Church is a multi-site church that currently has five locations; all meet in schools.

School Case Study: Evergreen Community Church[4]

Evergreen Community Church began as a dream in the minds of pastors Brent Knox and Mark Darling. Mark and Brent decided they needed to create a church that would be different. They wanted a church people would look forward to each week. As they wrestled with some ideas and sought God, they came up with the vision for Evergreen Community Church. With a core of approximately 120 people,

Evergreen officially opened its doors in June of 1988 at the Oak Grove School auditorium in Bloomington. In 1994, Evergreen added their second location in West Minneapolis. Over the years, Evergreen has continued to keep up with the changing times, meeting personal and spiritual needs even as they have grown and expanded to other locations throughout the Twin Cities. Evergreen now has five locations in urban and suburban areas of Minneapolis, Minnesota, with over 3,000 attending weekly.

Brent Knox, Lead Pastor at the Bloomington location, was asked, "After fifteen years of meeting in schools, what are the pros and cons for using a school for church planting?" Among the pros for meeting in a school, Knox listed:

1. Much cheaper than owning and/or operating a 24/7 facility.

2. Neutral and familiar setting for the unchurched.

3. Less facility headaches.

4. Tells the community the church is conserving resources.

On the other hand, he also shared the following cons in using a school for church planting:

1. Limits outreach options to the community.

2. Without a building, the church tends to fly under the radar. The church is "hidden" within a school building. The community forgets the church exists.

3. Limits ministry excellence, especially to children and youth.

4. Ministry hardship—setting up children's ministry, technical equipment (sound, lights, video), and first impressions (hospitality, welcome) every Sunday.

Theaters

A growing trend for church plants in recent years has been movie theaters. The explosion of the megaplex (ten or more theaters at one location) in the last decade has created incredible capacity with opportunities for multitheater use.

Theaters are typically in prime locations with great accessibility. Parking is in abundance. Seating is exceptional with great sight lines. Large theater complexes allow for expansion and/or intimacy depending on the crowd size or venue choice. Food and drink is typically allowed within the facility. In addition, many theater companies hope to partner with church plants as a source of additional revenue for their businesses.

One of the biggest challenges with the theater option is appropriate space for children's ministry. Churches need creativity to create a clean and safe environment for children. At Life Journey Church in Bakersfield, California,[5] the large space located in front of the screen in one of the theaters is sectioned off with baby gates. Rolled up carpet is stored behind the theater screen and brought out each week to cover unclean movie theater carpet. Creativity can transform almost any space.

Time constraints on Sunday morning limit service time flexibility. Movie showings as early as 11:30 a.m. on a Sunday can be challenging for church attendees who want to linger after the services. Seating configuration designed for presentation rather than participation or interaction also can pose a challenge for more interactive services that attract postmodern generations. Sound deadening in the theater can minimize the energy level of the experience.

Theater Case Study: National Community Church[6]

On January 7, 1996, National Community Church launched with 19 people in a school in Washington DC. Nine months later the school was condemned because of fire code violations and NCC became homeless. It took two months before the small band of missionaries found a new home. On November 17, 1996, NCC held its first service in the movie theaters at Union Station. Union Station is home to nearly 150 retail shops and restaurants. Located four blocks from the Capitol, it is one of the most accessible and visible places in DC. Nearly 100,000 people pass through the station each day. By virtue of its location, NCC has its own metro stop, bus stop, and train depot. "We've had people come to church during a layover on Amtrak and get back on the train headed in a totally different direction spiritually." Approximately one-quarter of the congregation gets to church via metro. And when NCCers exit church, they can choose from forty food court restaurants or hang around and catch a movie. On September 21, 2003, NCC launched its second location in the Regal Theaters at Ballston Common Mall and now has over 750 people in weekly attendance at its two locations. It is the dream of National Community to have a location at every Metro stop with a theater in the entire Washington DC area.

Mark Batterson, Lead Pastor, was asked, "After seven years of meeting in a theater, what are the pros and cons for using a theater for church planting?" Batterson shared the following pros for meeting in a theater:

1. An overflow of comfortable seats.

2. The screen, in most cases, is postmodern stained glass—it's how we tell the story in pictures and video.

3. We want to be in the middle of the marketplace, and a theater really is the marketplace of ideas in our culture.

4. It's also helpful meeting in a place people frequent anyway. It eliminates one major excuse people use to not attend church—"I've never been there before."

5. Accessibility and visibility—We don't have to tell anybody where NCC is because everybody already knows.

Batterson's cons for meeting in a theater include:

1. Gum.

2. Time constraints—We don't feel the same freedom to extend services.

3. The set up and tear down is tough, but we've made the theater semipermanent (equipment and materials stored behind the screen, speakers installed, etc.).

4. I think children's ministry is a little bit of a challenge, although in some ways it's cool to have a theater for kids.

Centers, Storefront/Warehouses and Existing Church Buildings

Additionally, you can find churches meeting in a variety of places including community centers, storefronts, warehouses, and existing church buildings. The following are mini case studies for each viable option.

Community Center Case Study: Community Christian Church[7]

The South Campus of Community Christian Church in Romeoville, Illinois, was born in 1998 out of a developer's dream to infuse the community he experienced through a small group into the real estate developments he created. As part of a master planned community, a 27,000 square foot community center was constructed to bring the residents of the development together. Community Christian Church was involved in the design of the facility where its South Campus would meet weekly for celebration services. Over 800 people now attend this location each weekend.

What are some pros for meeting in this type of facility for worship?

1. High level of involvement with residents.

2. Usage agreement with owner allows great flexibility.

3. Establishes permanency in a location you don't own.

4. Very cost effective.

On the other hand, potential cons for starting a church in a community center would include:

1. Limited amount of space for children's programming.

2. Nonweekend schedule conflicts with other programs.

Storefront/Warehouse Case Study: Jacob's Well Community Church[8]

After searching various locations such as schools and theaters, Dave Richa and his team decided to maximize impact while minimizing expenses. Jacob's Well Community Church was launched in January 2002 with two Saturday evening services and a unique partnership with Northern Hills Christian Church. Northern Hills was living out their church planting dream by allowing Jacob's Well to meet in their storefront location on Saturday nights, where they met on Sunday mornings. Northern Hills had land purchased and was in the process of initiating construction of their permanent home. In April 2003, Northern Hills moved into their permanent facility and Jacob's Well took over the lease for the storefront location and added two Sunday morning services. Jacob's Well now runs just over 400 people each weekend.

Pros for meeting in a storefront/warehouse, as experienced by Jacob's Well Community church, include:

1. Minimal set-up required.

2. Weekday presence and programming available.

3. Location within high traffic area.

Cons for meeting in this facility include:

1. Long-term cost of lease.

2. Conflict with retail schedules other than Sunday.

Existing Church Building Case Study:[9] Community Christian Church

In September 2002, a church with a 160-year history made the decision to focus on legacy in lieu of longevity. As the church decided to cease operation, it also decided to donate its 35-year-old facility and land to Community Christian Church. Over the course of six months the facility was rehabbed and modified in preparation for the launch of its West Campus. In March 2003, the West Campus was launched with two Sunday services. Today over 450 people celebrate weekly in this existing church facility.

Community Christian Church (West Campus) reported the following pros for meeting in an existing church building:

1. 24/7 ownership of the facility.

2. Limited weekly facility transformation required.

3. Extensive weekday programming opportunities.

They also reported the following cons for meeting in an existing church building:

1. Expense of facility rehabilitation or live with existing condition.

2. Limitations of existing architecture.

3. Limited off-street parking.

Weekday/Office Space

At some point every successful church planter will have to decide if and/or when to acquire permanent or weekday space. Most church planters choose to be fiscally responsible early in the life of a new church plant and utilize existing facilities such as a basement, garage, or room in a house for the team's office space. When the time comes for weekday or office space outside the home, one should first look for cheap or free space. Unused offices or idle retail space exists in almost every community. Relationships within the church or community may yield this space for little or no cost. As time goes by, expanded weekday space may be necessary to continue to impact your local community. Use of an experienced commercial real estate agent will expedite finding the various options. Before you sign a lease or purchase space, make sure you understand the local zoning laws and the costs associated with renovating the space to meet your specific needs.

Permanent Space

From the first Sunday people will ask, "So, when are you going to get a permanent facility?" Take your time. Establish the church as an impact player in the community. Be creative. Look to the future. Pray for direction. Ask for the impossible. Then build or buy.

Conclusion

From the beginning of time, God has dwelt in many different locations—from a mountain to a tent to a temple. He has used many interesting spaces to fulfill His mission—the belly of a fish, a pagan king's palace, and even a manger. The initial meeting place of a church plant is important, maybe even critical. Go for the best facility possible. And remember, if we are to fulfill the Great Commission, there will have to be a multitude of new churches in schools, theaters, community centers, restaurants, hotels, warehouses, and storefronts. Plus, we will still have to ask God for the ability to do church in a barn.

God has used many interesting spaces to fulfill His mission—the belly of a fish, a pagan king's palace, and even a manger.

---

[1] See Acts 13–28 for a detailed account of Paul's missionary journeys.

[2] Ed Stetzer, *Planting New Churches in a Postmodern Age* (Nashville: Broadman and Holman, 2003) 242.

[3] For more information on portable church equipment, check out **www.church-equipment.com**.

[4] See Evergreen Community Church's web site at **www.evergreencc.com** for more information regarding the history and current programs of this multicampus church.

[5] For more information on Life Journey Church, see their web site at **www.lifejourneychurch.com**.

[6] National Community Church currently has two locations that meet in theaters along the Metro rail system of Washington, DC. Further information about this dynamic ministry can be found at **www.theaterchurch.com**.

[7] Check on Community Christian Church at **www.communitychristian.org** for more information on this creative and thriving ministry.

[8] For more information on Jacob's Well Community Church in Thornton, Colorado, visit their web site at **www.jacobswell.cc**.

[9] Visit **www.communitychristian.org** to learn more about the West Campus ministry of Community Christian Church in Montgomery, Illinois.

Dr. Bob Harrington is the founding and senior minister of Harpeth Community Church in Franklin, Tennessee, and the Director of Planter Care for Stadia in the Southeast Region of the United States. He received his Doctor of Ministry degree in Evangelism and Church Growth from The Southern Baptist Theological Seminary in Louisville, Kentucky, just before Christmas 2003. He is also the husband of Cindy and the proud father of Ashley Rose and Robert Chad. He also plays hockey every week with his pagan buddies.

Outreach Evangelism and Church Planting

*I*n 1996 I left an established church in the Nashville, Tennessee, area to plant Harpeth Community Church in Franklin, a city just south of Nashville. I had dreamed of planting a church for many years, and now the opportunity was mine. I could lead lost people to Christ in a contemporary, cutting-edge setting! Ever since I became a Christian as a university student I had considered myself a very evangelistic person. I had helped win my parents, two of my sisters, various friends, and many other people to Christ. It never occurred to me that I was, in reality, not that great at evangelism.

Being the conscientious church planter that I was, I wanted to make sure that I was properly assessed (even after I had already started the work!). So, I set up an assessment interview with Dr. Charles Ridley, the pioneer of assessment tools for church planters. I thought that I would breeze through the assessment and, if anything came up, it would be just some minor weakness. To my surprise, according to Dr. Ridley, I was significantly weak in evangelism.

For a few years after my conversion, I was determined to be a very evangelistic person. But I slowly developed an orientation around church—all of my best energies were invested in the people I knew or met there. Even though I was regarded as a very evangelistic person, church had become the primary place where I met the people that I led to Christ. Until Ridley's assessment, I didn't get it. To be a truly evangelistic person, I needed to follow Jesus and actually go out and find lost people (Luke 15).

To be a truly evangelistic person, I needed to follow Jesus and actually go out and find lost people (Luke 15).

My new church coaches told me that it was a standard policy for church planters to spend up to *fifty percent* of their time building evangelistic relationships. That sounded like a daunting task to me. Who would I make connections with? What would I do? Where could I tastefully make such connections? When would I find the time? Why had I been so blind to such an incredible need?

It is now six years later. By God's grace I have effectively answered these questions and learned how to do outreach evangelism. But my experience as a coach of church planters and a student of evangelism shows me that, like myself, few church leaders really know how to be evangelistic. Almost every Christian thinks (as I did) that he or she knows how it should be done, but only a handful really "do it." I now know better. I have learned that those who "really do" outreach evangelism live by four key principles.

The "Intentionality" Principle

If you want to reach lost people, it must become your constant goal.

The most important principle that you will ever learn about effective evangelism is intentionality. If you want to reach lost people, it must become your constant goal. Intentionality is making evangelism a top priority in all activities, relationships, and contacts with unchurched people.[1] You must purposefully and constantly live with this end in mind. I like the way Ed Stetzer puts it:

> Without intentionality, evangelism remains undone. Intentionality causes the planter to plan for personal evangelism and leads to the creation of a strategy that is characterized by a high level of commitment to reach the unchurched. The staff members at many new churches hold one another accountable for building relationships with the unchurched.[2]

Effective evangelistic leaders intentionally "invest and invite."[3] They "invest" in relationships with lost people, so they can "invite" them into a life changing relationship with Jesus Christ.

If you closely examine denominations, churches, and individuals that are successful at evangelism, you will find, without exception, that they all made evangelism the top ministry priority. In the early 1990s, Charles Kelly set out to determine why the Southern Baptists were the fastest growing Protestant Denomination over five decades. Kelly tells us what he learned: "Southern Baptists have found evangelism to be the logical foundation of their denominational identity and the single most important driving force in their practice."[4] Southeast Christian Church in Louisville, Kentucky, is arguably the largest and most evangelistic church in North America (half of those attending came from an unchurched background). Their senior leader, Bob Russell, tells us how they did it when he writes, "Our primary call is to preach the gospel and bring people to salvation in Jesus."[5]

Thom Rainer and his research team investigated evangelistic church leaders. He writes, "If there was a single characteristic that separated the pastors of effective [evangelistic] churches from other pastors, it was the issue of accountability in personal evangelism."[6] A whopping 43% of pastors established some type of accountability for their own personal evangelism in evangelistic churches, compared to 2% in nonevangelistic churches. The apostle Paul describes the Intentionality Principle in 1 Corinthians 9:19-23:

> Though I am free and belong to no man, I make myself a slave to everyone, to win as many as possible . . . I have become all things to all men so that by all possible means I might save some.[7]

This principle is timeless—throughout history, those who effectively reached lost people lived by the intentionality principle.[8] You can learn a lot about evangelism, but the first thing you must do is master the "Intentionality Principle." You will not be a consistently evangelistic church planter and the church you are establishing will not have long-term success in reaching lost people under your leadership if you do not learn and implement this principle.

Action Plan for the Church Planter

- Meditate upon how you can best spend *up to 50%* of your prelaunch time intentionally building relationships and reaching out to unchurched people. You will need to spend more time meeting people, building relationships, and sharing your faith than you think. Spend more time on evangelism than anything else.

- Consciously build relationships by going to the same gas station, the same restaurants, the same copier place, etc. A new church in Florida intentionally made Starbucks, Borders, and Barnes and Nobles Booksellers their offices before the church launched. They developed relationships with the waiters/waitresses and then, when the church was launched, these non-Christians happily agreed to help by serving as greeters and ushers.

- Intentionally build relationships with non-Christians: join sports teams, coach little league, or find unknown golf partners. A church leader in Washington State joined the Rotary Club. He became good friends with many of the businessmen in the area. Several came to the church and became Christians.

- Ask your leaders to join you in being accountable for evangelism every week. Make sure that you hire staff members with a track record in evangelism and ask them to be accountable for evangelism on a weekly basis.

- Get your launch team to come up with projects and group activities that enable you to relationally connect with unchurched people. Steve Sjogren has some good projects to try in his book, *101 Ways to Reach Your Community*.[9]

- Make evangelism your priority when you develop budgets, ministries, and plans for the new church. Make sure that you spend more money on evangelism than anything else and make sure that evangelism is one of the primary purposes of *every ministry*.

The "Community First" Principle

Think for a few minutes about this principle before you accept or reject it. Ed Stetzer describes it well: "The first conversion is the conversion to community. With few exceptions, people come to Christ after they have journeyed with other Christians—examining them and considering their claims."[10] If we are even modestly to replicate the process which the disciples experienced at the feet of Jesus, then we must invite spiritual seekers into the life of our community before they become Christians.[11]

Relationships—like those that Jesus had with the twelve, and Paul had with his converts—are essential because they provide the context in which seekers can examine the truth claims of the gospel.

It is also in the context of relationships that seekers can be touched by the love of Christians. Jesus told us there is one significant item by which unbelievers could know that we are His disciples: "A new command I give you: Love one another. As I have loved you, so you must love one another. By this all men will know that you are my disciples, if you love one another" (John 13:34-35). When in community with us, non-Christians will experience the truth of the gospel.

> ## When in community with us, non-Christians will experience the truth of the gospel.

John Rambo is one of the world's leading authorities on the psychology of religious conversion. He sums up the importance of relationships in the conversion process:

> When loving friends and family affirm the worldview, life-style, and goals of a shared religious organization, this reinforcement is crucial to the creation of a "real" world. Overall, relationships provide an environment of security that nurtures, supports, encourages, and sustains the new life of the convert.[12]

The likelihood that a person will experience a conversion is directly related to the strong attachment that this person has to one or more committed believers. Statistically, it is a fact that the conversion rate increases when there is continued and intensive interaction between non-Christians and their Christian friends.[13] The "community first" principle shows us that the involvement of unchurched people in the church—before they become Christians—is one of the most important elements in outreach.[14]

> ## Involvement of unchurched people in the church—before they become Christians—is one of the most important elements in outreach.

Action Plan for the Church Planter

- Purposefully and regularly create social entry points into the church—social gatherings, small groups, and special outings are essential connection points for spiritual seekers.

- Purposefully find places where non-Christians can help out in the ministries of the church before they become Christians. Establish which jobs only Christians can perform, and open up the rest to your non-Christian friends.

- As you have the resources, create special small groups which meet the needs of unchurched people in social settings. Many have found the following groups to be effective—Divorce Care,[15] Financial Peace University,[16] Dynamic Marriages,[17] Quest For Authentic Manhood,[18] and others. The people who attend these groups naturally become part of the community of the church.

The "Process" Principle

Faith development—for most people—is a process. It was true in the Bible, and it is true today.[19] Instantaneous or sudden conversions, like that of the apostle Paul, are rare. This is seen through an in-depth study of the disciples, especially in the Gospel of Mark. Richard Peace shows how it works in his book, *Conversion in the New Testament*. He writes, "If . . . you understand conversion to be a process that unfolds over time, as it did for the Twelve, then your question to others is apt to be 'Where are you in your spiritual pilgrimage and with what issue are you wrestling when it comes to God?'"[20]

Many evangelical Christians continue to present the gospel to non-Christians and call for an immediate response. In a culture where basic Christian assumptions predominated, this approach was often effective, but such a culture is rapidly disappearing in North America. Most non-Christians now need time to process the implications of the gospel. You must develop a model that helps people to process the overarching message of the Bible while considering the basic claims of Christ.[21]

The Engel Scale is a popular model used to help people see conversion as a process.[22] As the scale shows, a conversion is first preceded by "mini-decisions" or "small steps" that lead up to the decision to surrender to Christ. Look at the bottom of the scale and see how people process the faith and move up to a commitment, as God leads them.

```
            + 5 Stewardship
          + 4 Communion with God
        + 3 Conceptual and behavioral growth
      + 2 Incorporation into Body
    + 1 Postdecision evaluation
New birth
  -1 Repentance and faith in Christ
    -2 Decision to act
      -3 Personal problem recognition
        -4 Positive attitude towards gospel
          -5 Grasp implications of gospel
            -6 Awareness of fundamentals of gospel
              -7 Initial awareness of gospel
                -8 Awareness of a supreme being, no knowledge of gospel
```

If someone starts the "faith journey" at −8, it is unwise to try to move that individual all the way to −1 in one sitting. He or she will likely have a negative reaction. Instead, we are well advised to help the individual process the claims of Christ by moving one step at a time, from −8 to −7, then from −7 to −6, and so forth.

There have been other modifications of the Engel scale,[23] including the Gray Matrix[24] and the Stetzer Evangelism Journey.[25] Recently, a modification of the Engel scale has been proposed by Thom Rainer and his research team.[26] The Rainer scale delineates where unchurched people are in the process of coming to Christ and what people need at each step.[27] According to Rainer, there are approximately sixty-one million Americans who are very open to Christianity. These are the most receptive people, and wise church planters will quickly learn how to find and make connections with them.

> Wise church planters will quickly learn how to find and make connections with the most receptive people.

Action Plan for the Church Planter

- As you develop relationships with unchurched people, try to gain a sense of where they are in spiritual matters. Make it your goal to invite them to move in a journey one step at a time as they process the faith. Resist the urge to rush people!

- Encourage people to get involved in the church before they commit themselves to Christ. Many church plants utilize nonchurch people to be greeters, ushers, musicians, and setup personnel. Take risks in this area, and the rewards will be great.

- Develop specific processes, classes, and stages for those who attend the church. Constantly invite them to move closer to Christ—while creating specific places (special sermons and membership classes) and times (monthly baptismal services) in which you boldly proclaim the gospel.

- Invite unchurched people to take special courses that are designed to help them process the claims of Christ. Courses like the British *Alpha Course*[28] or the new *Exploring Christianity*

Course[29] are designed to help people process the claims of the gospel in a group setting. These courses are built around the understanding that conversion is a process.

The "Word" Principle

The Bible teaches that people come to faith in Christ because of the teaching of God's Word. Unchurched people must call on Christ to be saved, but they must first hear about how to be saved through the teaching of the Word of God.

> How, then, can they call on the one they have not believed in? And how can they believe in the one of whom they have not heard? And how can they hear without someone preaching to them? . . . Consequently, faith comes from hearing the message, and the message is heard through the word of Christ (Rom 10:14-17).

Too many church planters get focused upon music, drama, and the like—as if these things are the substance of what is effective in a new church. It is supremely important that you focus upon the Word. In Isaiah 55:11, God says it will "not return to me empty, but will accomplish what I desire and achieve the purpose for which I sent it."[30] As a church planter, make the Word your authority; show people that you are basing your beliefs upon what it says. Our world is craving grace-driven clarity. Teach the Bible!

Focus upon the Word. Our world is craving grace-driven clarity. Teach the Bible!

Thom Rainer's studies in *Effective Evangelistic Churches*,[31] *High Expectations*,[32] and *Surprising Insights from the Unchurched*[33] all confirm this same principle—unchurched people want to know what the Bible says and how it applies to their lives. They do not want us to water down the faith, but they want us to help them understand it, make sense of it, and show how it makes a difference in our lives. Doctrine is very important to unchurched people.

Action Plan for the Church Planter

- Provide Bibles for newcomers. If you can, provide everyone with the same Bible and then give them a page number so they can follow along with you.

- Provide a "basic beliefs" class where you explain the elementary teachings of the Bible.[34] The *Purpose-Driven Church* describes how you can create a membership class, but include basic Christianity material in it too.[35] It is important that you develop a class like this so that you can show people what the Bible says about becoming a Christian.

- In all small groups and classes, make it a practice to use the Bible and ask everyone to bring their Bible. Provide Bibles in all settings for newcomers.

Concluding Thoughts

When we first started Harpeth Community Church and I realized the daunting task of becoming the church's leader in outreach evangelism, I panicked. But I then learned by God's guidance what I had to do. I fasted, prayed, and then developed an action plan. In addition to developing relationships with unchurched people in all kinds of different contexts, I developed a focus. My son and I both love hockey (we are Canadians after all!), and there were few committed Christians in community hockey. The newly focused commitment was easy. Instead of just focusing on enjoying hockey and talking to a few people at the rink (which is what we had done), we decided that we would purposefully reach out and work at developing significant friendships with the players and their families.

> I fasted, prayed, and then developed an action plan.

I signed on as the coach of a couple of teams. My son, a very good hockey player and a committed young Christian, and I joined together in the mission. We hung out with the boys and their families. We traveled with them to play hockey in surrounding cities. We joked with them, played with them, and we all became close friends. Because we stepped out and formed relationships with them, it was easy to invite them to the new church and youth groups. By God's grace we intentionally "invested" in relationships with them, "invited and involved" them in the life of the church even though they did not yet believe, gave them space and time to process the claims of the gospel, and showed them what the Bible taught.

Many families ended up becoming a part of the church. In the second year that I coached, over half the families on the team became regular attendees at the church. Many became Christians. We became known in the early years as the "hockey church." By the time that happened, I finally got it. I had learned how to do outreach evangelism. Now I am convinced that with God's help you can do it too!

---

[1] To catch the passion for the "intentionality principle," read Mark Cahill's *One Thing You Can't Do in Heaven* (Stone Mountain, GA: Mark Cahill Self-Published, 2003); available at **www.MarkCahill.com**.

[2] Ed Stetzer, *Planting New Churches in a Postmodern Age* (Nashville: Broadman and Holman, 2003) 187-188.

[3] Ibid.

[4] Charles S. Kelly, *How Did They Do It? The Story of Southern Baptist Evangelism* (New Orleans: Insight Press, 1993).

[5] Bob Russell, *When God Builds a Church* (West Monroe, LA: Howard Publishing, 2000) 251.

[6] Thom Rainer, *Surprising Insights from the Unchurched* (Grand Rapids: Zondervan, 2001) 162.

[7] All Scripture quotations are taken from the *New International Version* unless otherwise stated.

[8] "I look upon this world as a wrecked vessel," D.L. Moody said, "God has given me a lifeboat and said to me, "Moody, save all you can"; see William G. McLoughlin, *Revivals, Awakenings, & Reform: An Essay on Religion and Social Change in America* (Chicago: University of Chicago Press, 1980) 144. Spurgeon stated, "If you think you are going to win souls, you must throw your soul into your work, just as a warrior must throw his soul into a battle, or victory will not be yours. . . . Indeed it is a race. As such, nobody wins unless he strains every muscle and sinew"; see C.H. Spurgeon, *The Soul Winner*, reprint ed. (Springdale, PA.: Whitaker House, 1995) 203-204. It may be an overstatement, but Billy Graham stated the common refrain of evangelistic people: "My one purpose in life is to help people find a personal relationship with God"; see Russ Busby, *Billy Graham: God's Ambassador* (Minneapolis: Billy Graham Evangelistic Association, 1999) 1.

[9] Steve Sjogren, *101 Ways to Reach Your Community* (Colorado Springs: NavPress, 2001).

[10] Ed Stetzer, *Planting New Churches in a Postmodern Age* (Nashville: Broadman and Holman, 2003) 193.

[11] For more information, see Robert Coleman's book, *The Master Plan of Evangelism*, 2nd ed. (Grand Rapids: Fleming H Revell, 1994).

[12] Lewis Rambo, *Understanding Religious Conversion* (New Haven, CT: Yale University Press, 1993) 109.

[13] Ralph Hood, Richard Gorsuch, and Bernard Spilka, *The Psychology of Religion: An Empirical Approach* (Englewood Cliffs, NJ: Prentice-Hall, 1985) 213.

[14] See Dennis Hollinger, "The Church as Apologetic: A Sociology of Knowledge

Perspective," in *Christian Apologetics in the Postmodern World*, ed. by Timothy R. Phillips and Dennis L. Okholm (Downers Grove, IL: InterVarsity, 1995); and George Hunter, *The Celtic Way of Evangelism* (Nashville: Abingdon Press, 2000).

[15] For more information, visit [on-line] http://www.divorcecare.org.

[16] For more information, visit [on-line] http://www.daveramsey.com.

[17] For more information, visit [on-line] http://www.familydynamics.net.

[18] For more information, visit [on-line] http://www.mensfraternity.com.

[19] Lewis Rambo, "Theories of Conversion: Understanding and Interpreting Religious Change," *Social Compass: International Review of Sociology of Religion*, 46 (1999): 259-271; and Scott Thumma, "Seeking to Be Converted: An Examination of Recent Conversion Studies and Theories," *Pastoral Psychology*, vol. 39 (1991): 185-194. See also Hood, Gorsuch, and Spilka, *Psychology*.

[20] Richard Peace, *Conversion in the New Testament* (Grand Rapids: Eerdmans, 1999) 286.

[21] D.A. Carson, *The Gagging of God* (Grand Rapids: Zondervan, 1996); Graeme Goldsworthy, *According to Plan: The Unfolding of Revelation of God in the Bible* (Downers Grove, IL: InterVarsity, 1991); and Hollinger, "Church as Apologetic."

[22] This model is discussed in Bill Bright and Mark McCloskey, *Tell It Often, Tell It Well* (San Bernadino, CA: Here's Life Publishers, 1985); and in James F. Engel and Wilbert H. Norton, *What's Gone Wrong with the Harvest* (Grand Rapids: Zondervan, 1975).

[23] Jim Peterson has produced the most comprehensive program for evangelism training based on the realization that conversion is a process; see the video training course, *Living Proof: Evangelism* [Video Series] (Grand Rapids: Zondervan, 1997). Peterson has also written a book along these lines, but it is not as helpful in understanding conversion as a process as the video series. See Jim Peterson, *Living Proof: Sharing the Gospel Naturally* (Colorado Spring: NavPress, 1989).

[24] http://www.thegraymatrix.info.

[25] Stetzer, *Planting*, 192.

[26] See Thom Rainer, *The Unchurched Next Door* (Grand Rapids: Zondervan, 2003); and Thom Rainer, "Trendline: An Overview of Interesting Developments in the Church," *Rainer Report* (January, 2003) 3.

[27] Thom Rainer, "Newest Insights on the Unchurched/Faith Stages" (classroom lecture notes, 80514 - *Doctor of Ministry Seminar in Evangelism and Church Growth*, January 2003, class lecture).

[28] Many of us have major theological concerns with the Alpha Course (for example, never once does the course discuss hell), but it is very popular, having been tried by over 2.5 million people. See Nicky Gumble, *How to Run the Alpha Course* [Video Training Program] (New York: Alpha North America, 2001), and his written material in *How to Run the Alpha Course*, rev. ed. (New York: Alpha North America, 2001).

[29] *Exploring Christianity* is a new course for unchurched people and spiritual seekers that I created under Dr. Thom Rainer as part of my Doctor of Ministry program at The Southern Baptist Theological Seminary in 2003. We have witnessed *significant* success in the course through the field-testing in 2003. For information contact me at BobHarrington@aol.com.

[30] Bryan Chappell has a good discussion on this point in the first chapter of his book, *Christ-Centered Preaching* (Grand Rapids: Baker, 1994).

[31] Thom Rainer, *Effective Evangelistic Churches* (Nashville: Broadman and Holman, 1996).

[32] Thom Rainer, *High Expectations: The Remarkable Secret to Keeping People in Your Church* (Nashville: Broadman and Holman, 1999).

[33] Thom Rainer, *Surprising Insights*.

[34] You can obtain a sample of what we use entitled, *Basic Christianity*. Contact me at **BobHarrington@aol.com**.

[35] See Rick Warren, *The Purpose-Driven Church* (Grand Rapids: Zondervan, 1995).

Debbie Jones has directed the Children's Ministry at First Christian Church in Johnson City, Tennessee, since 1999. This exciting ministry touches over 300 children and their families. She has twenty-five years of local church experience working with children and has conducted children's ministry workshops and seminars throughout the United States. Debbie was the founding Children's Minister for Princeton Community Church (PCC) in Princeton, New Jersey. She also teamed with her husband Tom to start both PCC and SouthBrook Christian Church in Centerville, Ohio. Debbie graduated from Milligan College in 1977 and is the mother of two college age children.

Lisa Jones was the founding Children's Director for Christ's Church of the Valley, a new church in the suburbs of Philadelphia. Under her direction the Children's Ministry grew from her own children to over 200 (fifth grade and under) each week. Along with her husband Brian, Lisa was an integral part of planting two churches, one in a Philadelphia suburb and the other near Dayton, Ohio. Lisa taught as a public school teacher for many years and received her elementary education degree from the University of Cincinnati. She and her husband Brian have three wonderful little girls.

Strategies for Creating a Dynamic Children's Ministry

On December 6, 1992, Princeton Community Church (PCC) was born. Over 300 area residents showed up that day. One couple came with their little girl. This particular couple had not been regular attendees in a church for many years. Although they grew up in a church, they became disconnected and disinterested over the years. However, when their daughter came into the family picture, they decided that maybe she needed exposure to church and spiritual teaching. They began their family journey with PCC because they loved their daughter. Deep down, they knew she needed something more.

> Creating an excellent Children's Ministry in a new church may be the most important thing you do to ensure the success of your church plant.

Creating an excellent Children's Ministry in a new church may be the most important thing you do to ensure the success of your church plant. We've seen new churches that place a strong emphasis on ministering to kids and families and those that don't. Without exception, the churches that value children are much more effective.

250

Jesus was the first role model of valuing children and we, the church, should follow His lead.

At a recent Children's Ministry conference, the keynote speaker of a well-known megachurch said, if he had only one staff hire to make, it would be a children's pastor. His comment reinforces our conviction that Children's Ministry is so much more than babysitting or simply serving the nonbelieving adult population. Together, we could tell you many stories of people who have regularly attended our churches because their kids wanted to come back! It is so exciting to see the kids teaching their parents what they're learning, resulting in the parents themselves beginning to seek after God.

You might be thinking, "Yeah, I'm with you, but how do I build a strong Children's Ministry when I don't even have a church yet?" Without a doubt, faith is the most important virtue in developing a new church and its individual programs. You must pray and have faith like never before, or your dreams of an awesome Children's Ministry will never be realized.

Big Picture

The first thing you need to do is plan what your Children's Ministry should look like after it is well developed. Don't be afraid to dream big. While it is important to consider basics such as how many classes to launch or how to acquire volunteers, also ask, "What makes kids want to go to Disney World?" Once you put this foundation in place, vision planning and action steps naturally follow.

Plan what your Children's Ministry should look like after it is well developed. Don't be afraid to dream big.

Atmosphere and Structure

When children walk into a class at church, you want them to think, "Wow, I want to be here!" In addition, you want parents to walk into your Children's Ministry area, hear Christian music that's age appropriate, and trust this child-friendly, exciting space as a place their children will want to be. With new churches in particular, meeting spaces are often rented or leased. In these cases, how do you convert a school, movie theater, or hotel ballroom into an inviting place for kids? It's easier than it sounds with the help of Velcro and duct tape!

If the rental facility will allow you to store equipment on site, fall down on your knees and thank God. Many new churches are forced to transport their equipment each week. If that's your situation, invest in sturdy cabinets on wheels that can hold large plastic containers. You can buy them pre-made from church planting suppliers, contract a local carpenter to build some, or better yet find an engineer/carpenter from a supporting church to do the job. A word of caution: although most supply companies will try to convince you that their equipment is absolutely necessary, sometimes being creative with the resources God has already given you is the best and least expensive solution. Unfortunately, new church budgets, especially Children's Ministry budgets, are never large enough. With that in mind, be creative. Look at what God has already given you, and creatively use those resources for the good of His kingdom. You'd be surprised what passionate, innovative people can slip under a movie theater screen. You would also be surprised to see how generous people are when it comes to giving to a new church's children's ministry.

To create "atmosphere," consider hanging posters, banners, and pictures that relate to classroom lessons. Place items around the room that tie into your current teaching theme(s). In your preschool rooms, invest in toys like Little Tykes' play sets. Also, either purchase or rent baby swings, toddler tables, boppies, interactive toys and a changing table for your nursery. Many toy suppliers will donate these items to a worthy cause. We also suggest equipping your children's spaces with TV/VCR combos, rolls of carpet, child-sized tables and chairs, gates or protection barriers, and basic supplies like crayons, scissors, glue, Play-Doh, paper, and either a stereo or a small portable sound system.

Many new church planters ask, "How many classrooms should we start with?" That's a great question, and it is highly dependent on your specific situation. Although there are several rotational methods currently in practice, from our experiences in new church plants, you can always start with the essentials. Begin with a nursery, toddler class, preschool class, and an elementary age division. Then expand based on the needs of your young congregation.

By using this classroom structure and a monthly rotation for teachers and helpers, it's more feasible to grow the ministry, teach the children, and retain volunteers. The concept of teachers only teaching once a month is tough for some to embrace. Many times, however, this strategy is more effective. Many once-a-month teachers are more excited about serving; therefore they put 150% effort into their lessons because they are able to attend "big church" three out of four Sundays a month. Their creativity level is incredibly high. For example, to illustrate the story of Noah's ark, one of our volunteer teachers brought in live animals instead of simply reading the story to the kids. Additionally, it's a lot easier to recruit volunteers for one Sunday a month than to ask people to commit to every Sunday.

Recruitment

One of the toughest jobs of any children's director is recruitment. Far too often, people have had negative experiences when working with children in a church, and for good reason. For example, as leaders we are so happy to have a smiling, loving adult to serve in our toddler room that we often fail to properly train them. Worse yet, we're so thrilled that someone is willing to serve with the fifth graders that we leave them there *all alone* until they quit. With obstacles like these to overcome, our ability to recruit can be downright hard. Consider the following suggestions when recruiting Children's Ministry volunteers.

Ask sister churches to send teams of volunteers for the first two or three months.

♦ Ask sister churches to send teams of volunteers for the first two or three months. At Christ's Church in the Valley, for example, servants drove almost five hours to volunteer on Sunday mornings. After receiving outside assistance, make sure to overemphasize appreciation for your volunteers.

♦ Recruit close family and friends—people you know you can trust and who believe in your vision. Involve them early in your church plant, and both parties will be blessed.

♦ Recruit local college students to assist in the classroom. Many universities and school-sponsored organizations or clubs require students to complete community service hours before graduation.

♦ Invite people to get involved within weeks of your grand opening. People want to be a part of something that's exciting and growing.

_____

Invite people to get involved within weeks of your grand opening.

♦ Most importantly, share your vision for the ministry with newcomers who are beginning to seriously explore and connect with your church through prelaunch activities. However, be careful not to invite burnout in these individuals. Consider implementing a rotating lead teacher system that enables your people to serve and still be fed. Volunteers can't lead if they aren't getting fed themselves. Like it or not, many of the people who volunteer early on are not Christians _yet_. In the early days of Christ's Church in the Valley, we had just divided into small groups when one of the volunteers yelled out, "Hey, Lisa, what page is Romans 8:28 on?" It was an incredible moment—volunteers were learning right along with kids. That particular story is an example of a child leading a parent. Both of her children committed their lives to Christ shortly after the church opened, and she was baptized a couple of years later. Isn't that amazing?

Networks

Whether you're a veteran Children's Director or a rookie, networking is necessary in order for your ministry to not just survive, but thrive. Whether you have experience in education or not, attend children's conferences, subscribe to educational magazines, and, most of all, spend time with veteran Children's Ministers. Learn from the experts!

Networking is also a valuable tool for new church planting. Despite limited resources, continuous networking provides unlimited opportunities to raise the level of excellence in ministry. For example, resources for extra programs such as Christmas musicals or VBS are often limited. After examining all of your options, consider networking with an established church to acquire their old Christmas sets or VBS materials. The level of generosity extended for the benefit of the kingdom might surprise you. Sometimes just asking for "hand-me-downs" provides ways for a new church to raise its level of excellence in order to reach children in today's culture.

Networking opportunities are everywhere. For example, each month area children's ministers from various church affiliations in Tennessee come together to share ideas, support each other's ministry, and plan training for an annual conference. They share sets, equipment, ideas, and new resources.

A third way of networking could result from asking churches to adopt your ministry by meeting your needs. For example, I (Debbie) remember trying to find a way to provide our teachers in Princeton with basic supplies (crayons, scissors, construction paper, and other needs). I prayed and asked the Lord to help me find these materials for our teachers. Within a couple days, Southland Christian Church in Lexington, Kentucky, called and asked if we would be their mission project for their VBS. "Sure!" we said, not even fully understanding what a *big* answer to prayer this was. I immediately sent a list of supplies that our teachers needed, mentioning only the basics. To our church's delight, Southland Christian Church provided 1000 packages of each desperately needed supply. There is no doubt—God provides! After establishing your church plant's ministry, look for ways to share your acquired resources with others in need, especially other new church plants. That's what Southland did with PCC, and what PCC later did for other new churches.

Resources do not have to always be within your church congregation. They don't even have to be in your own town. Churches from across the nation can be used by God to meet your needs and raise your level of excellence through networking.

Context

Knowing to whom you are ministering is important in any church, but it is especially true in a new church plant. In addition to acquiring general demographic research, spend time with the people in your community in order to understand and reach them. A Midwestern girl, Lisa, learned firsthand the importance of knowing her culture's language. Just after moving to the northeast, she asked a salesman where the "pop" was in his convenience store. He had a look of horror on his face and said, "We don't sell *that* here." She then replied, "You don't have any Coke?" "No, never," was his indignant response. In a final effort to get what she came for, Lisa asked, "How about Pepsi, or Sprite?" "Oh!" he said with a great sigh of relief, "You mean *soda*." Learn your new home's culture by becoming familiar with the lingo, idiosyncrasies, and values. In other words, don't ask for "pop" in the northeast unless you are prepared to receive some confused responses.

"Where do the kids hang out? What's in the community that attracts the local kids?"

To become familiar with your church plant's environment, ask "Where do the kids hang out? What's in the community that attracts the local kids? Is it the mall, skateboard park, swimming facilities, tennis courts, art centers, or some other place? What's the economic situation of your kids? What is the educational background of your families? What are the educational expectations of parents for their children? In what activities do the people participate?" Some areas of the country have a grand football tradition, while others play primarily field hockey and lacrosse.

Being able to answer these questions will assist you in designing programs. For example, in the northeast, kids often attend several area camps during the summer (and not one of them is church camp). So, instead of calling a summer program "Vacation Bible School" or "VBS," a new church plant in the northeast might call their camp "Kids' Camp." This simple semantic change connects with people in a way that the traditional titles would not. Making simple, cultural adjustments to your methods and language may attract children to God.

Registration and Security Systems

In today's society, we must be very concerned about security issues. Some churches are afraid that if you ask people to fill out a guest registration form or require parents to regularly sign their children in, they'll become upset. Quite the contrary! If you get your hand stamped at Chuck E. Cheese to make sure the right kid goes home with the right parent, then it shouldn't be surprising that churches also develop security systems for their children's programs. Some type of sign-in/sign-out system allows you to reassure parents and protect the ministry. In a new church, this is especially helpful since everyone is new, including staff and volunteers.

Although there are many possibilities for implementing an effective sign-in/sign-out system, make sure your final product appeals to children. They are your ministry audience. For example, when a family walks through your church doors, do they see large signs that have the Children's Ministry name and logo? This would help them know where to go. When they register their child, do the sign-in sheets match their child's nametag, which matches the child's security card, which matches the large classroom sign in the hallway? Kids are empowered (and parents are pleased) when they can match the animal on their nametag to the animal greeting them in front of their classroom. These are all great examples of how to make your Children's Ministry security system both effective and kid-friendly.

Screening volunteers is a challenge when the church is young and dollars are few. As a necessary precaution, take time to research and explore the different methods of screening volunteers. Establish systems within your ministry that protect every child and the church. Parents will be comforted and you'll be confident knowing that you've done everything possible to provide a safe place for children to learn about their loving Heavenly Father.

Outreach

It's pretty much common knowledge that most people commit their lives to Christ as a child or youth. That being the case, Children's Ministry is an excellent place to labor for the cause. Taking your ministry outside the walls of your church will do wonderful things for your young congregation. First, it encourages all the new believers and those still on the fringe to bond together. One of the best ways to get to know someone is to work side by side toward a common goal. Second, it exposes the community to your church. You may feel like you've sent out more postcards, hung more flyers, and advertised more than the last presidential hopeful, but there are many people in your community who still don't know you exist. Although somewhat discouraging, it's true.

Christ's Church in the Valley's most effective evangelistic event is Kids' Camp. They take the idea of a basic Vacation Bible School and jazz it up—a lot! They develop a theme based on what is hot with older kids. Weeks before the event, church volunteers plaster the community with signs and send home registration forms through the school system. If the Girl Scouts can do it, so can the church. They've had a "Survivor" week, learned about "X-treme" faith, and gotten a little wet during their "Splashdown" adventure. The church holds Kid's Camp at community-centered locations like parks or schools. They sing the most popular Christian music, play wacky games, communicate biblical lessons through multimedia and drama, and demonstrate God's love to hundreds of kids each summer. Their church members have even begun scheduling vacation time around camp because they want to be a part of something that makes a lasting difference. Using basic contextualization, Kid's Camp reaches hundreds of children for Christ each summer.

Strategically choose outreach opportunities. Some will be big. Others will be small, yet important. Host parties to celebrate and invite relationship building among the kids and volunteers. Organize seasonal events that are very easy for unchurched people to attend, such as a harvest party or picnic. They come to eat and have fun but end up discovering Christians are normal people who possess incredible hope.

Leadership

When you hear the word leadership, do you get excited or become intimidated and overwhelmed? If God has called you to lead, then be the best leader you can be. It may take some learning, and it will definitely involve "mess ups" along the way. Find out what your leadership style is, know what your spiritual gifts are, read books, and listen to people who are great at what you do. Keep digging, and you'll grow in this most important area. The truth is, the ministry you oversee will only be as good as your ability to lead it.

If God has called you to lead, then be the best leader you can be.

One of the best ways to lead is by casting the vision God has placed on your heart. Sometimes we are so saturated in work that we don't take time to listen to where God may be leading us. Dream a little. What do you want your ministry to look like? How do you measure success? Begin praying about these things. Ask for creativity, direction, energy, guidance, resources, and wisdom. God will answer you.

Passionately share your vision. People want to know.

Once you know where you are going, gather people around you and passionately share your vision. Divide the mission into attainable goals. Offer training sessions, share ideas, show videos, and tell stories of how other churches have done it. People want to know where they're going, why it's important, and how to get there. When people are excited about the vision, they yearn for your guidance. Sometimes you can spell it out for them step-by-step. Other times, you can only explain what you want to accomplish. Remember, this is a team effort. Don't make the mistake of trying to look good at the expense of the ministry's growth. Share your ministry visions with others in detail.

A very simple way to build your ministry team is through regular meetings. Whether through training sessions, seminars, or luncheons, meet with your team. Simply getting together with your key leaders is energizing in itself. When gathering with your team, recast the vision. Collectively recall where you have been, share and celebrate successes, plan immediate action items, and then look to the future. Invite ideas and encourage feedback. When you build collaboration into the team's environment, other team members won't be angry when their ideas don't get implemented. Also, a volunteer may offer a practical suggestion that you never would have considered on your own. Remember, we accomplish more together than alone.

Realizing that we can't do it alone can be tough, but investing in the lives of other leaders is the only way to grow. Value the people God has given you. Nurture them through encouraging words and notes. Genuinely love them. Spend time with your team. Have fun, eat, laugh, share, and listen to them. When you do this, your personal growth will match, if not exceed, the growth of the ministry. It is an amazing thing to watch someone you've led begin to lead others. That's when you can smell the flowers, bask in the sunshine, and plow along with others on the greatest journey ever.

Conclusion

We began this chapter by telling you about a family that came to our church's first service in Princeton, New Jersey. Through the years, that family grew in their love for the Lord and His church. It was one of the highlights of our ministry in Princeton, therefore, when one Sunday we witnessed the baptism of the mom and dad of this family. What was even more exciting was to see mom and dad then baptize their daughter. This family now has a prominent leadership role at Princeton Community Church. The mom is on the Leadership Team. The dad leads the Drama Ministry, and their daughter is a leader in the youth group. It all began because of a new church's commitment to excellence in Children's Ministry. We could tell many more life changing stories like this one. You too will experience these same gratifying, God-honoring stories. So for now, *Just go for it!* Children's ministry is worth every effort you make.

Paul Williams is the longtime President of the Orchard Group, a church planting non-profit organization in the Greater New York City area. The Orchard Group has been a pioneer in creating partnerships for church planting in the Northeastern United States. Paul is also Editor at Large for *The Standard*, a Christian periodical, and can be seen as a regular host of the Worship Network. Paul and his wife Kathy are the parents of three grown children.

Preaching in the New Church

He was one of the brightest young church planters I had ever encountered. Well-educated, enthusiastic, and full of passion, he had drawn a great team together to plant a church in an influential Midwestern city. The postcards had been mailed, 50,000 of them, five times. Savvy enough to get free media attention, this senior minister had wrangled a front-page story in the newspaper. A reporter and photographer were at the first service, planning a follow-up article. The children's ministry had state-of-the-art security for the young families that attended. The worship team had practiced until they sounded like they had been together for years. Everything was ready for the launch. Everything, that is, except for one single critically important element—the sermon.

By the looks on most faces in the audience, the sermon preached that morning was not great. It wasn't even good. It was just okay. As I left the service, the church planter asked, "So, how'd you think everything went?" Years ago, early in my church planting ministry, I harshly judged a first Sunday sermon of a very capable church planter. I learned from that encounter that there is a time to confront, and there is a time to stay silent. "All in all, a great morning," I replied. I waited several weeks to have a deeper conversation with the young church planter.

When we met the next month at a church planting conference, I asked the young man how he had planned for the first service of

261

his new church. He gave me all the details of the planning stages, from first envisioning the inaugural service, to the final "test-drive" the Thursday evening before the opening Sunday. "And did you preach your sermon on that 'test drive?" I asked. "No," he said, "I didn't have the sermon done yet. I was just too busy." "How many hours do you think you put into that sermon?" I asked. With a sheepish grin, the young minister answered, "Honestly, probably three or four hours. I was just too busy."

At this point, I invited the young man into a meeting room at the hotel, pulled out two chairs and we sat down face to face. "How many hours do you think you and your staff put into the planning and preparation for the first service?" I asked. "Cumulatively, I'd guess hundreds," he answered. I continued, "And what was the single most time-consuming element in that service itself?" "The sermon," he replied. "Right. Forty minutes of a sixty-five minute service."

> **"Do you think a three-hour time commitment was adequate for the portion of your first service that occupied over 60% of its total time?"**

Pulling my chair closer, I asked my most important question: "Do you think a three-hour time commitment was adequate for the portion of your first service that occupied over 60% of its total time? If you look at all of your detailed planning, you devoted the least amount of time to the most time-consuming, and arguably, the most important element of the entire service." A light of recognition came into the young man's eyes, and we talked for quite a while longer.

I ended our conversation with these words: "Remember, you can't preach more than who you are, and no sermon is done until you truly own it—until it has cooked so long in your soul that you're ready to preach from the overflow. I don't care who you are. You can't do that in three hours."

Begin with the Message

Screenwriter and script editor Bart Gavigan says the easiest place to fix a movie is at the beginning, with the script. Let a bad script slide because you have a great director or well-known actors, and you might enjoy a big opening night, but the movie will die at the box office. Why? Because when it's all said and done, it's not about the production values, the location, the budget, or even the actors. It's about the story. A great story will cover a multitude of movie production sins. But a lousy story can't be put back together by all the king's horses and all the king's men. So it is with a sermon.

Back in the 1990s a study was done in one large new church, asking why visitors returned a second time. By far, the number one answer was "Because I liked the minister and his sermon." The number two answer was "I loved the worship." Number three? "My kids liked the church." Over the years I have heard anecdotal story after story that confirms those findings. People come to church because a friend invited them or because they responded to a great advertising piece. They come back because they identified with the minister and the message. There is no single element more important to the new church than the sermon. No other single element has the power to define the pathway of a new congregation.

People come back because they identified with the minister and the message. There is no single element more important to the new church than the sermon.

Over fifteen years ago Dr. Charles Ridley, an industrial psychologist, identified several key areas of ministry function for an effective new church planter. While thirteen areas were identified as important, five were considered "knockout factors," meaning a church planter needed to have at least rudimentary skill in each of the five areas. As the years have unfolded, at Orchard Group Church Planting[1] we have confirmed those five "knockout" areas and slightly redefined them:

1. Vision

2. Inner Motivation

3. Ability to Relate Well to the Unchurched

4. A Leader People Are Willing to Follow

5. A Spouse Committed to Church Planting

There is one single element critical to three of the five—preaching.

Vision

Rick Warren's best-selling book, *The Purpose Driven Life*, tells us one thing for sure—Americans are looking for a purpose beyond themselves. They want to give themselves wholeheartedly to something or someone who can bring meaning to their lives. There is no better way to rally people around a life-sustaining purpose than through a soul-stirring message.

When you think of Martin Luther King, Jr., what phrase comes to mind? "I have a dream." Of course! We can all see the grainy black-and-white film footage and those stirring words. When you think of the 1988 presidential election, what vision phrases of George H.W. Bush come to mind? "A thousand points of light." "A kinder, gentler America." "No new taxes." Years after Bush left office, most can still rattle off his vision statements without much thought, because they were compelling and memorable.

Now, what were George Bush's vision statements in the 1992 election? Having a hard time, aren't you? Maybe now we understand better Bill Clinton's victory against an incumbent president. President Bush didn't have a compelling vision for his second term.

Speaking to the Houston Press Club a number of years ago, Peggy Noonan, speechwriter for both George H.W. Bush and Ronald Reagan, was comparing the two. She said that Bush was a supremely decent man for whom she had great respect. When the Berlin Wall fell, she and others asked Bush what kind of speech he wanted them to write. His reply? He said he wasn't going to give a speech. He didn't want to "rub it in."

Noonan said that was the kind of man Bush was—a supremely decent fellow. He was able to develop a strong NATO coalition because he genuinely cared about developing relationships, one at a time. He missed something important, however. For the better part of the century, as Americans, we huddled together against the fear of Communism. Once that fear imploded before our very eyes, however, we wanted someone to affirm that the threat was gone and that we could celebrate. We wanted to hear from our president. Noonan went on to say that's why we still remember the words Ronald Reagan spoke after the Challenger space disaster, "They've slipped the surly bonds of earth to touch the face of God." We remember those words she paraphrased from John Gillespie Magee's poem, "High Flight," because we wanted someone to speak a word for us in the midst of our collective grief.

A visionary seizes the moment for the collective good of his or her audience. We want someone to put words to our collective thoughts. We want to be inspired, and called to serve a greater good. It's more than writing for a sound bite. It's writing to inspire.

The sermons that touch us most deeply are those that echo the words of Pascal, "The heart has its reasons that reason does not know." They stir the heart and touch our souls in the deep places where we are seldom moved. They tap into a collective need to serve, praise, and honor our Lord and Creator.

Ability to Relate Well to the Unchurched

When unchurched individuals come to a new church, they often don't really know why they are there. They experience a vague discomfort they don't understand. They are looking for answers, but often the questions haven't been formed in their mouths yet. The person who comes to a new church is looking for a language, for someone to speak the word they would speak if they had a vocabulary to speak it.

The visionary preacher speaks the word the listener has been searching for. The seeker says "Yes, yes. That's how I feel. Exactly."

The visionary preacher is one step in front of the audience. Two steps in front, and communication doesn't take place. The preacher's message is too obscure, or too didactic, disconnected from the life of the listener. If the preacher is stepping exactly with the audience, then communication is also difficult. The audience wonders if the preacher really has any insight they couldn't have discerned themselves over a cup of coffee and the morning newspaper. No, the preacher's message should be one step in front of the audience, saying, "I know how you're feeling. I had those feelings just yesterday. Here's where you might think about turning next."

A Leader People Are Willing to Follow

In the early 1990s Rick Rusaw and I completed a Master's degree thesis in which we compared the results of a particular psychological testing tool to thirteen important factors of church planting. Almost as an afterthought, we asked the church planters we had studied to score themselves in the five "knockout" factors of church planting. Almost every person who completed our test and survey acknowledged that the most difficult of all five factors was getting people to "buy into" their vision for the new church.

There is no doubt that the character of the church planter has more to do with effectiveness in this area than any other single item. Where is the best place for the church planter to communicate character and journey? From the pulpit, of course.

> ## The new church audience wants a preacher who is transparent, but not too transparent.

The new church audience wants a preacher who is transparent, but not too transparent. D.H. Laurence said, "a writer sheds his sickness in his writing." Overly transparent preachers can shed their sickness in their preaching. The audience wants to know you deal with the same struggles they face. On the other hand, they don't want to hear too many details about those struggles.

If the new church audience hears a preacher who is respectful of their time, having adequately prepared a thoughtful message that meets the listener where he or she lives, it won't be long before the listener is ready to follow the leader on a spiritual journey. That person will look to the leader and through the leader to the Christ who motivates the preacher.

The Age of Reason Is behind Us and The Age of Story Is upon Us

For a couple of centuries preachers have been able to primarily focus on preaching the truth, first and foremost, without a deep regard for style, technique, or illustration. During the Modern Age, with its focus on right thinking and scientific certainty, the best preaching was didactic, focused on deep exegesis, with an emphasis on learning the facts of the Bible.

> ## The focus has moved from "facts" and "right thinking" to "right relationships."

With the Modern Age behind us, however, and the arrival of what is currently called Postmodernism, trends are changing. Led by new discoveries in quantum physics and other cutting-edge fields, the focus has moved from "facts" and "right thinking" to "right relationships." In fact, some scientists now say the only ultimate reality is relationships. What does that mean for the preacher? It means we are in the age of the Great Commandment: loving God and loving one another. It's all about relationships.

If a new church truly is reaching unchurched people (which unfortunately is not often the case), those people are probably more interested in hearing the *stories* of faith than they are in hearing the *rules* of faith. They will be more responsive to the narratives of the Gospels, the book of Acts, or the Old Testament than they will be to hearing the Ten Commandments. It doesn't mean we should abandon sound doctrinal preaching. It just means we'll be doing it in a new way.

We are in the Age of Relationships, and there is no better time to return to the speaking style of Jesus than now. Jesus taught in parables. He asked questions and seldom made the answers obvious. A biblical story, well told, is marvelous in the new church. It reaches the listener at his or her own level. A child hears the story at its most basic level. An unchurched individual hears their "beginner's struggle" in the details. A seasoned saint finds a depth to the story even the preacher doesn't grasp. Stories find their own level, and are a marvelous place to start in the new church environment. Two narratives for every three messages is not a bad ratio.

The Psalms also should not be overlooked in preaching in the new church. Long before people know why they have wandered into a new church, they feel the need to praise someone or something. In fact, that's often why they've come to the new church in the first place.

On the other hand, people also come to a new church when they feel the heat, when life is not going well. That of course, brings us to the other half of Psalms, the Psalms of lament. Both Psalms of praise and lament, incorporated into worship and preaching, will speak effectively to the Postmodern seeker.

A year's worth of narratives or Psalms without the practical instruction of the New Testament epistles, however, would be unbalanced. Just remember that in the current environment, story reigns. The epistles of Paul take on far greater meaning when put in historical context, particularly when it can be done in a narrative way.

This is the age of story. You don't have to look any further than the movie theater box office to see that a good script will beat out a technologically savvy, but weak-storied movie every single time.

The Sacred Desk

When I was a child, I was playing with a rubber ball in the church auditorium late on a Sunday evening while Dad attended to an emergency elders meeting in the church office. I was tossing the ball back and forth with one of my friends when the wife of one of the elders cautioned me. "Be careful around the sacred desk," she said. The "sacred desk"? I'd never heard a pulpit called that before. I tucked the phrase away in my memory bank, and continued my game of catch far away from the front of the church auditorium. The phrase, however, stayed with me; the "sacred desk."

Whether it's a glass pulpit, a music stand, or no stand at all, there is a fear that should grip us all when we step behind the "sacred desk." Every one of us should be trembling in our wing tips when we stand to preach. We should tremble because so much is at stake. We should tremble because, even on our best days, we really aren't up for the task. God has still given us this ministry of reconciling the creation to the Creator, and so we give it all we've got. Sometimes it's laughable, imminently forgettable. We know our words won't make it past the Sunday buffet line at the local restaurant.

Other times we hear words coming from our mouths that we know we didn't form, don't have the wisdom to form, and don't even fully understand. It is at those moments that we understand why we tremble so. We tremble because the Spirit Himself is trying desperately to speak through us, and at that particular moment, we have risen to the occasion enough to get out of the way and let Him speak His heart through our mouths. It is at those moments that we realize just how holy and crazy and marvelous it all is, this greatest of all privileges, the privilege to preach the Gospel of Jesus Christ.

---

[1] The Orchard Group is a church planting organization that focuses their efforts on the Northeastern United States (**www.orchardgroup.org**).

Brent Foulke and **Mark Wilkinson** planted Christ's Church of the Capital District together in 1992. Both coming from worship leading backgrounds, they formed a unique partnership of sharing preaching and worship leading during the church's formative years.

Brent Foulke continues to serve as Lead Pastor of Christ's Church of the Capital District in Albany, New York. While leading Christ's Church to become a growing and reproducing church, Brent has helped oversee more than two dozen new churches, and currently serves as a Vice President of Orchard Group (formerly "Go Ye" Chapel Mission). Brent and his wife Kay have four children between 12 and 18 years old.

Mark Wilkinson is Founding and Lead Pastor of Journey's Crossing, a Christian Church in Gaithersburg, Maryland. One of the fastest growing and largest church plants in the region, Journey's Crossing has grown to around 500 in weekly attendance in just two years. Mark and his wife Barbara are the parents of four girls, ages 15, 13, 11, and 7.

Worship

I entered Christ's Church for the first time on Easter Sunday of 1996, mostly as a courtesy to my brother who had been inviting me for some time. I was expecting a typical church experience, and hoping it would go quickly so I could get home and back to everyday life. What I found was something altogether different—a place with an uplifting sense of community and people who loved praising God through music. Never before had I equated music, especially great music, with church. In some spiritual way, the music of the band that morning touched my life. I couldn't get enough. I loved it! I came back the next weekend, then the next, and the next.

While attending regularly, something amazing happened—I got it! The messages were relevant to my life, and God reached out and touched me. I was married in that church later the same year, and baptized there (along with my wife) two years later. Eventually I joined the band that initially kept me at church and that, in some way, saved my life.

We are so fortunate to worship an awesome God! It is an incredible honor to be in His presence and feel His love. The songs we sing speak of His grace, love, and mercy—things we can all use a little more of. Like all gifts from God, they are life changing and meant to be used for His glory.

We are so fortunate to worship an
awesome God! It is an incredible honor
to be in His presence and feel His love.

Corporate Worship and Church Planting

In the current North American church, people generally experience God in church through weekend worship services before experiencing small groups or personal connection with church leaders or teachers. You have heard it said, "You only have one chance to make a good first impression." Since our primary concern in new church planting is reaching those who are far from God—in some cases people who are skeptical, recovering, or struggling with serious life issues—the first impression is the key to whether or not we accomplish the church's mission.

Because the large group corporate worship experience is often the first impression and entry point for the seeking unchurched person, it is important that you are strategic and clear in the design and implementation of each service. Worship style can be one of the greatest battlegrounds in the new church if you are unclear as to why you have chosen to do "church" in a particular way. Even before you recruit a core group and a team of musicians, it is important to clearly establish and share the church's chosen worship style. In many ways, effective, inspiring worship is critical for the success of a new church.

In many ways, effective, inspiring worship
is critical for the success of a new church.

Begin by understanding your target audience. Who is it you hope this new church will reach? Rather than trying to reach everyone in your community, define the "niche" you are passionate about and best equipped to serve. Often this is the group of people in close approximation to your own stage of life and personality type. Try writing out a description of the particular characteristics that are indicative of these people. Once you have clearly defined the kind of person(s) you want to reach, begin research in local demographics to further refine your understanding. What radio stations would these people enjoy? What type of shopping, schools, or recreational events would they prefer? What do they like to eat, wear or read?

While no one person will probably be a perfect match with this kind of grid, it is a helpful filter by which you can plan and evaluate your worship service's ability to connect with your intended target audience. Of course, it's important that the style of worship you choose be consistent with your goals and strategy in other ministry areas.

Blended Worship

Maximizing the new church's large group experiences requires every aspect of the weekend service to be blended artistically with the others. In order to accomplish this, the speaker(s) who delivers the spoken message in the service must be part of the planning, execution, and evaluation of the weekend worship service. Themes should be planned well in advance, and the development of those themes should be a collaborative process in which teachers, musicians, dramatists, videographers, producers, and other artists contribute. Many average speakers can be part of truly excellent worship services when they cooperate and leverage every gift given to the team by God.

A Shared Vision and Unifying Experience

You should expect musical style and worship
to be a source of deeply felt emotion.

Even the best plans and clearly explained ideas yield a diversity of expectations and wishes. In no place is this more evident than in the church. Because new churches not only attract the unchurched or spiritually sensitive, but also the disenchanted or disillusioned churched people, you should expect musical style and worship to be a source of deeply felt emotion. The church planter should realize it is usually only a matter of time before this dichotomy yields confusion and some conflict. Therefore, as early as possible in the recruiting and planning process, the vision and direction of the corporate worship experience must be clearly defined and often articulated. Beware of the temptation to use competent musicians and artists who don't share your vision. Though doing so fills a void, it dilutes the strength of the vision. Sometimes it may be difficult to fill certain ministry areas in the new church, but don't compromise your vision and goals when selecting leaders. We have a tendency to overestimate our ability to "change" someone and underestimate his or her ability to create dissension. The first priority when selecting staff and ministry leaders for a new church, therefore, is that they embrace the vision, including the approach to the corporate worship gathering. They may not "like" it personally, but if they can understand who the target audience is and why this approach has been selected, they can support the larger goal of intentionally reaching a community with the saving message of Jesus Christ.

> ## "Good worship affects the entire life and ministry of the church and extends to all activities."

"The worshipping church knows that good worship affects the entire life and ministry of the church and extends to all the activities in which the people of God are involved."[1] Among the large gatherings of any church, vision casting occurs most efficiently when passed from one voice to many ears. This occurs through the spoken word, but increasingly in our culture, it also happens through multisensory experiences. By using multisensory experiences in worship, we acknowledge and celebrate that every person has a slightly different spiritual pathway through which he or she connects most strongly with God.[2] Some will engage the Good News through speaking, and others through images, drama, testimony, music, or another form that communicates God's vision for His church.

Throughout the process, we must remember that God is by nature creative. He makes all things new and is the master of innovation and beauty. As artists who lead the church in worship, we too should value creativity and beauty. For the sake of expediency, we too often become people of mundane music and repetitious reprise. Worship very easily becomes formulaic and predictable, which is foreign to God's own character.

> ## Worship very easily becomes formulaic, which is foreign to God's own character.

What keeps us from becoming more creative? Often it is our own discomfort with that which is different. We settle into ruts based on taste or preference and ignore or avoid the very things that could help break our monotony. When it comes to creativity, diversity is our greatest strength! It may be more comfortable to surround your-self with people who share your mind-set, behaviors, and prefer-ences, but it's not the best environment for innovation. It is healthy to explore different music styles and artistic themes in order to expand the creative possibilities. Don't be afraid to listen to and share ideas with others, even if it takes you to places that are foreign or uncomfortable.[3] When a team of artists massages different con-cepts in an environment of open acceptance and consideration, they have the opportunity to join God in the creative process. Not only does that give God pleasure, it also makes us more like Him!

Don't be afraid to listen to and share ideas with others, even if it takes you to places that are foreign or uncomfortable.

Maximizing our effectiveness as church planters and church leaders requires acknowledging that the spiritual experience of our congregation is a stewardship from God. For example, when David testified of God's saving grace, he also realized that the telling of his salvation would generate spontaneous singing and, therefore, result in the transformation of additional lives. Psalm 40:1-3 reads,

> I waited patiently for the Lord;
>   he turned to me and heard my cry.
> He lifted me out of the slimy pit,
>   out of the mud and mire;
> He set my feet on a rock
>   and gave me a firm place to stand.
> He put a new song in my mouth,
>   a hymn of praise to our God.
> Many will see and fear
>   and put their trust in the Lord.[4]

David was an Arts Pastor for the congregation of Israel. He viewed worship as evangelism. Church newcomers often begin their spiritu-al journey because of what they first experience in large group wor-ship. Spoken testimony (verses 1-2) or experience reflected in song (verse 3) may first capture their attention. Either way, the goal of new church plants is to share the Good News in ways that bring peo-ple who were once far from God into a relationship characterized by knowledge of, respect for, and surrender to our Almighty God. That's why we should plant churches that understand that the corporate worship experience is a core strategy for fulfilling the mission of the church. "If we truly understand what worship is, we will appreciate why worship services are an essential part of God's strategy for building the Kingdom and drawing others into it."[5]

The goal of new church plants is to bring people who were once far from God into relationship.

Transformation from Consumerism

The worship of God isn't just an "entry-level" experience. Our consumer-oriented society bombards us increasingly with the message, "It's all about you." Sadly, twenty-first-century America is driven by dissatisfaction and a constant pursuit of more—more pleasure, influence, power, and money. Almost every message we encounter places a self-centered worldview on display. When we gather as a congregation of celebrants, however, we acknowledge, "It's not all about me—it's all about God!"[6] Human beings have always needed a regular reminder of our dependence on God, and in new churches we must especially battle the egomaniacal "me" monster. God-honoring worship does just that, both for the new God-seeker and the battle-worn Christ follower.

In new churches we must especially battle the egomaniacal "me" monster.

Redeeming the Arts and Artists

Perhaps the most exciting transformation that happens through corporate worship services of a new church happens in those who plan, prepare, lead, perform in, and produce corporate worship. If we believe God authors truth and beauty, then we must also give Him the glory for beautiful music, compelling dialogue, amazing moments, and powerful lessons resulting from large group worship services.

In most new churches, people connect with the spiritual journey of the lead pastor and with the experience of the artists (including the pastor) who lead the church from the stage every weekend. Also, in most new churches, tremendous effort and resources are invested in the "grand opening" event that is designed to draw as many people as possible together for a worship service. Upon reflection, more resources should be devoted to developing the core artists that lead the weekend event. These musicians, actors, producers, and designers will do more to establish the new church than the best marketing campaign ever could.

Often those reached by a new church are seeking an authentic representation of faith and life. No more powerful witness to the "real life" transforming power of the gospel exists than the lives of those in the public eye at each weekend worship service. Not only does the style and content of the worship service speak volumes about the heart of the budding new church, but the people up front during the service also convey much to those in the crowd regarding who and what the new church is about. The expressions, dialogue, actions and skill of those "on stage" often say more about the church than any printed material. Fancy slogans and glossy publications can tote pithy sayings and worthy goals, but the question the first-time seeker is asking is, "Is this authentic?" "Do the leaders up front who represent this new church really live out the things they say they value?" A church can talk about grace and acceptance till it is blue in the face, but when the speaker makes an angry scowl or degrading comment to another team member who has just made a mistake, a message of "ungrace" will be shouted even louder!

The question the first-time seeker is asking is, "Is this authentic?"

Many new churches have observed their most rewarding stories of life-change in their instrumentalists, vocalists, and technicians that help execute worship services in the early days of the new church. Over time, every artist must be challenged to respond to the gospel. As the church begins, however, many of these challenges happen as the artists are providing musical and theatrical support for the evangelistic worship service!

Additionally, new churches that best use the arts and experience the most success with transforming worship often have strong staff influence in weekend worship celebrations. Often one or more staff members are musically gifted, and they strategically invest themselves in the weekend worship culture. Teams with little or no artistic ability must intentionally recruit volunteer musicians and other artists who can establish the worship environment for a new church.

From the beginning, developing the Arts Team, one life at a time, should be a high priority for the pastor and the church planting team. Invest in the personal journey of each worship leader, recognizing that the spiritual progress of the church is affected, in part, by the spiritual progress of its leaders. Each minute you invest in your worship staff is another minute you invest in your congregation. As church leaders, we are concerned with development—developing all people into Christ-followers.

Because of its visibility, the Arts (Worship) Team has an opportunity to become a standard-setting team for the whole church. Weekly opportunities for collaborative ministry create a laboratory for interpersonal development unequaled in other new church arenas. Sharing the spotlight, acquiescing to the leadership of others, independent preparation, flexibility, and patience are not natural traits of many artists, but they are absolutely necessary for successful Art Teams in the church.

Value-Based Teams

Jennifer Rutherford, the Arts Pastor at Christ's Church, designed a "Top Ten Values" list for her artists that serves as a valuable training outline for any new church plant.[7] Her suggested values are explained below in order of increasing importance.

10. **Own the Music.** Why? Owning the music gives us freedom to play, for others to worship, and for us to become better leaders because we respect others on the team who own it. The message of our music is life-changing. Therefore, owning it allows it to pierce our own hearts. "Own it" means to come prepared musically, technically, and spiritually with an understanding of the song's message. Choose music that will communicate specifically and powerfully to your audience each weekend.

9. **Be Ready for Growth.** As musicians, take risks, model humility, accept servant (rather than star) roles, and present a diversity of music. As servants of the kingdom, practice discipleship as commanded by Christ, mentor and cheer on the next generation of worship leaders, and welcome new musi-

cians to rehearsal. As a team member, be prepared. Preparation benefits not only your team, but also the congregation.

As a team member, be prepared. Preparation benefits not only your team, but also the congregation.

8. **Expect Transformation and Accountability.** Romans 12:1-2 says that we are transformed by the renewing of our minds. We can strive for transformation by asking ourselves questions about our daily routine and prayer life. Once we identify areas of growth, accountability helps us attain change. Inappropriate joking, pat answers, and time constraints inhibit your team from opening up. On the other hand, arriving on time, being sensitive to others, and being a good listener invites genuine, open relationships among team members. Accountability can happen as an entire group through prayer, or at other times one-on-one.

7. **Contribute Actively as a Participant.** Actively contributing means taking responsibility for yourself—asking for help when needed and independently taking advantage of resources (web sites, rehearsal CDs, and other tools). Participating, on the other hand, involves making suggestions during rehearsals that will help the team better serve one another and the church. Staying silent can lead to resentment. Find your own way to contribute to the band. God's character is active, not passive; we are created in His image.

God's character is not passive, and we are created in His image.

6. **Be a Team Player.** Team players are committed to resolving conflict. They regularly encourage one another. A team player doesn't care who gets the credit because he or she is committed to glorifying God at all times. Although worship may highlight individuals from time to time, overall, godly worship is about a collection of artists who value one another. It only takes one person with a misplaced perception of their importance to create negative tension and unhealthy competition on stage. Not only will it have disastrous effects on the team as a

whole, but also it will be a distraction to those we lead in worship. God is a jealous God, and He will not tolerate anyone else being the center of worship—not even if his or her singing ability or instrumental prowess is amazing.

God will not tolerate anyone else being the center of worship.

5. **Bring a Healthy Self to the Team.** Physically, spiritually, and emotionally, bring everything you have to God. This involves taking care of your body by eating properly, resting, and exercising on a regular basis. Also, exercise the spirit through regular prayer, confession, fellowship, and biblical teaching (see 2 Cor 8:5). Build meaningful relationships. Deal with pain and conflict in healthy, biblical ways. Care for your emotional health. Additionally, a team player will also be aware of how he or she spends Saturday evenings (or afternoons) in preparation for Sunday morning or Saturday evening commitment.

4. **Resolve Conflict Regularly.** Jesus' prayer for unity in John 17 expresses His desire to see His followers united in purpose and relationship. In Matthew 5 and 17, Jesus shows our responsibility to resolve conflicts with fellow believers. Dedication to biblical conflict resolution is a *must* for all worship teams.

3. **Pursue Excellence.** "Whatever you do, work at it with all your heart, as working for the Lord, not for men" (Col 3:23).

> During the days of the Old Testament, one of the ways people worshipped was through animal sacrifice. . . . God's people were admonished to offer the very best of their flock. In the New Testament, believers are encouraged to "continually offer to God a sacrifice of praise" (Hebrews 13:15). It is not overextending the metaphor to suggest that God continues to desire our contemporary vocal and instrumental "sacrifices" be characterized by the same spirit of bringing our best to the altar.[8]

"Pursuing excellence means we do our best with what we have to the glory of God."[9]

2. **Love One Another.** God tells us in 1 Corinthians 13 and in 1 John that we are nothing without love. Love propels us to

care for others, to grow in truth, and to celebrate our Heavenly Father, the Author of our lives.

1. **Above All, Worship Only God.** It is challenging to put aside worldly pleasures and instead pursue God alone when we feel empty. Television, food, recreation, and relationships sometimes replace a more fulfilling relationship with our Creator when we habitually turn to them instead of God. Only He can give us what we truly need. As worship leaders, we must worship only our God, and encourage others to do the same.

Conclusion

The worship service is the defining event of a new church in many ways. Planning an event each weekend that exalts God, communicates His truth, and attracts people is one of the most important things a church planting team does. Using diverse art forms can draw seekers toward God, form the culture of the new church, and remind the Christ-follower, "It's not about you!" In fact, worship is a process. It's a process that leaders evaluate each week as they serve God through their various gifts and abilities. It's a process of becoming more like Christ through sharing in His truth and grace, and a process of extending the kingdom to the unreached. Worship has the ability to connect people to God and His community of faith. Nothing pleases God more!

---

[1] Robert E. Webber, *The Worship Phenomenon* (Nashville: Start Song Publishing, 1994) 131.

[2] Gary L. Thomas, *Sacred Pathways* (Grand Rapids: Zondervan, 2000).

[3] If you really want to get "outside the box," take regular planned expeditions and forays in search of material, tools, tips and techniques that other worship teams around the world are discovering. Worship seminars and conferences put on by larger thriving churches of different denominations are great places to visit, observe, and learn new skills/ideas. Also, consider forming a network with like-minded artists and teams in your area where you can swap ideas and concepts. Not only will you find it to be a place of resourcefulness, but also it will be a source of encouragement and camaraderie outside your local situation. Fresh eyes and ears have a unique way of helping us solve problems and understand difficulties. You can even form teams within your local situation that encourage "green-light" thinking. Someone else's idea can be the catalyst to ignite a whole new way of approaching an idea or task.

[4] All Scripture quotations are taken from the *New International Version* unless otherwise noted.

[5] Sally Morgenthaler, *Worship Evangelism: Inviting Unbelievers into the Presence of God* (Grand Rapids: Zondervan, 1995) 46.

[6] Rick Warren, *The Purpose-Driven Life: What on Earth Am I Here For?* (Grand Rapids: Zondervan, 2002) 17.

[7] Jennifer Rutherford, http://lifechangechurch.com/music.

[8] Doug and Tami Flather, *The Praise and Worship Team Instant Tune-Up* (Grand Rapids: Zondervan, 2002) 9.

[9] Rory Noland, *The Heart of the Artist* (Grand Rapids: Zondervan, 1999) 132.

Jon Ferguson is one of the founding pastors at Community Christian Church, a multi-site church located in the west suburbs of Chicago. He plays a key role in identifying and developing small group leaders, coaches, and staff personnel. He serves as Teaching Pastor and leads and directs all Community Ministries (small groups for children through adults). The church has grown to a congregation of 3500 in attendance with over 225 small groups meeting all over the West and Southwest suburbs of Chicago. In addition, he was a national trainer for Serendipity Small Group Training and Pilgrimage (NavPress) Publishers. He is a cofounder of NewThing Network and serves on the Board of Directors for the Institute for Community. He has a Bachelor of Arts in Christian Education from Lincoln Christian College and a Master of Arts in Educational Ministries with an emphasis in Small Groups and Leadership Development from Wheaton Graduate School. He is married to Lisa, and they have two children.

Reproducing Biblical Community

We've built beautiful places, but we have yet to help people live beautifully in those places." That's what Bruno Bottarelli, Founding Partner of a property development corporation located in the Chicagoland Area said almost ten years ago. He continues: "This may sound harsh, but before I had a relationship with Jesus Christ and experienced biblical community, I wasn't concerned about how people lived in our developments. Experiencing real community gave me a whole new vision for my life's work." Bruno's personal experience of biblical community has had a dramatic impact on his development practices as well as how we do church at Community Christian Church.[1]

Real community building is a tremendous asset to the public and private sector, creating a safe, nurturing environment with happier, more productive people.

Bruno discovered that real community building is a tremendous asset to the public and private sector. From neighborhoods to small towns and small businesses to large corporations, genuine community creates a safe, nurturing environment that can lead to happier, more productive people. In a residential setting, a community that is safe and nurturing can lead to increased property values, greater retention, and a higher quality of life. In a business setting, relational collateral built through intentional community activities can lead to higher company earnings, decreased employee turnover, and a more satisfying work environment.

The adjacent graphic[2] conveys the progressive felt needs of almost any individual, community, or corporation: from *physical* needs like food and shelter to *informational* needs such as clear and consistent communication to *emotional* needs like belonging and friendship to a *spiritual* need of being part of something greater than oneself.

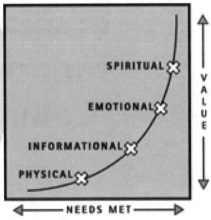

Christ-followers know that spiritual needs can only be experienced through a life-changing relationship with Jesus Christ and His church. When spiritual needs are met, participants begin to feel that they are part of something with eternal significance much greater than their everyday circumstances. As church planters, we are the custodians of a precious commodity that meets the physical, informational, emotional, and spiritual needs of people. The treasure we possess that meets these needs is biblical community. The principle that people's most basic needs must be met first before we can expect to earn an ear for the gospel applies to church planting in any context—urban, suburban, or rural.

As church planters, we are the custodians of a precious commodity—biblical community.

While the idea that providing people with a spiritual connection through Jesus Christ is of utmost value may be no surprise to church planters, it is surprisingly good news that the general "market" is beginning to discover that meeting needs on this level can greatly increase the value of a product such as real estate development. As Bruno and countless others have discovered, people have a longing for something more, the spiritual community God designed for every one of us.

Reproducing the Biblical Ideal

The Garden

God's dream from the very beginning was to satisfy humanity's physical, relational, emotional, and spiritual needs through community—a oneness vertically with God as well as horizontally between humans. That's what Adam and Eve experienced—complete unity and oneness with God and each other. Then look what happened: ". . . they hid from the LORD God among the trees of the garden" (Gen 3:8). When they sinned, their oneness with God and each other was gone, and God's dream for community disintegrated. Since then, God has been pursuing us over and over, giving us opportunities to experience that same community experienced by Adam and Eve in the garden.

It's no wonder we function best within the context of community. The Bible says we are created in the image of God—who Himself exists in community: God the Father, Jesus the Son, and the Holy Spirit. We are created to be in close relationship with others, and when we're not—when we're alone, we feel it, because God wired us up to feel like something is missing when we're *not* connected. Throughout Scripture God utilizes small group structures to provide care and to help people experience community with one another and Himself.

God wired us up to feel like something is missing when we're not connected.

Old Testament

The Nation of Israel was organized around large and small groups. The nation was divided into tribes, the tribes were broken down into families or clans, and the families or clans were subdivided into single-family units.

When Moses found himself running out of steam, on the verge of burnout and unable to meet the needs of the people he was commissioned to lead, his father-in-law, Jethro, suggested a small group system to better meet the needs of his people. He said,

> . . . select capable men from all the people—men who fear God, trustworthy men who hate dishonest gain—and appoint them as officials over thousands, hundreds, fifties and tens. Have them serve as judges

for the people at all times, but have them bring every difficult case to you; the simple cases they can decide themselves. That will make your load lighter, because they will share it with you. If you do this and God so commands, you will be able to stand the strain, and all these people will go home satisfied (Exod 18:21-23).

Notice the results Jethro promised: not only would Moses save himself from a nervous breakdown, but also the people he is leading would actually be more satisfied as well. A small group structure answered the need for increased care.

Jesus

In the New Testament, Jesus spent the majority of His time with His small group, the disciples. The primary focus of Jesus' ministry was investing in His small group, His missional team of disciples. When asked what was the greatest commandment, Jesus boiled it down to two things: love God, and love others (Matt 22:36-40). In the context of a small group we are able to best fulfill this two-part command that serves as a synopsis of all of God's teachings and a template for biblical community.

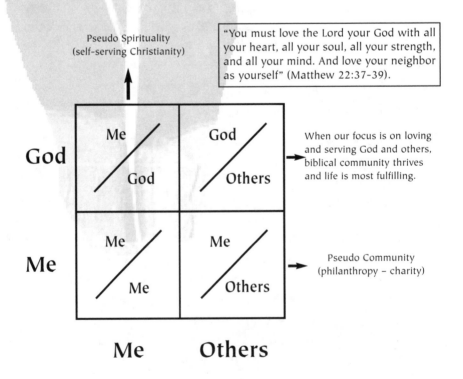

Pseudo Spirituality
(self-serving Christianity)

"You must love the Lord your God with all your heart, all your soul, all your strength, and all your mind. And love your neighbor as yourself" (Matthew 22:37-39).

God

| Me / God | God / Others |
| Me / Me | Me / Others |

Me

Me   **Others**

When our focus is on loving and serving God and others, biblical community thrives and life is most fulfilling.

Pseudo Community
(philanthropy – charity)

284

The Early Church

Finally, when we look at the early church in Acts 2, we read that they gathered in two places: "Every day they continued to meet together in the temple courts. They broke bread in their homes and ate together with glad and sincere hearts . . ." (Acts 2:46). The temple court was a public place, where large groups of people gathered.

The early church also met in homes. In homes, the church gathered in small groups to enjoy a meal together and the Lord's Supper. When we look at what are often called the "one another" passages pertaining to the activity of the church in the epistles, we are reminded of the necessity of small groups in facilitating the kind of community that God wants our churches to experience. Gil Bilezikian in *Community 101* writes, ". . . it should become obvious that the primary application of the biblical mandate for communal life can only take place in a context of closeness and togetherness. Necessarily, this spells 'small groups.'"[3]

The "one another passages" are reminders of the necessity of small groups in facilitating the kind of community that God wants our churches to experience.

Joseph Myers in *The Search to Belong* challenges the church's approach to building community through small groups. He writes: "So often our small group models encourage *forced belonging.* We surmise that putting people into groups will alleviate the emptiness so prevalent in our fast-paced culture."[4] While his challenge is an important one, when the options are considered, small groups remain the most effective way to care for people, help them develop into committed Christ-followers, and foster the kind of caring community that is so attractive to the outside world. The call to community goes beyond providing meals in a time of crisis and borrowing each other's leaf blowers to being the living and breathing body of Jesus Christ to one another.

Bottom line—small groups *are* optional, while community is *not.* Until another effective method emerges, let's get people connected through small groups.

Small groups are optional, while community is not.

So, how do small groups in a new church become transforming communities? While there are many experiences that contribute to biblical community, three emerge from the description found in Acts 2:42-47. They are *Celebrate, Connect, and Contribute.* At Community Christian Church, we expect anyone who considers themselves part of our church family to celebrate, connect, and contribute weekly. These experiences are imbedded into the life, activities, and DNA of our church.

Reproducing Experiences

Celebrate

The group of people who formed the very first Christian community was a celebrating community. Acts 2:46 says, "they worshiped together . . . each day . . ." (NLT), and then the very next verse continues to describe this celebrating community. They "shared their meals with great joy and generosity—all the while praising God" (Acts 2:47, NLT). Did you catch that—"all the while praising God"? Celebration wasn't a weekly event; it was a *lifestyle* and an integral part of community life. The first Christian community celebrated the great things God was doing in their presence.

> Celebration wasn't a weekly event; it was a lifestyle and an integral part of community life.

Small groups need to celebrate. We are called to "rejoice with those who rejoice" (Rom 12:15). In small groups we can celebrate the simplest of blessings, like a job promotion or a birthday. We can also celebrate the more significant "wins" in life, like a restating of wedding vows or the adoption of a child.

Connect

Another popular word that characterizes the kind of community people long for is the word "connect." The first church community was unequivocally and tightly connected to one another and to God. So connected, the Bible says they were together everyday: "Everyday they continued to meet together" (Acts 2:47).

In our fast-paced, fragmented lifestyles, the very thought of connecting daily seems absurd. Most of the people in our communities and churches would think, "You've got to be nuts! Celebration services once a week and small group meetings once a week or every other week is already a stretch. Yet you want to connect every day? Not a chance." But this kind of regular, even daily interaction was one of the dominant characteristics of this attractive community, the early church. Randy Frazee refers to this concept as "frequency." He writes: "If people are not willing to restructure their lives and their time to get to the heart of this characteristic of frequency—and trust me, it can be done—the experience of true community will continue to elude them. Unless we make these changes, we will never have the kind of community the 'First Church of Jerusalem' had, and we should stop pretending that we do."[5]

Contribute

The third word that characterizes this community of small groups is "contribute." Acts 2:44 says, they "shared everything they had" (NLT). Verse 45 says, "They sold their possessions and shared the proceeds" (NLT). This appears to have been a group of people who could stand up and say, "If you've got a genuine need, we will help you." The example of Barnabas who sold a piece of property and gave the proceeds to the church to help the poor (Acts 4:32-37) contrasted with Ananias and Sapphira who misrepresented their gift and ended up dead (Acts 5), provides a glimpse of just how seriously they took the call to "share everything they had."

Fortunately at Community Christian Church, we taught and encouraged people from day one that small groups are not optional. We were convinced biblically and practically that if we were going to be an impact church, the best way for people to experience life-change and to be cared for would be in the context of a small group. For new churches being established, this value must not only be part of your philosophy and strategy, but also it must be lived out by the people who lead the church—you and your staff.

How do we develop reproducing communities that are characterized by celebrating, connecting, and contributing? It begins with reproducing leadership.

Reproducing Leadership

Neal McBride discusses Jesus' work with His disciples by saying,

. . . the small group was Jesus' method for leadership training. He devoted Himself primarily to the task of developing a select group of men, the Apostles. His goal was to equip this small group of disciples to carry out the work of the gospel after He returned to the Father. Success was to be measured in terms of their future ministries, not in present achievements.[6]

The apostle Paul offers wise advice to the young church planter Timothy that remains as valuable today as it was then. He says, "And the things you have heard me say in the presence of many witnesses entrust to reliable men who will also be qualified to teach others" (2 Tim 2:2).

This passage has served as a theme verse for our strategy to reproduce small group leaders at every level and in every ministry— children, students, adults, and all others. We refer to it as the "2-2-2 Principle." We tell our leaders, "You have taken on the most important responsibility there is—pastoring, caring for, discipling and leading ten other people. It is a tremendous honor to be used by God to impact the lives of ten other people for eternity." Then we ask, "What if I told you that within the next five years you could impact the lives of over 300 people . . . while still caring for 10? Are you interested?"

"What if I told you that within the next five years you could impact the lives of over 300 people . . . while still caring for 10? Are you interested?"

How to Reproduce Leaders and Small Groups

We challenge every leader to identify and train an apprentice—someone he or she is working with and developing in order to become a leader. There is a simple process for developing an apprentice that gives him or her the opportunities to lead in a safe environment under the direction of a leader. You've likely seen something similar:

Step 1: *I Lead. You Observe. We Talk.*
Step 2: *I Lead. You Help. We Talk.*
Step 3: *You Lead. I Help. We Talk.*
Step 4: *You Lead. I Observe. We Talk.*
Step 5: *You Lead. Someone else Observes.*

When it comes to the tactical strategy for multiplying a small group there are basically three options:

1. An apprentice leader is released to start a new group with some members from the existing group.

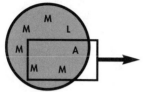

2. An existing leader is released to start a new group with some members from the existing group.

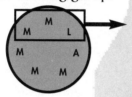

3. A Turbo Group is started where all members are apprentices, and they all are released to start new small groups.

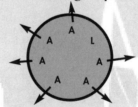

When faced with the reality of literally hundreds of people showing up for a grand opening celebration service, and only a handful of staff and a limited number of people in your core group available to lead, it will demand taking some leadership risks. God does not always send us 8s, 9s, and 10s on the leadership scale. These people are low-risk ventures. The risky ones are the 4s, 5s, and 6s, who flourish or fail when someone takes a risk on them.

Here's an example of a low-risk, high-return success story:

> My dreams led me to make a move, in the interest of my career path, to a Fortune 100 corporation where the growth in my career was "unlimited." God continued to bless me with success in my career and within a few years I was promoted to sales manager. With that promotion came a critical transition from winning sales campaigns to the full-time development and leadership of others. It also meant a move to Illinois.

My move led me to Community Christian Church. At CCC, I was exposed to a new level of leadership development in the church. I joined a small group and was soon invited to become an apprentice leader with Jerry. Jerry began meeting with me regularly and I was intrigued by the common concepts between the corporate leadership development I had received and the kind of development that took place at CCC. Ultimately the group was released to me as a leader and I was now simultaneously leading in the church and in my company. God continued to tug on me regarding the balance between these two roles and I began to wonder if maybe He had something else in store for my life besides the corporate ladder climb.

Tim eventually became a coach of small group leaders, and he now serves as our Director of Small Groups at our South Campus.

From day one of a church, small group leaders need to understand the difference between addition and multiplication. As a small group leader, if you simply equip and release one leader from your group every year for five years, you will have 6 leaders. However, if you release one new leader every year, and each leader releases a leader every year, and each of those leaders releases a leader every year and so on, and so on, you will have 32 groups, capable of reaching over 300 people in just five years. Bottom line—we cannot settle for addition!

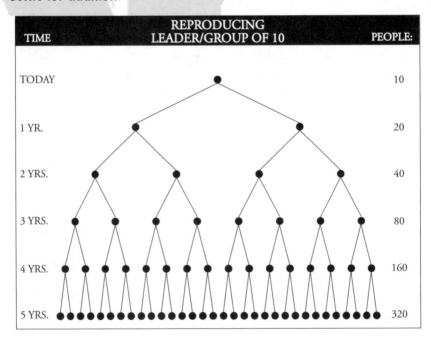

TIME	REPRODUCING LEADER/GROUP OF 10	PEOPLE:
TODAY		10
1 YR.		20
2 YRS.		40
3 YRS.		80
4 YRS.		160
5 YRS.		320

In the process of writing his book, *Natural Church Development*, Christian Schwarz conducted thousands of surveys in hundreds of churches all over the world, and compiled a list of over 170 defining variables that contribute to a healthy church. His research concluded that if he had to narrow it down to a single most common contributing factor—the consistent thread that ran through the most healthy churches—it was that they had small groups that multiplied.[7]

Reproducing Leadership Requires Relational Coaching

Developing a leadership layer of nonpaid coaches has been an ongoing challenge for us at CCC. And from conversations with pastors and leaders from other churches implementing a small group strategy, it is clear that this is a continual struggle. The temptation is to solve the problem through additional staffing. The challenge really is providing care for small group leaders. We know that a small group leader, if left on his or her own to function independently without a coach or a group of supportive peers will not survive. Our experience indicates that it is only the highly motivated leader who will last more than six months without consistent care and accountability.

Every leader needs a coaching relationship.

We have put significant effort into developing this leadership role, realizing that in order for us to continue to grow, expand our outreach, and care for the number of people God continues to send us, we cannot afford to pay enough staff to carry out this task. Every leader needs a coaching relationship. Here is a model we are developing to better help us equip and release coaches to care for small group leaders:

New Model for Coaching[8]

Here are three recent discoveries concerning coaching:[9]

1. **The heart of coaching is a relational investment.** Our experience is that coaching only is effective when the relational contact between leader and coach is given first priority. The

temptation is to be tactical and emphasize trouble-shooting and skill development, at the expense of building a spiritual friendship. In their book, *Building a Church of Small Groups*, Russ Robinson and Bill Donahue conclude,

> Coaches are primarily lovers of leaders. Love is the overriding Christian virtue, and it must be expressed between leaders. A leader who is loved is a leader who will serve well for a long time. A leader who is loved is a leader who will respond to correction or training. A leader who is loved is a leader who can be given more responsibility, because he or she will receive it appropriately. So much of coaching is simply loving.[10]

2. A reasonable span of care for coaching is five leaders. At CCC, we figured that, as the church grew, our ability to raise up coaches would naturally improve. We were wrong, and we continue to cheat when it comes to span of care. The result is overburdening our coaches and staff with the responsibility of caring for more leaders than is reasonable. If a coach is *not* leading a small group, it is reasonable for him or her to care for up to five leaders.

3. Three tasks flow out of a relational investment. Once the spiritual friendship is well developed, three primary tasks will flow out of the relational investment. 1) *Equipping*—providing the leader with the necessary skills to effectively lead and shepherd a small group. 2) *Recruiting*—the task of helping the leader identify and enlist additional small group members or apprentice leaders. 3) *Serving*—the task of coming alongside the leader at times and leading with him or her. This may be done to help the leader develop in a specific area or walk the leader through a particular dilemma or challenge. The time and energy given to these tasks will vary in emphasis based on the individual needs of the leader (notice the dotted lines = flexibility).

Reproducing Friendships

At the heart of building community is developing caring spiritual friendships. Lyman Coleman, Founder of Serendipity House and one of the pioneers of the contemporary small group movement, developed a baseball diamond model to help us understand the process a group must undergo to become a real, caring community.[11] At Community Christian Church, we've adapted his model to assist small group leaders in helping their group members develop meaningful friendships.

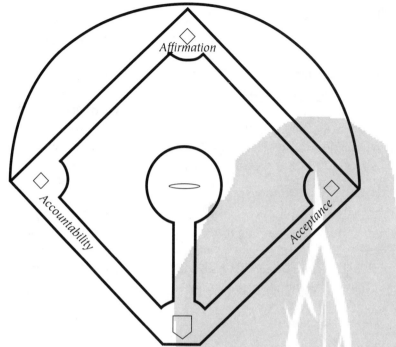

First Base

Similar to baseball and circling the bases, building a caring community begins with First Base. The word that best describes this stage of community building is *Acceptance,* and it primarily revolves around sharing your story and talking about the past. Storytelling has long been a part of building community. Through storytelling, a group will begin to learn about one another—the events in their lives that have formed them into the people they are today. As individuals are given the opportunity to tell their stories, they hopefully will discover an unmistakable acceptance that reflects the heart of Jesus.

Second Base

The word that best describes Second Base is *Affirmation.* At this stage of community building, the focus is on the present, identifying specific qualities or actions of group members from which you have personally benefited. Affirmation is a critical part of community building because sometimes at first base, in the getting-to-know-you stage, people will often share less than flattering stories or events from their past. Affirmation assures group members that they are loved unconditionally.

Third Base

After a group has shared their stories, and affirmed each other, they can be led into this stage of community building. The word associated with this stage of community building is *Accountability*. Here we mostly focus on the future—acknowledging areas in our lives in which we need to let God do significant work. Third base is sharing on a "deeper level." It involves the questions, "Where do you need to grow? Where is God calling you? What is keeping you from this change in your life?"

Home Plate

Genuine biblical community is the longing of every human heart. Most of us can identify times and places where we've experienced it, but it still is nearly impossible to define. We no more arrive at biblical community than we do Christlikeness. It is an ongoing journey of relational connectedness that can't be explained outside of the Holy Spirit's work when we come into a relationship with Jesus Christ and His church.

Reproducing Communities in Community?

So, what's the latest with Bruno? Bruno's journey led him and his business partner, Nick Ryan, to approach the leadership team at CCC with the idea of creating a place where people could not only live in beautiful places but live in those places beautifully. This dream led to the birth of CCC's South Campus in Romeoville, Illinois.[12] Through a partnership between Community Christian Church and the development corporation of which Nick and Bruno are founding partners, a new nonprofit organization was launched—the Institute for Community.[13]

Through this partnership, CCC was able to reproduce community on a scale never before dreamed possible. In 1998, the HighPoint Community was opened with CCC's South Campus meeting in the community center as a value-added commodity offering genuine community through small groups to the residents of this development. What started as a life-changing experience in a small group eventually led to a new way of developing single family and multifamily residential communities. What's next in building community? Who knows? But we cannot wait to see what new things God is dreaming up!

[1] Community Christian Church is a multi-site (one church meeting in many locations), small-group-based church that was started in 1989. Since that time the church has experienced considerable growth and now reaches 3500 people at its weekly celebration services and has over 250 small groups for children, students, and adults. In addition, the church has planted two churches and launched the NewThing Network as a catalyst for reproducing networks of mulit-site churches (**www.newthing.org**).

[2] Value Curve developed by Michael Basch, Founder of Federal Express.

[3] Gilbert Bilezikian, *Community 101* (Grand Rapids: Zondervan, 1997) 54.

[4] Joseph Myers, *The Search to Belong* (Grand Rapids: Zondervan, 2003) 68.

[5] Randy Frazee, *The Connecting Church* (Grand Rapids: Zondervan, 2001) 130.

[6] Neal McBride, *How to Lead Small Groups* (Colorado Springs: NavPress, 1993) 17.

[7] Christian Schwarz, *Natural Church Development* (Carol Stream, IL: ChurchSmart Resources, 1996) 33.

[8] Tammy Melchien and Janet McMahon, *Coaching Guidebook* (Naperville, IL: Community Christian Church, 2003).

[9] Editor's Note: For more information on coaching, visit John Wasem's chapter in this book.

[10] Bill Donahue and Russ Robinson, *Building a Church of Small Groups* (Grand Rapids: Zondervan, 2001) 149.

[11] Lyman Coleman, *Small Group Training Manual* (Littleton, CO: Serendipity Publishers, 1991) 16.

[12] Community Christian Church is a multi-site church and uses the term "Campus" to designate a church presence in a specific community. For more information see related chapter on multi-site church development.

[13] For more information on the Institute for Community, visit their web site at **www.instituteforcommunity.org**.

In 1987, **Glen Schneiders** was called by the churches of Lexington, Kentucky, to start Crossroads Christian Church. The church was founded on November 15, 1987. Crossroads is presently in its third building program on their 36-acre campus. Glen has been married for 30 years to the former Marilyn Hammond. They have two grown daughters, Jodi and Jennifer.

Developing the Leadership Culture

*L*eadership development never happens accidentally. I learned this important lesson in the early years of our new church. I had a very young, inexperienced staff, and I found myself increasingly frustrated that they were not more assertive leaders. They were tentative at times, and at other moments were like bulls in a china shop. "Why didn't they just step up and lead?" I kept asking myself.

One day as a staff member and I were making a hospital visit, it hit me. Actually, I made the visit while he was in the hospital bathroom having a panic attack! It was not that he did not want to make the visit, but rather felt unprepared and needed coaching from me.

For the first time, I viewed staff leadership deficiencies as my failures in leadership development. The staff had great hearts and were committed to our church's vision. They were the right people, but lacked experience. They needed someone to develop them as leaders.

> I now viewed staff leadership deficiencies as my failures in leadership development. They were the right people, but lacked experience.

I recalled my first hospital visit as a twenty-year-old. An elderly man in our church had major surgery and had just returned from the recovery room. I was not prepared for what I encountered when I entered his room. His wife, upset by the uncertainty of his condition, was seated apprehensively next to him. As I greeted her, I noticed that there were numerous tubes with all sorts of fluids secreting from his body. The sight of blood made me queasy, and the room began to spin. I asked her if I could pray with them. I knelt, placing my head on the bed, to keep from fainting! She thought I was deeply spiritual. I was just trying not to end up in the bed next to her husband. I couldn't get out of that room fast enough.

My second hospital visit was much different. Explaining my previous hospital experience to our elders, I was accompanied by one of them who led me around, and kept me shielded from the tubes, bags, and blood. I never lost consciousness, and slowly, after several visits, with the help of our elders, I felt more comfortable in those settings.

My young staff members needed the same support from me that I received from my elders. The issue was not desire, but rather confidence and competency. They needed someone to coach them.

I committed the classic mistake in leadership development. I hired someone to do a task, to take something off my plate. As soon as they walked in the door, I shoved it at them and expected them to figure it out. I failed to assess their abilities, to train them, or give them constructive feedback as they performed the task themselves. From my experiences, I realized that an important part of my role as lead pastor was to develop leaders and a leadership culture.

Creating a healthy leadership culture may be as important to the long-term viability of the church as anything done by the church planter. A significant part of the church planter's job is to provide a healthy environment for leaders to grow within the emerging church.

A significant part of the church planter's job is to provide a healthy environment for leaders to grow within the emerging church.

One of the first elders in our new church, when asked to serve, told me, "I don't believe I'm qualified." I promised to walk with him on his leadership journey. Sixteen years later he still serves as an elder. He recently told me it was my promise to walk with him and coach him that encouraged him to accept the role.

Jesus modeled leadership development. He made it a matter of first importance in the establishment of His kingdom. Jesus' first action, with a clear vision and sense of where He was going, was to call twelve others to come and follow Him. Jesus then spent significant time mentoring twelve men (and several vital but less publicly acknowledged women) for three years. He trusted the disciples with responsibilities, gave them opportunities to succeed and fail, and challenged them to learn through all experiences. He debriefed the experiences. He was their biggest fan and most loving critic.

> ## Jesus spent significant time mentoring twelve men (and several women) for three years.

Jesus never stopped teaching His disciples. Even as His time on earth ended, Jesus reminded them of the mission for which they were trained. His commission was a restatement of His vision, and it implied His confidence in their ability to implement it. At His ascension Jesus declared, "But you will receive power when the Holy Spirit comes on you; and you will be my witnesses in Jerusalem, and in all Judea and Samaria, and to the ends of the earth" (Acts 1:8).[1] Jesus reminded the disciples that they would not be alone; the Holy Spirit would walk with them and would take His place in ongoing leadership development.

Like Jesus, the church planter must make identifying potential leaders a high priority from day one. The future of your church and the Church universal depends upon this. Place time on your calendar for developing leaders.

In the busyness that comes with new church work it will be easy to defer leadership development to the back burner. If that happens, developing leaders will be formed without your input, and your church will have to live with the results. If you want to maximize effectiveness, and minimize heartache, time spent with leaders must begin from day one.

Jack Welch, former CEO of General Electric, spent thirty percent of his time doing leadership development with emerging leaders at GE. Welch realized that the distinguishing factor that would set them apart from their competition was not their product, but their people.[2] There is no substitute for quality leaders. One distinguishing factor in healthy new churches is a climate where leadership development is an ongoing part of the strategy.

The Pareto Principle states, "A minority of inputs produces a majority of results."[3] It has become known as the 80:20 rule.

(Twenty percent of people control eighty percent of the world's wealth.) While originally applied to economics, the 80:20 rule has been expanded to include leadership development. Leaders are encouraged to spend eighty percent of their time with the twenty percent that will make the greatest difference. Make sure the difference makers have your ear and your calendar.

Jesus gathered the core before He ever considered the crowd.

Jesus gathered the core before He ever considered the crowd. Often He dispersed the crowd so He could teach the core. If you want the crowd to grow, you must spend time consistently with the core. Bill Hybels notes, "Leaders learn best from leaders."[4] There are certain tasks that cannot be delegated. Leadership development is one of those tasks.

Characters of Potential Leaders
Potential leaders must exhibit integrity.

You can teach skills, but you cannot teach integrity. Yet too often we look first at a person's skill level, and try to ignore their character deficiencies. Bob Russell said, "Leadership begins with who we are not what we do."[5] Russell continues, "It is easier to train a person of character to do the job you want than to turn a talented person into someone who is trustworthy."[6]

Yet many have fallen guilty to the recruitment of skill with the hope that the integrity issue will fall in line. And most have learned the hard lesson of having to de-hire or de-volunteer someone, now in a position of some power, because they lacked integrity. Often the fallout can get pretty messy because the hard work was not done on the front end.

Many have fallen guilty to the recruitment of skill with the hope that the integrity issue will fall in line.

When it comes to integrity, followers take their cue from the leader. If you exaggerate information or excuse questionable behavior, it trickles down to your followers. "Lived doctrine will make the difference between effectiveness and ineffectiveness in this spiritual landscape," says Sally Morgenthaler.[7]

Potential leaders must be loyal to the vision.

Before you begin to recruit, the leader must be able to clearly articulate the vision. To what are you calling potential leaders? In the early days of church planting, one central vision supported by every leader is essential. There is nothing more potentially damaging than someone trying to rearrange the vision according to a personal agenda. Recruit leaders to the vision.

In the planning stages of our new church, I heard church growth expert Carl George say, "Don't be surprised if the first people to greet you are also the first people to leave you." I thought to myself, "Carl doesn't know what a likable guy I am. That will never happen!" Yet, within the first year, two of our largest givers and most influential leaders left over issues that concerned a redirection of vision. To waver on the vision for the sake of dollars or influence would have had lasting negative impact on our direction and future growth.

Potential leaders are born, not made.

Most people have a certain aptitude to develop some leadership skills, but God gifts fewer to lead. Romans 12:6-8 reads, "We have different gifts, according to the grace given us . . . if it is leadership, let him govern diligently. . . ." It is the church planter's job to discover potential leaders and place them in an environment that will stimulate growth.

> It is one thing to lead from the power associated with salaries and promotions and demotions; it is another to lead volunteers.

Henry Ford noted, "To ask who should be the leader is like asking who should sing tenor in the quartet. The tenor should sing tenor, of course; and the person who is gifted to lead should lead."[8] Just because someone is recognized as a leader in the marketplace does not necessarily transfer to the church. It is one thing to lead from the power associated with salaries and promotions and demotions; it is another to lead volunteers. Also, exercise caution appointing someone to a leadership position because they have led in another church. Sometimes those who are power-hungry or who have been dysfunctional leaders in an established church will view a new church as a place to finally get his or her way. I like to have a chance to watch potential leaders over time to see how they respond in areas where they are asked to serve, not lead. I watch how they are with others who serve alongside them. Some people feign great respect for the leader, but demonstrate little respect for his or her peers. This should be a red flag.

Potential leaders must possess a humble spirit.

Are potential leaders more interested in the title and power, or are they truly being called by God to serve? Jim Collins in his book, *Good to Great*, says that the two characteristics of truly outstanding leaders are "a paradoxical blend of personal humility and professional will (their ambition is first and foremost for the institution, not themselves)."[9]

Another way to look at this: potential leaders may have great skills, but are they team players? How will each one mesh with the other members of the team? How often have you heard championship athletic teams talk about team chemistry as a reason for their success? The superstar mentality grates against the servant leader example of Jesus.

Keys to Developing Leaders
Don't Shortcut the Selection Process for Potential Leaders.

You will pay in the long run for shortsighted personnel decisions (paid and unpaid). In the early days of church planting, the tendency is to fill slots with "warm bodies," and often we have to do that. But as you do, assess which people have the capacity to lead. Don't hand over control too quickly; it is much harder to reclaim it.

"Nothing will take more of your time and energy than hiring the wrong person. And nothing will help your ministry more than hiring the right person."[10] This applies as much to unpaid leaders as paid leaders, except that sometimes it can be harder to de-hire the unpaid leader because you cannot take away compensation!

David Cottrell concurs,

> If you hire tough, it will be a whole lot easier to manage the right people. The decision you have to make is to hire tough and manage easy, or hire easy and manage tough. I can assure you that the best thing to

do is to take your time on the front end so that you can enjoy having the right people on your team.[11]

That word "enjoy" in Cottrell's statement is huge. Church plants are hard work. Placing the right people in the right roles makes life much more enjoyable for the whole team.

Jim Collins, in an interview about his book *Good to Great*, observes,

> We learned that people are *not* the most critical asset. The *right* people are. So much so that great companies will put picking the right people ahead of picking the right strategy. . . . So these great companies were bipolar—they were great places to work for the right people. But they were terrible places for the wrong people. . . . Great company leaders didn't see it as their objective to make it a great place to work. There was an absence of motivational programs. That's because they had the right people: those who wanted to be part of an environment that succeeds and wins, and whose values connected with the values of the institution.[12]

When potential leaders want to leave, sometimes you need to let them. They may have reached the realization that this is not the right place for them.

Look for the Teachable Moments.

Don't do a task alone when someone can join you in the experience. When you speak or travel, take someone with you. Use your travel time to mentor. Isn't that what Jesus did as He traveled the dusty roads of Judea? When we started our new church, I was a young trustee at a Bible College. Three to four times a year I would travel to trustees' meetings with two respected, veteran ministers in our area. I used that time to ask them questions and also listen to them discuss the issues their churches were facing. I learned so much by just being with them.

Use travel time to mentor.
Catch leaders doing things
right and encourage them.

Catch developing leaders doing things right and encourage them. Do this over and over so that when you need to make constructive assessments you have earned that right. Don't allow your only points of contact to be for correction. Defend in public, correct in private.

Provide Planned Learning Opportunities.

Expose developing leaders to good resources. If I read an outstanding book, I will discuss the key points I learned with other leaders. Often we will go through leadership books together. Some of the best money you can spend is for leadership conferences with seasoned leaders and developing leaders attending together. Make sure that your developing leaders are exposed to models of what God is doing in leading churches and businesses.

Let Developing Leaders Lead.

Give developing leaders a chance to lead. Provide an environment that gives them a chance to succeed, but make the tasks significant enough to encourage them to give their best efforts.

When Jesus sent out the twelve, "He gave them power and authority" (Luke 9:1). He gave them instructions on what to take, where to go, what to say, what to do, how to handle conflict, and why to expect resistance. Then it says, "When the apostles returned, they reported to Jesus what they had done. Then he took them with him and they withdrew by themselves" (Luke 9:10). Jesus gave the disciples something meaningful to do. He gave them a high-stakes challenge. The disciples preached, and they healed the sick. You must give developing leaders exciting opportunities where they can make a difference in someone's life. And you must give them honest feedback to help them excel.

Final Thoughts on Developing a Leadership Culture

Be continually on the lookout for new leaders. Watch for those who are at midpoints in careers and are ready and able to move from success to significance. They have a certain flexibility that their marketplace success has created that allows them to consider opportunities to use their resources and skills for Kingdom advancement. But they will not see the church as a viable place for use of those skills unless you have them on your radar screen.

Also scan the horizon for emerging leaders. Many are challenged to do something different with their lives than to climb the ladder of success that has left their parents unfulfilled. Young people are looking for a meaningful cause for which to give their lives. This means youth ministries must also develop a leadership culture.

Continue to be an active learner. Where do you go to be challenged? You cannot lead leaders if you have stopped growing. Ask annually of yourself and from other key leaders, "Am I still the right person to lead this mission?"

As your church grows, you will have to be more selective with whom you spend your time, even among your growing leadership circle. Failure to do this will stifle the growth potential of the church and emerging leaders.

As the church grows, the organization will have to be fluid enough to adopt and adapt to new leadership structures. Some who led in the early days of your church will not "get promoted" to new levels of responsibility. Recognizing this early on and helping people to understand their strengths and weaknesses can help ease some of the pain associated with the necessary changes of a growing church.

Someday you will be gone, and the effectiveness of what you have done will be measured by how well the church survives and thrives in your absence. Great leaders help mentor their successors and provide a solid core of leaders to assist the church for years to come.

Jim Collins states that great leaders "set up their successors for even greater success in the next generation."[13] Wouldn't it be wonderful if the church grew mightily in your absence under the hands of capable leaders that you helped to develop?

Hebrews 13:17 says, "Obey your leaders and submit to their authority. They keep watch over you as men who will one day give an account." One day God will ask you to give an account for the way you managed your leadership gift and the leadership gifts of those that God placed around you. May God find you faithful.

---

[1] All Scripture quotations are taken from the *New International Version* unless otherwise noted.

[2] Bill Hybels, *Courageous Leadership* (Grand Rapids: Zondervan, 2002) 133.

[3] Pareto Principle, "80:20 rule," http://www.paretplaw.co.uk/principle.html.

[4] Bill Hybels, 2003 Leadership Summit, Barrington, Illinois, August 7, 2003.

[5] Bob Russell, *When God Builds a Church* (West Monroe, LA: Howard Publishing, 2000) 75.

[6] Ibid., 91.

[7] Sally Morgenthaler, quoted by Dan Kimball, in *The Emerging Church* (Grand Rapids: Zondervan, 2003) 52.

[8] Henry Ford, quoted by Russell, *When God*, 81.

[9] Jim Collins, *Good to Great* (New York: Harper Publishing, 2001) 20.

[10] Russell, *When God*, 91.

[11] David Cottrell, *Monday Morning Leadership* (Dallas: CornerStone Leadership Institute, 2002) 57.

[12] Jim Collins, "*Good to Great*'s Leadership Model Looks Familiar to Christians," in *Christianity Today*, posted March 14, 2003, http://www.christianitytoday.com/ct/2003/110/51.0.html.

[13] Collins, *Good to Great*, 39.

Mike Decker is the lead church planter for Three Strands Christian Church, a new church in Greenville, South Carolina. Mike is a graduate of Concordia College, Emmanuel School of Religion, and most recently, the South Carolina Criminal Justice Academy. Mike lives in Greenville with his wife, Kathleen, and his two children, Benjamin and Samantha.

A veteran church planter and pastor for over twenty years, **Dr. Tom Jones** is a widely sought after new church development coach, consultant, assessor, seminar leader and teacher, and mentor. He has a Doctor of Ministry Degree from United Theological Seminary in Dayton, Ohio, with an emphasis in church planting. Tom received his Master of Divinity Degree from Emmanuel School of Religion and his Bachelor of Arts Degree from Milligan College. Among other things, he now directs the Supervised Ministerial Experience (SME) Program, teaches in the Christian Ministries area at Emmanuel School of Religion in Johnson City, Tennessee, and is Director of Recruitment and Assessment for Southeast Stadia, a national church planting movement. Tom and his wife Debbie led the church planting teams at SouthBrook Christian Church in Dayton, Ohio, and Princeton Community Church in Princeton, New Jersey. They have two children, Melanie and Tom. Tom can be reached at **jonest@esr.edu**.

Growing Pains:
Managing Conflict in Church Planting

Introduction

We're having a baby!" As any parent can attest, that statement is one of the most exciting and reality-changing exclamations that can be uttered. I (Mike) know, because I just lived through the arrival of my second child—a girl. When my wife informed me we were pregnant again, I was ecstatic. As the news spread through our circle of family and friends, everyone seemed to catch "baby fever." Suddenly, everyone was interested in children, and as a result, baby names, gender preference, and the ultimate hope that this one would get lucky and look like my wife, seemed to be all anyone wanted to talk about. We were excited too. We put the nursery back together, started re-collecting all of the gear necessary to care for an infant, and began the process of selecting names. My wife attended baby showers and celebrated the joy of the impending arrival as we waited anxiously and excitedly for the birth of our little girl. When the day finally arrived, we were on top of the world. Things went well at the hospital, and by the time we made it home we were convinced my wife had given birth to the perfect baby. That theory lasted about three hours. Our daughter wasn't sure she really liked to eat, and it was obvious that she had serious disdain for

306

extended periods of sleep. In order to get her to sleep, you had to hold her in exactly the right position and if you changed that position, even to breathe, she let you know behavior of that nature was not acceptable. Having been parents once before, we weren't exactly shocked, but we were quickly reminded that having an infant around the house wasn't perfect. It wasn't easy, and it certainly wasn't without some measure of conflict.

The same is true in the establishment of new churches. In fact, the phrase, "We're planting a new church," produces some of the same responses as, "We're having a baby." In the days leading up to the start of the church everyone is excited and filled with dreams of what the new church will be like. As the vision is fleshed out, the name is selected, and the pieces start coming together, people are thrilled as they anxiously await the birth of the church. When the day finally arrives and the church is born, everyone is on top of the world, and they find themselves secretly thinking they may have done it—they may have planted the perfect church. Unfortunately, the church won't be perfect. At some point in the church's early life someone won't like something, or there will be a problem that leads to a disagreement and suddenly it's there—conflict.

Conflict is a normal part of the human equation.

Conflict is a normal part of the human equation, and it should be no surprise that the history of God's people in Scripture reflects that reality. In the New Testament book of Acts, we learn a great deal about how the early church managed conflict, a fact that is of particular interest and value to present-day church planters and church planting organizations. Like the early church and families with newborns, new churches experience a number of growing pains. No matter how hard you try to keep it from occurring, conflict in new churches is unavoidable; it's a part of life. It's not a matter of "if," but rather "when." As Jim Van Yperen puts it, "If death and taxes are the first two certainties, then conflict is the third. Life requires conflict. It is an essential part of God's redeeming plan."[1] Kenneth Haugk echoes that opinion,

> Conflict is a fact of life throughout society, including the church. Conflict that hones the edge of an organization and keeps it mindful of

and true to its purposes is healthy. An organization with no conflict at all (and we don't know of one) must have either no purpose at all, or at best a very frivolous one.[2]

As new church planters, or as members of existing congregations, we must understand and accept the inevitability of conflict.

The book of Acts records the establishment of many new churches, and as you would expect, there is considerable conflict. As a result, Acts has become a textbook on how to handle conflict in the church. For our purposes we will look at two incidents: the disagreement between Paul and Barnabas in Acts 15 and the more serious conflict regarding Ananias and Sapphira in Acts 5. Both are extremely instructive and helpful for learning how to handle conflict in a new church setting.

> Acts has become a textbook on how to handle conflict in the church.

Paul and Barnabas: Acts 15:36-41

Acts 15 is seen by some as *the* conflict story of the early church. Early in the chapter we see that a controversy arose when a group of men from Judea traveled to the church in Antioch and taught that salvation could not be secured by Gentiles without circumcision. Church planters Paul and Barnabas expressed significant disagreement and were sent by their commissioning church in Antioch to discuss the issue with the mother church in Jerusalem. After considerable debate, the Jerusalem Council resolved the question by relaxing the requirements for Gentiles, and sent both a written response and messengers to confirm the Council's findings. The decision that came from this meeting was perhaps the most important one made by early church leaders, and it arose from conflict.

The second conflict in Acts 15 is the disagreement between church planting team members Paul and Barnabas. Verse 39 says, "There arose such sharp disagreement that they parted company."[3] The key word in this sentence is *paroxysmos*, meaning "sharp disagreement, irritation."[4] There is a sense the conflict carried a strong emotional quality to it.[5]

What was going on between Barnabas and Paul? During the debate at the Jerusalem Council, they were united. Then, without much time having elapsed, they were in such difference of opinion they disbanded their successful church planting team. What happened? Were they not spiritual enough? Were they no longer a part of God's will?

In taking a closer look at the situation, the conflict centered on John Mark. Paul suggested that the church planting team "visit the brothers" (verse 36) where they had previously preached and established churches. The language in verse 36 suggests a sense of oversight and inspection of the young churches. Barnabas desired to have John Mark, his nephew (Col 4:10), join the team, but Paul strongly disagreed.[6] Family ties are strong, but Barnabas was also a people-person. He was an encourager and mentor (Acts 4:26). He saw value in investing time in the young John Mark regardless of past failures.

In contrast to Barnabas, Paul was a task-driven person and was adamant that John Mark not be allowed to become a part of their church planting team. He had deserted Barnabas and Paul on an earlier trip (Acts 13:13), and their mission was too important "to enlist someone who might prove unreliable."[7] The writer Luke seems to agree with Paul. His description of John Mark's departure from the church planting team communicates a sort of apostasy or abandonment of ministerial work.[8] The mission to which the church planting team had been called was not a matter of human strategy or motivation, but a matter of divine commission. "Commitment to it was therefore not a matter of personal taste."[9]

From our church planting experience, another issue that plagues church planting teams also may have been an underlying problem in the conflict between Paul and Barnabas. All church planters experience a great deal of physical, emotional, and spiritual stress as they go through the process of starting churches. Many church planting teams underestimate how these pressures impact the relationships represented on the team. Likewise, Paul and Barnabas would have experienced the same kinds of stress, and in addition to the normal pressures of church planting, they had just participated in the heated debate that took place at the Jerusalem Council. Does it not make sense that the constant stress eventually took its toll on the relationship between Barnabas and Paul? We believe so. We also believe this is an issue present-day church planters must take into consideration.

So who was right, Paul or Barnabas? Perhaps both were right and wrong, and God used this conflict to further His kingdom. Barnabas was right to champion John Mark and give him a second chance. We know he must have succeeded in his mentoring of John Mark, as later even Paul comes to appreciate and love John Mark. Certainly, every church planter should have a John Mark or a Timothy to mentor in church planting. However, Paul's commitment to the task of fulfilling his church planting mission to reach the Gentiles is commendable. He saw the assignment as too important to risk failure because of the lack of commitment on the part of a team member. Without Paul's singleness of mind, how successful would the expansion of the church have been?

> ### Every church planter should have a John Mark or a Timothy to mentor in church planting.

A number of observations can be made about the Barnabas and Paul conflict. First, conflict occurs amidst even the best of church planting teams. Here we have two giants of the faith, yet they had a difference of opinion so serious that they dismantled their team. Second, this kind of conflict can be handled in a way that glorifies God and is not destructive to the church. Paul and Barnabas agreed to disagree and parted amicably. There was no backbiting nor slander, but rather mutual respect resulting in the commissioning of two teams instead of one. Two teams allowed for both John Mark and Silas to be added to the ministry of church planting, which enabled more work to be accomplished. Third, both men kept the mission of the church in focus, found a way to fulfill it, and at the same time remained true to their own personal convictions.

> ### Conflict occurs amidst even the best of church planting teams.

Ananias and Sapphira: Acts 5:1-11

One of the first serious conflicts in Acts is found in the fifth chapter: the story of Ananias and Sapphira. As you will remember, the members of the early church shared all of their resources and sold property from time to time to help other members of the community. Acts 5 records a married couple, Ananias and Sapphira, who sold land and brought the money to Peter. They did not, however, surrender all of the proceeds, but tried to give the impression they had. Ananias came before Peter and laid the money at his feet in an act of submission and dedication, but Peter saw into Ananias's heart and knew he was lying. Peter reminded Ananias he didn't have to sell the land or give all of the money, but because he lied, there was trouble. Peter explained that in their selfish attempt at self-promotion, Ananias and Sapphira hadn't just lied to the church; they had lied to the Holy Spirit. When Ananias heard these words, he fell down dead and was carried off and buried. A few hours later Sapphira came to Peter, not knowing what had happened, and instead of being greeted with thanks, she was grilled by Peter as to the amount of money they had received for the land. When she substantiated her husband's story, Peter announced to her that she had attempted to deceive the Holy Spirit, and as a result she too fell down dead. Luke goes on to explain that as a result of this, a great fear came upon the whole church as well as everyone who heard the story.

This was obviously a serious conflict. This isn't a difference of opinion as we saw with Paul and Barnabas. It was not a conflict over strategy, methodology, or style; this was a matter of sin. Ananias and Sapphira were not having a misunderstanding with the "faith promise" committee concerning a pledge; they were guilty of secrecy, collusion, and attempting to deceive the Holy Spirit. Ananias and Sapphira had lied to God, and what was at stake was not simply their integrity; it was the integrity of the entire body. Luke describes Ananias using language previously reserved for Judas Iscariot (Luke 22:3). Satan filled Ananias's heart, and Ananias had violated the integrity and character of the entire community. Witherington writes, "Luke sees this story not just as being about human greed and duplicitous actions but about an invasion of the community of the Spirit by the powers of darkness by means of Ananias."[10] Luke Timothy Johnson adds,

> The community was constituted as "one mind and heart" by the Spirit of God. It was the Spirit that led them to call nothing their own and share all their possessions. But this couple "falsified the Spirit" in the first place by their breaking the unanimity of intention; they "colluded" in their action. They were hoping that by counterfeiting the ges-

ture, they could both partake of the community life and "hold back something of their own."[11]

The *koinonia* of the early church was being threatened,[12] and it was serious business.

Conflict that threatens the koinonia of the church has to be handled quickly and well.

This was a terrible conflict for the early church to face, and though it's sad to admit, it is the type of conflict we often face in the new church setting. Churches are filled with imperfect, sinful people, and as a result there are going to be serious conflicts. Conflict that threatens the *koinonia* of the church has to be handled quickly and well. Unfortunately, we least desire to deal with this type of conflict. When conflict of this nature occurs, we are tempted to overlook or rationalize it for fear that confronting it might derail a young church. Allowing conflict born of sin to run its course in a church, especially in a new church, is to allow sin the opportunity to infect so much of the church that it becomes wholly ineffective at fulfilling its purpose. Its health and very life are threatened. Allowing conflict of this nature also means permitting the Church to be stripped of its *koinonia*, identity, and power. As a result, the Body of Christ becomes a warped caricature of God's intended design. Allowing conflict born of sin to go unchecked for the sake of comfort or convenience produces a victory for Satan and a deathblow to the very foundation of a community that initially held so much promise. Just like a serious disease can easily bring death to a newborn baby, this kind of unchecked conflict can bring death to a new church.

Serious conflict like that of Ananias and Sapphira has to be confronted. We suspect there are times when we all wish we had Peter's incredible prophetic insight. There are probably even times we secretly wish that God would handle the sources of conflict in our churches as swiftly and as definitively as He handled Ananias and Sapphira. In doing so, fear might grip everyone else in our flock prone to causing problems. Fortunately, judgment doesn't always come as quickly as it did in this case.

What, then, is the best way to handle this type of conflict in a new church setting? Despite all the books and articles that exist on handling conflict in the church, the best advice is still found in

Matthew 18:15-17. As Jesus instructs us, when conflict arises we should do our best to handle the matter privately and confront the individual one-on-one. If that doesn't work, Jesus commands us to confront the individual again, this time in the presence of witnesses. If the matter still is unresolved, we are to go before the leaders of the church, who will have the task of trying to lead that person to repentance, forgiveness, and reconciliation with the one offended and the greater body of Christ. The goal is always reconciliation.

The best advice is still found in Matthew 18:15-17.

We all understand this process, its potential, and its benefits. What if the person will not repent, however? What if the person refuses to acknowledge the sin? Regarding these cases, the apostle Paul instructs, "As for a man who is factious, after admonishing him once or twice, have nothing more to do with him, knowing that such a person is perverted and sinful; he is self-condemned" (Titus 3:10-11, RSV). "Factious," refers to a person who sets up warring parties. The person is threatening the *koinonia* of the church. While this might seem a bit extreme, that's exactly what a person who refuses to repent is doing—drawing a line and pitting a battle between the community of light and the influence of darkness. As we have explained, that simply cannot be tolerated in the church. However, when exercising the option of exclusion from the community, we must be extremely careful to always seek reconciliation and restoration. Sometimes, as in the case when Paul provided direction for the church in Corinth, people do come to repentance. Sometimes, people refuse and suffer the consequences. While the latter always hurts, and it is difficult to remove yourself physically and emotionally from someone you love, the integrity and health of the baby church has to be the primary consideration. Conflict born of sin cannot be overlooked or rationalized for the sake of comfort or convenience. Handling serious conflict is difficult, but absolutely necessary, particularly in vulnerable new churches where the stakes are so high.

When exercising the option of exclusion from the community, we must be extremely careful to always seek reconciliation and restoration.

Preventive Measures to Reduce Conflict in Church Planting

As we have illustrated, conflict is an inevitable reality of church planting. All church planters should understand and accept that fact from the outset. We must, however, do more than simply accept the inevitability of conflict. In addition, we must become proactive and take steps before the doors ever open to reduce potential sources of conflict. Here are some important things to consider when developing a plan to handle conflict:

1. Like Paul and Barnabas, present-day church planting teams should possess a sense of God's call about their mission. This helps to keep conflicts regarding personality, strategy, and other issues in perspective.

2. It is important for church planting teams and organizations to understand there will be conflict. When that fact is accepted, there is little surprise when it happens.

> It is important to understand there will be conflict.

3. All church planters should undergo professional church planting assessment. This exercise usually provides psychological testing, team building exercises, personality profiles, various simulation modules, and projects that allow for valuable input about an individual's or team's potential success. Quality assessment will not and should not eliminate all conflict. However, it will reduce conflict, helping teams to understand each other so future conflict can be dealt with in healthy ways.

4. Written mission, vision, and value statements reduce conflict. It is important that church planting teams know what is important to the team, how they will accomplish the mission, and how they will relate to one another. This is not to say that there is never healthy discussion about these issues. In fact, healthy conflict around core beliefs leads to open discussion that leads to sharpened understanding.

5. Team building is also an important task that must never be left for later. All too often church planters get involved in the urgent

activities required to start a church, but they pay little attention to fostering the relationships of team members.

Team building is a task that must never be left for later.

6. Finally, new churches should unwaveringly commit to high biblical standards when resolving conflict. As we mentioned earlier, it is hard to improve on the clear teaching found in Matthew 18.

Conflict is a natural part of life. It will happen in every new church. It's not a matter of "if," but a matter of "when." When conflict happens in the new church plant, don't run away from it. Instead, appropriately take care of it in ways illustrated in Scripture and emphasized in this chapter. Your new church will be better for it.

---

[1] Jim Van Yperen, "Conflict: The Refining Fire of Leadership," in *Leaders on Leadership*, ed. by George Barna (Ventura, CA: Regal, 1997) 241.

[2] Kenneth C. Haugk, *Antagonists in the Church* (Minneapolis: Augsburg, 1988) 31.

[3] All Scripture quotations are taken from the *New International Version* unless otherwise noted.

[4] Ben Witherington, *The Acts of the Apostles: A Socio-Rhetorical Commentary* (Grand Rapids: Eerdmans, 1998) 472.

[5] Luke Timothy Johnson, *The Acts of the Apostles* (Collegeville, MN: Liturgical Press, 1992) 282.

[6] Ibid.

[7] Warren W. Wiersbe, *The Bible Exposition Commentary*, Vol. 1 (Wheaton, IL: Victor, 1989) 466.

[8] Witherington, *Acts*, 472.

[9] Johnson, *Acts*, 282. See also 1 Cor 9:16-18.

[10] Witherington, *Acts*, 215.

[11] Johnson, *Acts*, 287.

[12] Witherington, *Acts*, 215.

Tom and Nona Lohr are ministering at CrossPointe Christian Church in Albuquerque, New Mexico, where Dr. Lohr is the Founding Pastor and Nona serves as Worship Leader. The Lohrs served with Tom and Debbie Jones on the new church planting team in Princeton, New Jersey, in the early 1990s. They have served other churches in Tennessee and West Virginia. Nona has performed music professionally, taught private music lessons, and worked as a public school teacher. Dr. Lohr received his Doctor of Ministry degree in Marriage and Family Therapy from Eastern Baptist Theological Seminary and M.Div. from Emmanuel School of Religion. Tom and Nona both have degrees from Milligan College and are the parents of two boys, Ben and Will.

When You Hit the Church Planting Wall

*T*he marathon is the toughest race to run. Not only does it measure 26.2 miles in length, which is enough to make anyone wonder why a person would choose to run it, but also, at the twenty-first or twenty-second mile, most runners "hit the wall." At this point, the runner's body goes into rebellion because it has used up all its stored energy. It begins to burn fat and muscle. The last six miles or so become a battle of will. Your body wants to stop, while your mind wants to finish the race.

During the yearly New York City Marathon, more than 30,000 runners leave Staten Island and head across the Verrazano Bridge continuing through all five boroughs of New York City. The world-class runners finish in roughly two hours and five minutes, and the rest of the field will fall in somewhere after that. I (Tom) ran the race in 1991 and finished in four and a half hours. Most people finish somewhere before the six-hour mark. However, the last place runner in 2003 finished in twenty-nine hours and forty-five minutes. Her name is Zoe Koplowitz. You might be thinking, "I could walk that race faster than that without any training!" Although you might be right, you're probably not 55 years old with diabetes and multiple sclerosis.[1] In order to finish the race, Zoe used two purple crutches. After the race, Zoe was asked how she managed to finish. She responded, "I think the ultimate lesson is you just keep going until you get it done; you do whatever it takes."[2]

So it is with church planting! We need to approach it with Zoe Koplowitz's attitude. We need to "just keep going, get it done, do whatever it takes," even when we hit the church planting wall.

When We Hit the Wall

The "wall" we hit was during our third year at CrossPointe. We started CrossPointe Christian Church in November of 2000 in Albuquerque, New Mexico, with 241 people. The people came as a result of five mailings of 60,000 cards each. We eventually leveled off with an average attendance of 150 people. The first year went fairly well, but during the second year we lost a couple of families. This scared us, and we wondered if that might be the "wall." It wasn't. In fact, it wasn't even close. Our "wall" began with my (Nona) being diagnosed with cancer. When the diagnosis came out of the doctor's mouth, I could not think anymore. I heard nothing else she said. The room started spinning, and I was flung into a deep, dark world. I was glad Tom was there to listen, although I'm sure he was experiencing the same disillusionment as me.

Immediately, the needs of the church went on the back burner. I had to cancel our church Christmas program, which was heartbreaking for me. I have a deep desire to see the church grow, and I knew that canceling would hurt our growth. We had no choice. I had to have surgery on December 10, and, at that time, no one could take my place. I made it through the surgery and found I was truly blessed. The cancer I had was "Ductal Carcinoma in Situ," which means it was contained in a duct. It had not spread. All the cancer was removed, with no trace found in any of the lymph nodes. I did not have to endure radiation or chemotherapy. We rejoiced, thinking all was well, but we weren't through the wall yet.

The year 2003 began, and again I did not feel well. I continued working as hard as I could, but was sick constantly. Finally, in May, my part-time teaching job ended. I spent time on the couch thinking that all I needed to do was rest. My health did not improve. Although I visited several doctors for blood tests, they could find nothing wrong. Finally, through prayer and talking to friends, I found a doctor who diagnosed me with a swollen and inflamed liver due to food allergies (caffeine, yeast, and dairy products). I began to wonder what I could eat. Sandwiches? Bread? Coffee? Milk? Ice Cream? I changed diets and slowly got better. Just when I was beginning to think it was over, I had an allergic reaction to medications the doctors had given me. It was a violent reaction, and it took my body several weeks to recover.

Before I could recover completely, I caught a viral bronchitis that would not go away. To make a long story short, I was bedridden for almost six months. As I was trying to get over the bronchitis, I discovered that in addition to my food allergies, I was allergic to household chemicals and fragrances such as fingernail polish, Pine Sol, and Downy. Tom took over the laundry chores, recognizing that I was too sick. On top of all that, I couldn't sleep at night. The doctor prescribed a medication to help me sleep, but all it did was create some terrible side effects. I didn't realize it was the medication until my body entered another terrible tailspin that took two months to overcome. During these months, I became very discouraged, as well as angry with God.

It seemed like I was never going to get well, and it made no sense. I was trying to do something good—to win people to Christ—but I couldn't do anything. I prayed for healing, but God was silent, and I stayed sick. I missed several Sundays at church and was unable to prepare for band rehearsals (an important element of the worship leading position I held). Gradually, I began to realize that I could not keep going this way. We had two options: I had to get well, or we would have to leave CrossPointe. Our dream of starting and growing a real and vibrant church was going up in smoke.

We were also going through the most difficult time we had ever experienced at the church. It was the summer, which is always hard because attendance and offerings both go down. Five or six families moved away, and several others left the church due to marriage problems or not agreeing with our vision. It was terrible. This was the wall, the never-ending wall.

One of the families that left the church was very special to us. We had spent hours with them and had given them several hundred dollars from our own pocket as well as from the church's funds. The husband was an alcoholic, raised in a fatherless home, and had a terrible anger problem. Tom counseled him for countless hours, and I ministered to his wife. On multiple occasions Tom went immediately to their home when the husband was in a fit of rage. He even went to buy diapers when the wife did not have a car. So, why did they leave? He quit coming to church, so she decided to go to a church where several of her friends attended. It was a shock. We had built a relationship with them. We loved them dearly and thought they loved us. It broke our hearts. We felt betrayed and used.

Shortly after that, another family left due to the same kind of circumstances. This trend continued with family after family. We began to wonder if God wanted us to stay at CrossPointe. What were we doing wrong? Was He trying to give us a message? Did He want us to move on? We had had good relationships with these people. What was happening? Then we remembered Jesus. When He needed his friends most, one denied Him, one betrayed Him, and the others ran away. So, why did we think people would treat us differently? We certainly weren't perfect. The Bible says to rejoice in all sufferings. Our sufferings couldn't begin to equal the sufferings of Jesus or Paul. How many crosses had we hung on? How many years had we spent in prison? What reasons for complaining did we really have?

The Bible says to rejoice in all sufferings. Ours couldn't begin to equal those of Jesus or Paul.

We prayed, studied our Bibles, and sought God's leading. Slowly, I got well. I'm still not sleeping perfectly, but I'm feeling 100% better. We're not through the wall yet. The church has not been able to pay our retirement for several months, and we may have to take a salary cut. As I type these words, we are considering downsizing our home and selling our car. That's okay. After all, Jesus had no material possessions. We are hoping to stay here to help the people who are still so dependent upon us. We are asking God to send more people to enable the church to grow numerically and spiritually. So, what has kept us going? Why didn't we leave?

Preparing To Hit The Wall

There are three major reasons: commitment, training, and nourishment. Without them, no one can make it through the church planting or marathoning walls. Both walls are inevitable. In order to make it, one has to be committed. In a marathon, for example, the commitment to run the race has to occur long before you get to the starting line. It is going to be tough. It is going to be painful. It is going to be tiring. There are no maybes about it! A person has to be prepared mentally and physically to "run through" those challenges. If you've not decided to do whatever it takes to finish the race, you won't. If you've left the door open even a crack for the possibility that you will quit, then when you get a cramp, develop a blister, start the uphill portion of the course, or hit the wall; you'll quit.

> **Without preparing for commitment, training, and nourishment, no one can make it through walls. If you've not decided to do what it takes to finish, you won't.**

The same is true for church planting. Tom and I were committed to planting a church in Albuquerque. We had helped plant Princeton Community Church in Princeton, New Jersey, six years before with Dr. Tom Jones, who was the lead planter. We enjoyed it and had hoped to someday plant one of our own. Then the right time came. We began considering a church plant and began praying earnestly for God's leading. We checked several plants and finally decided on Albuquerque. It seemed like that was where God wanted us. It was not an easy decision because we had never lived west of the Mississippi, and both of our families lived in the east. We made the commitment to raise funds, however, and the financial support came. We truly believed God wanted us here.

The commitment to God's work in Albuquerque is helping us now. It would not be easy to quit because we still have hopes and dreams for a church named CrossPointe to exist in 100 years. We want to see hundreds and even thousands of people make a commitment to Jesus Christ. That won't happen if we leave now.

As noted earlier, no one can get through the wall in a marathon without training. One must train for several months in order to run a marathon. One must be mentally and physically prepared. Usually a runner begins training about a year before the race date. The training starts by running every other day for shorter distances with one day being a longer day. Week by week, the mileage must be increased with the longer day increasing from five to seven to ten miles until the peak of twenty-one or twenty-two miles is reached. This must be at least a month before the race. Through this training process, one must learn to trust that he or she can actually finish the marathon. One must also learn to recognize areas of weakness. A runner's feet tend to blister in the same spots. So tape must be put on those spots before the race. Shoes must be broken in and comfortable. The underarm area tends to chafe, so the runner puts Vaseline there so the underarms won't get raw and bleed. The preparation becomes an extension of the race and what it takes to finish. There is no way to finish the race without getting ready for it.

The preparation becomes an extension of the race.

The same is true for church planting. We received a lot of training before starting CrossPointe in Albuquerque. We attended numerous seminars and have continued to attend them since our start. Our work at the church plant in Princeton helped us immensely. We knew what it was like to set up and tear down every Sunday. We knew how to store the equipment. We had been through it. The seminars also helped us because at least we knew walls existed, and that we would hit one eventually. From other people's experiences, we learned what to do and what not to do. We also were fully aware of our weaknesses, so we put bandages on those spots. We purified ourselves spiritually, mentally, and physically before starting CrossPointe, and we have continued to look at ourselves deeply each day in order to see where we need to improve.

During the darkest hours, Scriptures like these pulled us through the pain: "Let us not become weary in doing good, for at the proper time we will reap a harvest if we do not give up" (Gal 6:9).[3] "Consider it pure joy, my brothers when you face trials of many kinds, because you know that the testing of your faith develops perseverance" (Jas 1:2-7). Philippians 4:6-7[4] was a great help, as was Romans 8:28.[5] We decided to be thankful because good things can come out of bad circumstances, and there really were many reasons to be thankful. We also knew from Philippians that God's peace comes from praying and putting the situation into His hands, not from having prayers answered our way. So we prayed and received peace. Our training has helped us immensely, but we still need nourishment from friends and family to survive.

Without nourishment, one cannot make it through the wall in a church plant. The same is true for a marathon. Water and food are made available along the racecourse for all the runners. In order to keep from dehydrating, runners must take in fluids before they know they are needed. If a runner waits until his or her mouth is dry or a leg cramp develops, then it's too late. Dehydration has already begun. Fluids have to be taken from the first water stop through the end of the race. Foods, such as orange-wedges, are also made available and should be eaten as the race proceeds. A racer won't notice the need for nourishment in the first two-thirds of the race; but, when he or she hits the wall, the extra fuel makes finishing possible.

Without nourishment, one cannot make it through the wall in a church plant.

Before we hit the wall, and since then, we have desperately needed nourishment from our Christian friends and family. We have received it. During my illness, people from CrossPointe brought food and gifts. I was flooded with cards and phone calls from everywhere. It was just what we needed. I have never felt so loved. Tom and I have a gel group (small group) that meets weekly. These people constantly thank us for being here and helping them find their way back to God. They thank us through their prayers and in their worship of God.

Several recovering addicts attend CrossPointe. They are now helping each other by forming a gel group. The leaders are very excited and are constantly telling me stories about the progress of the participants. We have also helped numerous couples hold their marriages together. They also express their gratitude in many ways. This is nourishment—real, vital, spiritual nourishment. Without it, we could not go on.

Exciting things have also begun to happen. The general manager of a secular radio station saw our signs along the road and decided to give us a call. He wanted to air our worship celebrations every Sunday. Wow! Great News! Tom and I are also preparing a call-in radio show on marriage and parenting that will air every Saturday for 30 minutes on the same station. We are so excited! What a great way to help people and CrossPointe at the same time.

We are hoping to make it through this wall. We do recognize that God may decide He wants us elsewhere; but, until we know that for sure, we are going to keep pressing on. We pray the words we have written will help you when you "hit the wall." Remember to be committed before you start, train relentlessly, and rely on the nourishment from your church, family, and Christian friends to get you through. May God bless your journey.

Remember to be committed before you start, train relentlessly, and rely on nourishment from church, family, and friends.

---

[1] Multiple Sclerosis is a degenerative disease of the central nervous system.

[2] Deepti Hajela, "Last New York City Marathon Runner Crosses Finish Line—on Monday," *The Sacramento Bee*, 3 November 2003, Associated Press.

[3] All Scripture quotations are taken from the *New International Version* unless otherwise noted.

[4] "Do not worry about anything, but in everything by prayer and supplication with thanksgiving let your requests be made known to God. And the peace of God, which surpasses all understanding, will guard your hearts and your minds in Christ Jesus" (NRSV).

[5] "We know that all things work together for good for those who love God, who are called according to his purpose" (NRSV).

A 1985 graduate of Cincinnati Bible College, **Charlie McMahan** is the Senior Pastor at SouthBrook Christian Church in Centerville, Ohio. The SouthBrook Church has nearly 3,000 attendees on a given weekend. He and his wife, Sherry, and children, Jordan and Austin, have been in ministry at SouthBrook from 1992 to the present.

Phase 2 of Church Planting

My wife Sherry, our children, Jordan and Austin, and I were excited when we left Kentucky in 1992 and moved to Centerville, Ohio. We had prayed for seven years for the right opportunity to open a new church. We felt we were wired for new church work, and it looked like God had finally answered our prayers by sending us to a new church plant which had been in operation for about six years.

We came with the strong notion that God had led our family to Centerville for reasons only He knew. Tom and Debbie Jones had planted Centerville Christian Church in 1986 and built a community with an impressive foundation of excellence and a "whatever-it-takes" attitude.

As I recall, our first Sunday was a cold and snowy January day. I felt a sense of optimism. Even with Tom and Debbie gone, the church was primed for growth. Something special was about to happen here. This place had the right DNA. These people were willing to "lay it on the line."

But on that first Sunday only 72 people attended. The church had seen much higher attendance, but the relocation of the Jones family to Princeton, New Jersey, had left some skeptical. After all, this was a young church with no building, populated mostly with young adults. Add to that a wet-behind-the-ears preacher who had been in Kentucky for seven years, and it was safe to say people were a little uncertain. These Dayton suburbanites were wondering if I had a decent pair of shoes before I came north.

We were worshiping at the Seventh Day Adventist facility in Centerville. The church building seated about five hundred people, and with only 72 in attendance the pews were sparsely populated. We had a comfortable attendance. By that I mean everyone had room to lie down in their pew if they felt so inclined!

I remember thinking, "Uh-oh, we've got to pray as if everything depends on God and work as if everything depends on us." And that's what we did. That little group of 72 was the right 72. They were get-it-done people willing to take a risk.

In 1992 most of them signed a loan agreement, putting their homes at risk so we could build our first building. In the fall of 1993 we started a Sunday service designed to reach out to people who didn't like church, those in the community who were finished with organized religion. As Rick Warren[1] has said, our appeal was, if you've had it with organized religion, come and join us, because we're disorganized religion. We had prepared for a year and a half for that moment, expecting big results for that new service in our new building.

Fifty-seven people showed up.

Once again, we faced an uphill battle, clearly needing to spend more time than ever on our knees and working even harder than we already had been. The service that started with 57 people in 1993 has grown to more than 2,800 people in 2003 worshiping over six services in a tiny twenty-thousand-square-foot facility.

Why has our approach worked? We certainly haven't arrived, but in evaluating SouthBrook's early days I ask myself that question often.

I was told countless times that we wouldn't succeed.

I was told countless times that we wouldn't succeed. I heard, "This church won't work," "Your building is too small," "Your budget is too limited," "You can't grow a church targeted at people who don't like church because they won't give to it," "You're too different, too sick, too weird!" But at this point, we've been through relocation, three building programs, a name change, the loss of key staff, severely limited space and parking, and yet the church continues to prevail. It's crazy! Why is it happening?!

Jesus said in Mark 4:26-27, "This is what the kingdom of God is like. A man scatters seed on the ground. Night and day, whether he sleeps or gets up, the seed sprouts and grows, *though he does not know how.*"[2]

Lyle Schaller said that once a church is past 35-40 people, "the natural, normal, and predictable institutional pressures begin to work in the direction of reducing that number. The larger the size of the congregation, the more fragile it is in institutional terms."[3] Social dynamics are in constant opposition, working against its growth. No wonder it feels like a growing, prevailing church is an act of God. It is.

No wonder it feels like a growing, prevailing church is an act of God.

One reason for the church's growth is that when God is up to something, you can't stop Him. The Joneses and Sherry and I have always had strong convictions that God's leading hand and transcendent purpose are on our church, now called SouthBrook Christian Church.

To paraphrase 1 Corinthians 3:6, the Joneses planted, we watered, but God made it grow. That said, the first task I faced was a critical assessment of the church and its culture. Max DePree wrote that the first task of the leader is to define reality.[4] Based on an honest assessment of who we were and where we were, we made four commitments that would define our church.

The Joneses planted, we watered, but God made it grow.

We didn't write down these strategic commitments at the time, but looking back, these points aligned us with *both* the needs of the south Dayton community and the blessing of God.

We will teach for life change.

In phase two of church planting, the most critical decision concerns what is taught. On the heels of that is the decision about how to teach.

Teaching the Bible practically, passionately, and personally spawns life in people. This is foundational. Bill Hybels[5] compared it to pitching in baseball. There's an old adage that pitching is 90% of baseball. Nearly all championship baseball teams have good pitching. Skillfully teaching the Bible is core to growing the church. It is what catalyzes change in individual's lives and in the church as a whole.

Teaching the Bible practically, passionately, and personally spawns life in people.

I decided early on to leverage my teaching strength to its maximum level. I devoted large chunks of time to reading and research. I listened to tapes. I memorized Scripture. I made teaching Scripture the highest priority.

The decision about what to teach and how to teach it creates simplicity.

The decision about what to teach and how to teach it creates simplicity. Like a football team that knows its identity is to establish the run first, this decision allows the church to form its identity around something that was core to what Jesus was about—clear, relevant, creative, and transformational teaching.

This decision also allows for the work of the Holy Spirit. Today we have a number of gifted teachers at our church, and it's amazing how many times they've been asked, "Do you have our house bugged? How do you know what is going on in our home?" We don't have houses bugged, but when the Bible is taught in relevance to our culture, the Holy Spirit goes to work. He is aware of needs of which we couldn't possibly be aware. It's almost eerie, especially to people in the church who don't even believe the Bible yet and can't explain how we can speak directly to them!

We will establish mission integrity.

Mission integrity is about everything in the church flowing in one direction—toward the mission. Around here, we say that February 1993 was the month that saved SouthBrook. After going through a year of intense evaluation, we decided there were enough "normal" churches in Dayton. In the upstairs office of a building we were renting, we decided there needed to be a church that was *radically* committed to reaching people who didn't like church.

We believe our mission is to help people who don't like church learn to live and love with Jesus Christ forever. That's our brand. That's our main thing, and the mantra here is that the main thing is to keep the main thing the main thing.

Mission integrity creates simplicity in decision-making. Every decision we make is filtered through our mission statement: "To bring unchurched people into a saving and serving relationship with Jesus Christ." Decision-making was easier when the church was smaller and less complex. It's not as easy today and won't be as easy in the future. That's what makes mission integrity vitally important.

Southbrook Christian Church—Centerville, Ohio
Our Mission
To bring unchurched people into a saving
and serving relationship with Jesus Christ.
Our Vision
To be a front porch for greater Dayton,
a biblical epicenter of creativity, community,
compassion, and life change through Jesus Christ.

Mission integrity also creates resourcefulness. This is critical in the early days when you don't have much money! It helped us decide where to risk resources and where not to. If an opportunity didn't serve the mission, we generally didn't go there. It is a waste of resources, which is not only poor stewardship, but also nonnegotiable when you're as money-poor as we were and still are.

Finally, mission integrity creates impassioned volunteerism. When we live the mission, say the mission, and share the mission, it creates a snowball of passion. People want to give themselves to a purpose that transcends this life. They become passionate about doing their part to reach the people they care about. I believe our high rate of volunteer participation is largely a result of our mission integrity.

Make sure your mission flows out of your heart, and then speak and lead from that heart. What comes from the heart goes to the heart. People are looking for people with heart and passion. A clear, relevant, biblical mission statement that flows from who you really are creates the heart of passionate volunteerism.

However, there's a downside to our mission, and that is a nonantiseptic atmosphere. It's not "clean" at our church. We're full of spiritually immature, unhealthy people. That's good, but it creates challenges.

People start their journey with Christ pretty far to the left on the spiritual maturity continuum. If you come to our church, you'll get to do something Jesus did: hang out with "sinners, thieves, and whores."

Mike Stephens, a member of our church, was talking to his neighbor and the conversation drifted to where they went to church. The neighbor told him where she attended and then he told her he was a part of the SouthBrook community. There was an awkward pause and then she said, "Oh . . . that's the church that will let anybody come, isn't it?" That's our mission alive and well.

"Oh . . . that's the church that will let anybody come, isn't it?"

Our mission means that many people who aren't Christ-followers are not only allowed to serve, but are encouraged to serve. Why? Most people get served and loved into the kingdom in the context of community service.

We will be leader-driven.

Like many flourishing churches, our church is not a classic democratic system. We don't vote on anything. (People vote with their backsides and their bucks, true, but they don't get to vote on leadership issues.) Our church is leader-led, beginning with our Leadership Team.

This came out of a radical change that began in 1993, very early in the second phase of our growth. At that time the church experienced some tumult due to the transition away from eldership. Beginning in 1992 we took a year to evaluate our structure of leadership and decided that the Scriptures are more concerned about the *function* of plural leadership rather than the exact *form*. So we disbanded our eldership and eventually formed a Leadership Team, made up of a few of the previous elders and some key leaders from the church, both men and women. The change caused intense friction for a while. We lost some good people through this process, including some who previously were elders. But it was the right thing to do. While it was painful, it was also highly instrumental in our development as a church. The difference between calling our overseeing body a Leadership Team versus an Eldership was monumental. It may be semantics, but where we live the term "elder" implies control.

329

Since Leadership Team is equal to Eldership (from the New Testament term *presbuteroi* or elders) in definition and function, we moved in this direction with clear resolve. In our context the change was more effective because it spoke less of control and more of vision, direction, and macromanagement (versus micromanagement).

When the Leadership Team was unleashed in 1994, so was our church. Our church today in one sense is out of control because of this change. That was the point. Our Leadership Team oversees the big picture of vision and mission. From there, authority is decentralized to ministry leaders. This was a huge contributing factor to the growth of SouthBrook.

Would we be where we are with an eldership? Maybe. Maybe not. Because we were unconventional in structuring our overseeing body of leadership, we did not appeal to controlling types. We still don't. We've had more than a few confrontations where we've peacefully stood firm about our leadership structure.

How are we structured? We illustrate the leadership structure at SouthBrook using the mustard tree Jesus described in Matthew 13.[6] Our Leadership Team is the root system. Our pastors and administrators (most of whom are not paid staff) are the trunk. Our staff and ministry leaders are the branches. The Leadership Team resources the church, especially the staff. While the Leadership Team holds the staff accountable in a traditional way, the main emphasis is on being a resource center for the staff just as a root system is for the branches of a tree. It's an upside-down pyramid, in effect.

This organic concept of a leadership-driven structure was communicated well in a quirky book by Gordon MacKenzie entitled *Orbiting the Giant Hairball*. MacKenzie evaluated the leadership structure of the company he worked for, Hallmark Cards, and determined that pyramids are "tombs for dead people"![7] In a living, growing organism like a church we want leadership to be a source of service, life, and freedom. The decision early on to adopt this structure of leadership for our church was not easy. But it unleashed and empowered our church.

When the tree of the church is rooted in leadership that maintains and resources the mission, the tree grows, and, as Jesus said, "the birds of the air come and perch on its branches and find refuge."

We will be a church with intolerance for "religionism."

Since the American church has been plagued with a "form of godliness that denies its power," we determined early on to be a place that was intolerant of religion for religion's sake. We wanted our church to be a place based on *relationship, not rules*.

For years we've asked these questions over and over: What impresses God about a church? What is God about? Is God just the ultimate cold, religious ruler in the sky, or does He truly desire mercy more than sacrifice? In the Gospels, Jesus shows us over and over that God has no tolerance for religionism.

What impresses God about a church?

As a result, we believe religious activities like church attendance, tithing, and Bible reading are valuable when connected to relationships. But we believe they have little value when reduced to religious rituals. That belief doesn't make us unique. A lot of churches believe this. At SouthBrook, however, it's largely a realized value, not just an idealized one.

The fact that we don't take ourselves too seriously fleshes this out. Our mission is serious. There's a real heaven and a real hell and real people are going to one or the other forever. But I see more churches getting weighed down by religious, oppressive attitudes in which they take themselves too seriously. The result is an atmosphere of death, not life.

A few years ago I was riding back to Dayton with my then eight-year-old daughter, Jordan. She was commenting on a number of things from the life of an eight-year-old, and out of the blue she said the one thing someone in my position wants to hear. She said, "Daddy, I love being a preacher's daughter. Tomorrow is Sunday. I love Sundays."

"So do I," I said.

That was a compliment to our church. It's an understatement to say SouthBrook is not a perfect place, but my daughter was making a positive cultural statement about SouthBrook.

Around here we talk about the "church pew smell." The church pew smell is the oppressive, heavy dynamic that stifles a church's life and snuffs out its light. By God's grace we got rid of the church pew smell.

How? At first we intentionally went out of our way to appeal to the nonlegalistic mind and intentionally tried not to appeal to the legalist.

Additionally, a large part of the SouthBrook diet was intense servings of the principles of spiritual freedom in the book of Galatians. The teachings from Galatians have been critical to our church culture. They gave us motivation to be intolerant of anything legalistic and set us free.

The teachings from Galatians have been critical to our church culture.

We have people who wonder from time to time, if they come to a church like SouthBrook, does it count? Church isn't supposed to be this fun! And they don't want to get to heaven and hear God say, "Nice try, but you bought the off-brand with the designer tag, pal. Wish someone would have told you. Sorry."

The result? SouthBrook is an un-church. We have a church full of very nonchurchy people which creates a positive atmosphere of not only genuine repentance and surrender that flows out of relationship, but also a spirit of levity that makes us known for our laughter, love, and life.

I love Romans 8:15. It defines what I hope the spirit of our people will be. It says, *"For you did not receive a spirit that makes you a slave again to fear, but you received the Spirit of sonship. And by him we cry, 'Abba, Father.'"*

For me, that verse defines what the culture of a church should be like. When I read that, I think of the time when Tom Jones, a few friends, and I played golf in Princeton, New Jersey, at the TPC (Tournament Players Club) at Jasna Polana. The TPC at Jasna Polana was built on the Johnson estate of Johnson & Johnson Company fame (think baby powder). The family mansion was converted into a $50 million clubhouse. It was impressive, to say the least.

With that impressive mansion in mind, let's say that you were a homeless orphan. Lost. No home. And then the owner of this Jasna Polana estate adopts you. The owner of the estate becomes your new father. He says, "This is your home. It is safe. I want you to stay on the estate. Don't play in the street. The estate I've provided is big enough for you. Don't eat from the poisonous plants that could harm you. You'll get hurt. I don't want you to get hurt because I love you. And I know what's best for you, *so if you love me,* keep my commandments. But enjoy the yard. Live in it. You don't have to walk around in fear, wondering if there's a rule about playing on the swing set."

Does the Father want us to enjoy the field? Can we play in the trees? Does He want us to play the golf course? "Yes!" the father says. (He says this because he knows the Wise Father invented golf!)

Then the owner of the estate asks a critical question, "Now, you don't deserve all of this. Do you understand that?"

You would say, "Yes. Yes I do understand that I deserve none of this."

Then He says, "You know I provided this for you because I love you, and you were an orphan in the streets?"

"Yes. I don't doubt your love now, Father."

"So you know you didn't earn my love or earn what you've been given?"

"Yes."

"You know you're free to enjoy it?"

"Yes."

"One thing I ask. Enjoy it and serve your brothers and sisters with it, so that other orphans will want to come to my house, too."

When we know the Father's love, we will do that. We are free to choose Him and to love Him, and we don't have to cower in service before a Father who is abusive or unfair. Instead, we respect and honor a loving Father who is strong, and we choose to obey and honor Him.

He said, "If you love me, keep my commandments." We will love Him by doing the best we can to do His will, not our own. We don't have to be religious around Him because He just wants us to love Him. It's about a relationship. And so we come under His rule, and we live in His estate, His Kingdom.

And that's the kind of church I dream SouthBrook can be.

---

[1] Rick Warren is the founding pastor of Saddleback Valley Community Church in Orange County, California. An expert in church planting strategies, Warren's lead-

ership has helped Saddleback's congregation grow to over 10,000 strong in attendance, and has played a pivotal role in the church's planting of over twenty-five other churches. Some of his writings include *The Purpose Driven Church*, *The Purpose Driven Life*, *Dynamic Bible Study Methods*, *Answer's to Life's Difficult Questions*, and *The Power to Change Your Life*.

[2] All Scripture quotations are taken from the *New International Version*.

[3] Lyle E Schaller, *The Very Large Church* (Nashville: Abingdon Press, 2000) 28.

[4] Max DePree, *Leadership Is an Art* (New York: Dell Publishing, 1989) 11.

[5] Bill Hybels is the senior pastor of Willow Creek Community Church in Southern Barrington, Illinois.

[6] "The kingdom of heaven is like a mustard seed, which a man took and planted in his field. Though it is the smallest of all your seeds, yet when it grows, it is the largest of garden plants and becomes a tree, so that the birds of the air come and perch in its branches" (Matt 13:31-32).

[7] Gordon MacKenzie, *Orbiting the Giant Hairball* (Shawnee Mission, KS: Opus-Pocus, 1996) 180.

Conclusion

I pray that the preceding chapters have accomplished three things in your mind in regard to church planting.

1. **The Importance of Church Planting.**

   If we are to be successful, as a strategically sent church fulfilling the Lord's mission, then the multiplication of God-honoring local churches will have to receive greater priority. Our mission is too important not to take our marching orders seriously. I challenge you, your church, and your denomination to be creative in picking up the pace in church planting. Individuals, local churches, associations of churches and all denominations must get serious about restoring the biblical principle of New Testament church planting. It can begin with you!

2. **The Recruitment, Assessment, Equipping, Deployment, and Care of Church Planters and Church Planting Teams.**

   Starting new churches is too important to the Kingdom not to be done wholeheartedly. Take a close look at the chapters in this book and follow their lead in recruitment, assessment, equipping, deployment, and care. You might not agree with everything written in this book, and that's okay. If we have encouraged you in any way to think critically and prayerfully about the church planting task, then we have accomplished at least part of our goal. Whatever you do, take time to ask the right questions, and pray that the Lord will lead you to the right answers. Don't take shortcuts. There are plenty of listed resources in this book to help get the job done effectively.

3. Church Planting Is All about Reaching Real People.

I'd like to conclude this book by introducing you to a few of my friends.

Marge is a grandmother of eight. When I first met her, she was a widow, lived by herself and was a severe diabetic. When Marge first came to our new church, she was rather suspicious of churches because a church she previously attended failed to meet her needs. Marge was old and ready to die. She had given up on life. When our new church introduced Christ to Marge and welcomed her with open arms, her life began to change. She no longer seemed ready to die, but alive. I baptized Marge on her 75th birthday. She became a dynamic participant in our community of faith. She loved her Lord and her church. When Marge heard I was leaving to start a new church in another part of the country, she looked at me with tears in her eyes and said, "You made my life." Where would Marge have been without church planting?

Dave was sitting at home one night when he received a telephone call. The caller, Martha, was part of our church's marketing efforts. (In the 1980s telemarketing was a successful new church strategy. I suggest you not use this strategy today.) Martha had actually dialed the wrong number, but took advantage of the situation and talked to Dave about our new church. Dave had been praying that God would give direction to his life, and help him find a church that would meet his needs. God answered Dave's prayer when Martha called. He came to our new church a week later and was soon baptized into Christ. Later, Dave left his secular job to enter seminary. He became the assistant editor for a religious periodical and now serves faithfully in local church ministry. Where would Dave be without church planting?

Laura was the first person we met after moving to a new town. The day we arrived at our new home, Laura knocked on the door, introduced herself, and gave us a bag of soft drinks welcoming us to the neighborhood. We didn't hear from Laura again until she stopped me one day in the yard and explained to me that she was a recovering alcoholic. It was another couple of months before I heard from Laura again. She had received five mailings about our new church. She saw my wife Debbie and yelled across the yard, "I'll see you Sunday." Within six weeks Laura became a Christian. Where would Laura be without church planting?

Jane was a Christian and began attending our new church shortly after it began. However, her husband, **Tom**, was not interested in church. Tom was a recovering alcoholic and cocaine addict. He believed in a Higher Power, but didn't have much use for church. Knowing he was a sports enthusiast, I invited him to play softball with our church team, which played in a rowdy, competitive nonchurch league. Through softball, golf, and our growing friendship, Tom accepted Christ and was baptized. Turn the clock forward fifteen years and you will find that Tom, Jane, and their two children are integral parts of the church. Tom is a leader in the church now. In fact, my wife Debbie and I witnessed his ordination into Christian ministry. His daughter attends a Christian college, and she too plans to enter vocational ministry. Where would Tom and his family be without church planting?

John was a sales executive for medical equipment. He had little use for God or church. His life was unfolding just fine. That is, until he was diagnosed with a brain tumor. God got his attention. John showed up at our new church one Sunday and found Jesus. Eighteen months later I conducted John's funeral, a celebration of John's graduation into a Christ-filled eternity. Where would John be without church planting?

Along with every author in this book, I could go on and on about real people who have been influenced in the name of Jesus by new churches. These individuals and families who did not know Jesus were saved from hunger, failed marriages, addiction, emotional scarring, shameful pasts, homelessness, abuse of all kinds, unemployment, and all the pain that goes with a sin-filled world. They were saved by Christ working in and through His church! Only He is the answer to all of these problems. All we need to do as a sent church is to multiply our communities of faith so that more people will come to know Jesus and His people! Do you agree? If so, what will you do about it?

Church Planting Bibliography

Compiled by

Dr. Thomas F. Jones, Jr.

Assoc. Professor of Christian Ministries and
Director of Supervised Ministerial Experience
Emmanuel School of Religion

Director of Church Planting Recruitment and Assessment,
Southeast Stadia

jonest@esr.edu
www.stadia.cc

John E. Wasem

Founding Minister of Suncrest Christian Church
in St. John, Indiana

Director of New Church Leadership Certificate Program
Lincoln Christian College and Seminary

www.churchleader.net

BOOKS THAT DEAL DIRECTLY WITH CHURCH PLANTING

Amberson, Talmadge R., ed. *The Birth of Churches: The Biblical Basis of Church Planting*. Nashville: Broadman Press, 1979.

Amstutz, Harold E. *Church Planter's Manual*. Cherry Hill, NJ: Association of Baptists for World Evangelism, 1985.

Appleby, Jerry L. *Missions Have Come Home to America*. Kansas City, MO: Beacon Hill, 1986.

Bailey, Keith M., ed. *The Church Planter's Manual*. Harrisburg, PA: Christian Publications, 1981.

Becker, Paul. *Dynamic Church Planting: A Complete Handbook*. Vista, CA: Multiplication Ministries, 1992.

Bright, Bill, and Mark McCloskey. *Tell It Often, Tell It Well*. San Bernadino, CA: Here's Life Publishers, 1985.

Brock, Charles. *Indigenous Church Planting: A Practical Journey*. Neosho, MO: Church Growth International, 1994.

_____. *The Principles and Practice of Indigenous Church Planting*. Nashville: Broadman Press, 1981.

Chaney, Charles L. *Church Planting at the End of the Twentieth Century*. Wheaton, IL: Tyndale, 1982.

Cole, Neil, and Paul Kaak. *The Organic Church Planter's Greenhouse Intensive Training Event Participants Notes*. Signal Hill, CA: Church Multiplication Associates, 2003.

Conn, Harvie M., ed. *Planting and Growing Urban Churches: From Dream to Reality*. Grand Rapids: Baker, 1997.

Cox, Michael, and Joe Ratliff. *Church Planting in the African-American Community*. Valley Forge, PA: Judson Press, 2001.

Dorr, Luther M. *The Bivocational Pastor*. Nashville: Broadman Press, 1988.

Durkin, Jim, Dick Benjamin, Larry Tomczak, and Terry Edwards. *The Church Planter's Handbook*. South Lake Tahoe, CA: Christian Equippers, 1988.

Estep, Michael R., ed. *Church Planting Strategy: The Great Commission*. Kansas City, MO: Nazarene Publishing House, 1988.

Faircloth, Samuel D. *Church Planting for Reproduction*. Grand Rapids: Baker, 1991.

Falwell, Jerry, and Elmer Towns. *Stepping Out on Faith*. Wheaton, IL: Tyndale, 1984.

Feeney, James H. *The Team Method of Church Planting*. Anchorage, AK: Abbott Loop Christian Center, 1988.

Francis, Hozell C. *Church Planting in the African American Context*. Grand Rapids: Zondervan, 1999.

Garrison, David. *Church Planting Movements*. Richmond, VA: Southern Baptist Convention, 1999.

Godwin, David E. *Church Planting Methods*. DeSoto, TX: Lifeshare Communications, 1984.

Hesselgrave, David J. *Planting Church Cross-Culturally: North America and Beyond*. 2nd ed. Grand Rapids: Baker, 2000.

Hiebert, Paul G., and Eloise Hiebert Meneses. *Incarnational Ministry: Planting Churches in Band, Tribal, Peasant, and Urban Societies*. Grand Rapids: Baker, 1996.

Hill, Monica, ed. *How to Plant Churches*. London: MARC Europe, 1984.

Hurn, Raymond W. *The Rising Tide: New Churches for the New Millennium*. Kansas City, MO: Beacon Hill Press, 1997.

James, Joseph F. *On the Front Lines: A Guide to Church Planting*. Winona Lake, IN: Free Methodist Church, 1987.

Jones, Ezra Earl. *Strategies for New Churches*. San Francisco, CA: Harper and Row, 1976.

King, Fred G. *The Church Planter's Training Manual*. Harrisburg, PA: Christian Publications, 1993.

Lehman, James H. *Thank God for New Churches*. Elgin, IL: Brethren Press, 1984.

Lewis, Larry L. *The Church Planter's Handbook*. Nashville: Broadman and Holman, 1992.

Malphurs, Aubrey. *Planting Growing Churches for the 21st Century*. Grand Rapids: Baker, 1992.

Mannoia, Kevin. *Church Planting: The Next Generation*. 2nd ed. Indianapolis: Light and Life Communications, 1994.

McGavran, Donald. "Reaching People through New Congregations." *Church Growth Strategies That Work*. Ed. by Donald McGavran and George F. Hunter, III. Nashville: Abingdon Press, 1980.

McNair, Donald J. *The Birth, Care and Feeding of a Local Church*. Wheaton, IL: Canon Press, 1973.

McNamara, Roger N., ed. *A Practical Guide to Church Planting*. Cleveland: Baptist Mid-Missions, 1985.

Moore, Ralph. *Starting a New Church: The Church Planter's Guide to Success*. Ventura, CA: Regal Books, 2002.

Moorhous, Carl W. *Growing New Churches: Step-by-Step Procedures in New Church Planting*. Cleveland: Baptist Mid-Missions, 1985.

Murray, Stuart. *Church Planting: Laying Foundations*. Scottdale, PA: Herald Press, 2001.

Nevius, John L. *The Planting and Development of Missionary Churches*. East Jaffrey, NH: Monadnock Press, 2003.

Nicholson, Steve, and Jeff Bailey. "What Does the Church Planter Look Like?" *The Cutting Edge*. Vol. 2, No. 1. Winter 1998.

Nikkel, James. *Antioch Blueprints*. Winnipeg, Manitoba: Canadian Conference of Mennonite Brethren Churches, 1987.

Patterson, George, and Richard Scoggins. *Church Multiplication Guide: Helping Churches to Reproduce Locally and Abroad*. Pasadena, CA: William Carey Library, 1993.

Redford, F.J. *Planting New Churches*. Nashville: Broadman Press, 1979.

Ridley, Charles R. *How to Select Church Planters*. Pasadena, CA: Fuller Evangelistic Association, 1988.

Robinson, Martin, and Stuart Christine. *Planting Tomorrow's Church Today*. Tunbridge Wells, UK: Monarch, 1992.

Romo, Oscar I. *American Mosaic Church Planting in Ethnic America*. Nashville: Broadman and Holman, 1993.

Rusaw, Rick, and Paul Williams. *Leadership and the Church Planter: A Master's Thesis*. Cincinnati: Cincinnati Bible College and Seminary, 1990.

Ruth-Heffelbower, Duane. *A Technical Manual for Church Planting*. Elkhart, IN: Mennonite Board of Missions.

Sanchez, Daniel R., Ebbie C. Smith, and Curtis E. Watke. *Reproducing Congregations: A Guidebook for Contextual New Church Development*. Churchstarting.net, 2001.

Schaller, Lyle. *44 Questions for Church Planters*. Nashville: Abingdon Press, 1991.

Sheeks, Bill F. *How to Plant a Church of God*. Cleveland, TN: Pathway Press, 1987.

Shenk, David W., and Ervin R. Stutzman. *Creating Communities of the Kingdom: New Testament Models of Church Planting*. Scottdale, PA: Herald Press, 1988.

Sjogren, Steve, and Rob Lewin. *Community of Kindness: A Refreshing New Approach to Planting and Growing a Church*. Ventura, CA: Regal Books, 2003.

Starr, Timothy. *Church Planting: Always in Season*. Fellowship of Evangelical Baptist Churches of Canada, 1978.

Steffan, Tom. *Passing the Baton: Church Planting That Empowers*. 2nd ed. Center for Organizational and Ministry Development, 2000.

Stetzer, Ed. *Planting New Churches in a Postmodern Age*. Nashville: Broadman & Holman, 2003.

Timmis, Stephen, ed. *Multiplying Churches: Reaching Communities through Church Planting*. Christian Focus, 2003.

Tinsley, William C. *Upon This Rock: Dimensions of Church Planting*. Atlanta, GA: Baptist Home Mission Board, 1985.

Towns, Elmer L. *Getting a Church Started*. Privately published in 1982 by the author, but available from the Fuller Bookstore.

Towns, Elmer L., and Douglas Porter. *Churches That Multiply: A Bible Study on Church Planting*. Kansas City, MO: Beacon Hill Press, 2003.

Wagner, Peter. *Church Planting for a Greater Harvest*. Ventura, CA: Regal Books, 1990.

Wilson, J. Christy Jr. *Today's Tentmakers*. Wheaton, IL: Tyndale House, 1979.

BOOKS THAT CONTAIN MATERIAL HELPFUL TO CHURCH PLANTING

Adizes, Ichak. *Corporate Lifecycles*. Paramus: Prentice Hall, 1988.

Aldrich, Joseph. *Gentle Persuasion*. Portland, OR: Multnomah Press, 1988.

_____. *Lifestyle Evangelism*. Portland, OR: Multnomah Press, 1981.

Anderson, Keith R., and Randy D. Reese. *Spiritual Mentoring: A Guide for Seeking and Giving Direction*. Downers Grove, IL: InterVarsity, 1999.

Anderson, Leith. *Dying for Change*. Minneapolis: Bethany House, 1990.

Anderson, Lynn. *They Smell Like Sheep: Spiritual Leadership for the 21st Century*. West Monroe, LA: Howard Publishing, 1984.

Arn, Charles, and Win Arn. *The Master's Plan for Making Disciples*. Pasadena, CA: Church Growth Press, 1982.

Arn, Win. *The Church Growth Ratio Book: How to Have a Revitalized, Healthy, Growing, Loving Church*. Pasadena, CA: Church Growth, 1987.

Arn, Winfield, and Donald McGavran. *Ten Steps for Church Growth*. San Francisco, CA: Harper and Row, 1977.

Austin, Nancy, and Tom Peters. *A Passion for Excellence.* New York: Warner Books, 1986.

Bakke, Ray. *A Theology as Big as the City.* Downers Grove, IL: InterVarsity, 1997.

Barker, Steve, Judy Johnson, Jimmy Long, and Rob Malone. *Good Things Come in Small Groups.* Downers Grove, IL: InterVarsity, 1985.

Barker, Steve, Judy Johnson, Jimmy Long, Rob Malone, and Ron Nicholas. *Small Group Leaders' Handbook.* Downers Grove, IL: InterVarsity, 1982.

Barna, George. *Evangelism That Works: How to Reach Changing Generations with the Unchanging Gospel.* Ventura, CA: Regal Books, 1995.

_____. *The Frog in the Kettle.* Ventura, CA: Regal Books, 1990.

_____. *The Habits of Highly Effective Churches: Being Strategic in Your God-Given Ministry.* Ventura, CA: Regal Books, 1999.

_____. *How to Increase Giving in Your Church.* Ventura, CA: Regal Books, 1997.

_____. *The Invisible Generation: Baby Busters.* Glendale, CA: Barna Research Group, 1992.

_____. *Leaders on Leadership: Wisdom, Advice and Encouragement on the Art of Leading God's People.* Ventura, CA: Regal Books, 1997.

_____. *Marketing the Church.* Colorado Springs: NavPress, 1988.

_____. *The Second Coming of the Church.* Nashville: Word, 1998.

_____. *A Step-by-Step Guide to Church Marketing: Breaking Ground for the Harvest.* Ventura, CA: Regal Books, 1992.

_____. *User Friendly Churches.* Ventura, CA: Regal Books, 1991.

_____. *What Americans Believe.* Ventura, CA: Regal Books, 1991.

Bast, Robert. *Attracting New Members.* New York: Reformed Church in America, 1988.

Bellah, Mike. *Baby Boom Believers.* Wheaton, IL: Tyndale House, 1988.

Bennis, Warren. *Why Leaders Can't Lead: The Unconscious Conspiracy Continues.* San Francisco: Jossey-Bass, 1989.

Biehl, Bobb. *Increasing Your Leadership Confidence.* Sisters, OR: Questar Publishers, 1989.

_____. *Master-Planning: The Complete Guide for Building a Strategic Plan for Your Business, Church, or Organization.* Nashville: Broadman and Holman, 1997.

Bilezikian, Gilbert. *Community 101: Reclaiming the Church as Community of Oneness.* Grand Rapids: Zondervan, 1997.

Blanchard, Ken. *Mission Possible.* New York: McGraw-Hill, 1997.

Blanchard, Ken, Bill Hybels, and Phil Hodges. *Leadership by the Book: Tools to Transform Your Workplace*. New York: Waterbrook Press, 1999.

Bosch, David J. *Believing in the Future*. Harrisburg, PA: Trinity Press, 1995.

_____. *Transforming Mission: Paradigm Shifts in Theology of Mission*. Maryknoll, NY: Orbis Books, 1991.

Bright, Bill, and Mark McCloskey. *Tell It Often, Tell It Well*. San Bernadino, CA: Here's Life, 1985.

Brown, Daniel A. *The Other Side of Pastoral Ministry: Using Process Leadership to Transform Your Church*. Grand Rapids: Zondervan, 1996.

Cahill, Mark. *One Thing You Can't Do In Heaven*. Stone Mountain, GA: Mark Cahill Self-Published, 2003.

Callahan, Kennon. *Effective Church Finances: Fund-raising and Budgeting for Church Leaders*. San Francisco: Harper and Row, 1997.

_____. *Effective Church Leadership*. San Francisco: Harper and Row, 1983.

_____. *Giving and Stewardship in an Effective Church: A Guide for Every Member*. San Francisco, CA: Harper and Row, 1992.

_____. *Twelve Keys to an Effective Church*. San Francisco: Harper and Row, 1983.

Campbell, Bruce. *Listening to Your Donors: The Nonprofit's Practical Guide to Designing and Conducting Surveys*. San Francisco: Jossey-Bass, 2000.

Cannistraci, David. *The Gift of Apostle*. Ventura, CA: Regal Books, 1996.

Carson, D.A. *The Gagging of God*. Grand Rapids: Zondervan, 1996.

Chandler, Russell. *Racing towards 2001: The Forces Shaping America's Religious Future*. Grand Rapids: Zondervan, 1992.

Chapman, Gary. *The Five Love Languages*. Chicago: Northfield Publishing, 1995.

Chappell, Bryan. *Christ-Centered Preaching*. Grand Rapids: Baker Books, 1996.

Cimino, Richard, and Don Lattin. *Shopping for Faith: American Religion in the New Millennium*. San Francisco: Jossey-Bass, 1998.

Cladis, George. *Leading the Team-Based Church: How Pastors and Church Staffs Can Grow Together into a Powerful Fellowship of Leaders*. San Francisco: Jossey-Bass, 1999.

Clegg, Tom, and Warren Bird. *Lost in America: How You and Your Church Can Impact the World Next Door*. Loveland, CO: Group, 2001.

Clinton, J. Robert. *Connecting: The Mentoring Relationship You Need to Succeed in Life*. Colorado Springs: NavPress, 1992.

_____. *The Making of a Leader*. Colorado Springs: NavPress, 1988.

Coleman, Lyman. *Small Group Training Manual*. Littleton, CO: Serendipity Publishers, 1991.

Coleman, Robert. *The Master Plan of Evangelism*. Old Tappan, NJ: Fleming H. Revell, 1963.

Collins, James, and Jerry Porras. *Built to Last*. New York: Harper Business, 1994.

Collins, Jim. *Good to Great: Why Some Companies Make the Leap and Others Don't*. New York: Harper Collins, 2001.

Costas, Orlando. *Christ outside the Gate*. Maryknoll, NY: Orbis Books, 1982.

Cottrell, David. *Monday Morning Leadership*. Dallas: Cornerstone Leadership Institute, 2002.

Covey, Stephen R. *The Seven Habits of Highly Effective People*. New York: First Fireside Edition. Simon and Schuster, 1990.

Crispell, Diane. *The Insider's Guide to Demographic Know-How: Everything You Need to Find, Analyze, and Use Information about Your Customers*. 3rd ed. Ithaca, NY: American Demographic Books, 1993.

Daft, Robert L., and Robert H Lengel. *Fusion Leadership: Unlocking the Subtle Forces that Change People and Organizations*. San Francisco: Berrett-Koehler Publishers, 2000.

Davis, Ron. *Mentoring: The Strategy of the Master*. Nashville: Thomas Nelson, 1991.

Dawn, Marva J. *Reaching Out without Dumbing Down: A Theology of Worship for the Turn-of-the-Century Culture*. Grand Rapids: Eerdmans, 1995.

DePree. Max. *Leadership Is an Art*. New York: Dell Publishing, 1989.

_____. *Leadership Jazz*. New York: Dell Publishing, 1992.

Donahue, Bill. *The Willow Creek Guide to Leading Life-Changing Small Groups*. Grand Rapids: Zondervan, 1996.

Donahue, Bill, and Russ Robinson. *Building a Church of Small Groups*. Grand Rapids: Zondervan, 2001.

Drucker, Peter. *The Age of Discontinuity: Guidelines to Our Changing Society*. New York: Harper and Row, 1968.

_____. *Innovation and Entrepreneurship: Practice and Principles*. New York: Harper and Row, 1985.

_____. *Managing the Non-Profit Organization*. New York: Harper-Collins, 1990.

Dunkin, Steve. *Church Advertising*. Nashville: Abingdon Press, 1982.

Dunn, William. *Selling the Story: A Layman's Guide to Collecting and Communicating Demographic Information*. Ithaca, NY: American Demographics Books, 1992.

Easum, Bill. *Leadership on the Other Side*. Nashville: Abingdon Press, 2000.

Ellis, Joe. *Church on Purpose*. Cincinnati: Standard Publishing, 1982.

Engel, James F., and Wilbert H. Norton. *What's Gone Wrong with the Harvest*. Grand Rapids: Zondervan, 1975.

Engstrom, Ted, and Robert Carson. *Seizing the Torch: Leadership for a New Generation*. Ventura, CA: Regal Books, 1988.

Erickson, Millard. *Christian Theology*. Grand Rapids: Baker, 1985.

Finzel, Hans. *Help! I'm a Baby Boomer*. Wheaton, IL: Victor Books, 1989.

Frazee, Randy. *The Connecting Church*. Grand Rapids: Zondervan, 2001.

Galloway, Dole. *20/20 Vision: How to Create a Successful Church*. Portland, OR: Scott Publishing, 1986.

George, Carl. *How to Break Growth Barriers*. Grand Rapids: Baker, 1993.

_____. *Nine Keys to Effective Small Group Leadership*. Mansfield, PA: Kingdom Publishing, 1997.

_____. *Prepare Your Church for the Future*. Tarrytown, NY: Fleming H. Revell, 1991.

George, Carl, and Warren Bird. *The Coming Church Revolution: Empowering Leaders for the Future*. Grand Rapids: Fleming H. Revell, 1994.

George, Carl, and Robert Logan. *Leading and Managing Your Church*. Old Tappan, NJ: Fleming H. Revell, 1987.

Gerber, Michael E. *The E-Myth: Why Most Small Businesses Don't Work and What to Do about It*. New York: Harper Business, 1995.

Gibbs, Eddie. *Church Next: Quantum Changes in How We Do Ministry*. Downers Grove, IL: InterVarsity Press, 2000.

_____. *I Believe in Church Growth*. Grand Rapids: Eerdmans, 1981.

Gilliland, Dean, eds. *The Word among Us, Contextualizing Theology for Mission Today*. Eugene, OR: Wipf and Stock, 2002.

Gladwell, Malcolm. *The Tipping Point: How Little Things Can Make a Big Difference*. Boston: Little, Brown, and Co., 2000.

Goldsworthy, Graeme. *According to Plan: The Unfolding of Revelation of God in the Bible*. Downers Grove, IL: InterVarsity, 1991.

Gorman, Michael J. *Cruciformity*. Grand Rapids: Eerdmans, 2001.

Green, Michael. *Evangelism in the Early Church*. Grand Rapids: Eerdmans, 1970.

Greenway, Roger S., and Timothy M. Monsma. *Cities: Missions' New Frontier*. Grand Rapids: Baker, 2000.

Grimm, Eugene. *Generous People—How to Encourage Vital Stewardship*. Nashville: Abingdon Press, 1992.

Grunlan, Stephen A., and Marvin K. Mayers. *Cultural Anthropology: A Christian Perspective*. Grand Rapids: Academie Books, 1988.

Guder, Darrell L., ed. *Missional Church: A Vision for the Sending of the Church in North America*. Grand Rapids: Eerdmans, 1998.

Hajela, Deepti. "Last New York City Marathon Runner Crosses Finish Line—on Monday." *The Sacramento Bee*, November 3, 2003.

Hamel, Gary, and Prahalad, C.K. *Competing for the Future*. Boston: Harvard Business School Press, 1994.

Harari, Oren. *The Leadership Secrets of Colin Powell*. New York: McGraw-Hill, 2002.

Haugk, Kenneth C. *Antagonism in the Church: How to Identify and Deal with Destructive Conflict*. Minneapolis: Augsburg Publishing, 1988.

Hayford, Jack, John Killinger, and Howard Stevenson. *Mastering Worship*. Portland, OR: Multnomah Press, 1990.

Hemphill, Ken. *The Antioch Effect: 8 Characteristics of Highly Effective Churches*. Nashville: Broadman and Holman, 1994.

Hendricks, Howard, and William Hendricks. *As Iron Sharpens Iron: Building Character in a Mentoring Relationship*. Chicago: Moody Press, 1995.

Hesselgrave, David J. *Communicating Christ Cross-Culturally: An Introduction to Missionary Communication*. Grand Rapids: Zondervan, 1991.

Hestenes, Roberta. *Using the Bible in Small Groups*. Philadelphia: Westminster, 1985.

Hickman, Craig R. *Mind of a Manager, Soul of a Leader*. New York: John Wiley and Sons, 1992.

Hillenbrand, Laura. *Seabiscuit: An American Legend*. New York: Random House, 2001.

Hollinger, Dennis. "The Church as Apologetic: A Sociology of Knowledge Perspective." *Christian Apologetics in the Postmodern World*. Ed. by Timothy R Phillips and Dennis I. Okholm. Downers Grove, IL: InterVarsity, 1995.

Hollister, C. Warren, and Judith M. Bennett. *Medieval Europe: A Short History*. New York: McGraw Hill, 2002.

Hood, Ralph, Richard Gorsuch, and Bernard Spilka. *The Psychology of Religion: An Empirical Approach*. Englewood Cliffs, NJ: Prentice Hall, 1985.

Hunter, George G. III. *Church for the Unchurched*. Nashville: Abingdon Press, 1996.

_____. *How to Reach Secular People*. Nashville: Abingdon Press, 1992.

_____. *Leading and Managing a Growing Church*. Nashville: Abingdon Press, 2000.

Hunter, George, and Donald McGavran. *Church Growth: Strategies that Work*. Nashville: Abingdon Press, 1980.

Hunter, Kent. *Your Church Has Personality*. Nashville: Abingdon Press, 1985.

Hybels, Bill. *Too Busy Not to Pray*. Downers Grove, IL: InterVarsity, 1988.

_____. *Courageous Leadership*. Grand Rapids: Zondervan, 2002.

Hybels, Bill, and Lynne Hybels. *Rediscovering Church*. Grand Rapids: Zondervan, 1995.

Hybels, Bill, and Mark Mittelberg. *Becoming a Contagious Christian*. Grand Rapids: Zondervan, 1994.

Johnson, Luke Timothy. *The Acts of the Apostles*. Collegeville: The Liturgical Press, 1992.

Kelly, Charles S. *How Did They Do It? The Southern Baptist Evangelism*. New Orleans: Insight Press, 1993.

Kenneson, Philip D., and James L. Street. *Selling Out the Church: The Dangers of Church Marketing*. Nashville: Abingdon Press, 1997.

Kimball, Dan. *The Emerging Church*. Grand Rapids: Zondervan, 2003.

Kotler, John. *Leading Change*. Boston: Harvard Business School Press, 1996.

Kraft, Charles H. *Communication Theory for Christian Witness*. Nashville: Abingdon Press, 1983.

Krzyzewski, Mike. *Leading with the Heart: Coach K's Successful Strategies for Basketball, Business and Life*. New York: Warner Books, 2000.

Kurian, George Thomas. *The Illustrated Book of World Rankings*. Amonk, NY: M.E. Sharpe, 1997.

Levell, Dorsey E., and Wayne E. Groner. *The Pastor's Guide to Fund-Raising Success: Step-by-Step Details That Will Improve Your Church's Donor Program*. Chicago: Bonus Books, 1999.

Levinson, Jay Conrad. *Guerilla Marketing for Free*. Boston: Houghton Mifflin, 2003.

Lewis, Robert. *The Church of Irresistible Influence*. Grand Rapids: Zondervan, 2001.

Lo, Jim. *Intentional Diversity: Creating Cross-Cultural Ministry Relationships in Your Church*. Indianapolis: Wesleyan, 2002.

Logan, Robert. *Beyond Church Growth*. Old Tappan, NJ: S. F. Revell, 1989.

Logan, Robert E., and Neil Cole. *Raising Leaders for The Harvest*. Carol Stream, IL: ChurchSmart, 1995.

Macchia, Stephen A. *Becoming a Healthy Church: 10 Characteristics*. Grand Rapids: Baker, 1999.

MacDonald, Gordon. *Ordering Your Private World*. Nashville: Oliver Nelson, 1985.

MacKenzie, Gordon. *Orbiting the Giant Hairball*. New York: OpusPocus Publishing, 1996.

Malphurs, Aubrey. *Advanced Strategic Planning: A New Model for Church and Ministry Leaders*. Grand Rapids: Baker, 1999.

Maxwell, John C. *Developing the Leaders around You*. Nashville: Thomas Nelson, 1995.

_____. *Developing the Leader within You*. Nashville: Thomas Nelson, 1993.

_____. *The Power of Partnership*. Vol. 14, No. 7. Atlanta, GA: Injoy Life Club, 1999.

McFalls, Joseph A. Jr. *Population: A Lively Introduction*. (53:3) Washington, DC: Population Reference Bureau, 1998.

McGavran, Donald. *The Bridges of God: A Study in the Strategy of Missions*. New York: Friendship Press, 1955.

_____. *Understanding Church Growth*. Grand Rapids: Eerdmans, 1970.

McIntosh, Gary L. *Staff Your Church for Growth: Building Team Ministry in the 21st Century*. Grand Rapids: Baker, 2000.

McIntosh, Gary, and Glen Martin. *Finding Them, Keeping Them: Effective Strategies for Evangelism and Assimilation in the Local Church*. Nashville: Broadman Press, 1992.

McKechnie, Paul. *The First Christian Centuries: Perspectives on the Early Church*. Downers Grove, IL: InterVarsity, 2001.

McLaren, Brian D. *Reinventing Your Church: If Your Church Could Start Over from Scratch What Would You Want It to Be?* Grand Rapids: Zondervan, 1998.

Melchien, Tammy, and Janet McMahon. *Coaching Guidebook*. Naperville, IL: Community Christian Church, 2003.

Mittelberg, Mark. *Building a Contagious Church: Revolutionizing the Way We View and Do Evangelism*. Grand Rapids: Zondervan, 2000.

Montgomery, Jim. *DAWN 2000: 7 Million Churches to Go*. Pasadena, CA: William Carey Library, 1989.

Morgenthaler, Sally. *Worship Evangelism: Inviting Unbelievers into the Presence of God*. Grand Rapids: Zondervan, 1999.

Mueller, Walter. *Direct Mail Ministry*. Nashville: Abingdon Press, 1989.

Murren, Doug. *The Baby Boomerang*. Ventura, CA: Regal Books, 1990.

Myers, Joseph. *The Search to Belong*. Grand Rapids: Zondervan, 2003.

Naisbitt, John. *Megatrends: Ten New Directions Transforming Our Lives*. New York: Warner Books, 1982.

Naisbitt, John, and Patricia Aburdene. *Megatrends 2000*. New York: William Morrow & Co., 1990.

Nanus, Burt. *Visionary Leadership: Creating a Compelling Sense of Direction for Your Organization*. San Francisco: Jossey-Bass, 1992.

Newbigin, Lesslie. *The Gospel in a Pluralistic Society*. Grand Rapids: Eerdmans, 1989.

Noland, Rand. *The Heart of the Artist*. Grand Rapids: Zondervan, 1999.

Oden, Thomas C. *Pastoral Theology*. New York: Harper & Row, 1983.

Orbitz, Manuel. *One New People: Models for Developing a Multiethnic Church*. Downers Grove, IL: InterVarsity, 1996.

Peace, Richard. *Conversion in the New Testament*. Grand Rapids: Eerdmans, 1999.

Penn, William. *Reflections and Maxims*. Publisher and date unknown.

Petersen, Jim. *Evangelism as a Lifestyle*. Colorado Springs: NavPress, 1980.

_____. *Living Proof: Sharing the Gospel Naturally*. Colorado Springs: NavPress, 1989.

Petersen, Jim, and Mike Shamy. *The Insider: Bringing the Kingdom of God into Your Everyday World*. Colorado Springs: NavPress, 2003.

Piper, John. *Desiring God*. Sisters, OR: Multnomah Books, 1996.

Pippert, Rebecca Manley. *Out of the Saltshaker and into the World.* Downers Grove, IL: InterVarsity, 1979.

Pocock, Michael, and Joseph Henriques. *Cultural Change and Your Church: Helping Your Church Thrive in a Diverse Society.* Grand Rapids: Baker, 2002.

Rainer, Thom S. *The Bridger Generation: America's Second Largest Generation, What They Believe and How to Reach Them.* Nashville: Broadman and Holman, 1984.

_____. *Effective Evangelistic Churches.* Nashville: Broadman and Holman, 1996.

_____. *High Expectations: The Remarkable Secret to Keeping People in Your Church.* Nashville: Broadman and Holman, 1999.

_____. *Surprising Insights from the Unchurched and Proven Ways to Reach Them.* Grand Rapids: Zondervan, 2001.

_____. "Trendline: An Overview of Interesting Developments in the Church." *Rainer Report.* (January 2003).

_____. *The Unchurched Next Door.* Grand Rapids: Zondervan, 2003.

Richardson, Rick. *Evangelism outside the Box: New Ways to Help People Experience the Good News.* Downers Grove, IL: InterVarsity, 2000.

Rambo, Lewis. *Understanding Religious Conversion.* New Haven, CT: Yale University Press, 1993.

Roberts, Wess. *Leadership Secrets of Attila the Hun.* New York: Warner Books, 1987.

Roembke, Lianne. *Building Credible Multicultural Teams.* Pasadena, CA: William Carey Library, 2000.

Rogers, Everett. *Diffusion of Innovations.* New York: The Free Press, 1995.

Roland, Allen. *Missionary Methods: St. Paul's or Ours?* Grand Rapids: Eerdmans, 1962.

Roof, Wade Clark. *A Generation of Seekers: The Spiritual Journeys of the Baby Boom Generation.* San Francisco: Harper and Row, 1993.

Russell, Bob, and Rusty Russell. *When God Builds a Church: 10 Principles for Growing a Dynamic Church.* West Monroe, LA: Howard Publishing, 2000.

Russell, Cheryl. *100 Predictions for the Baby Boom: The Next 50 Years.* New York: Plenum Press, 1987.

Schaller, Lyle. *Assimilating New Members.* Nashville: Abingdon Press, 1978.

_____. *Center City Churches: The New Urban Frontier*. Nashville: Abingdon Press, 1993.

_____. *Growing Plans*. Nashville: Abingdon Press, 1983.

_____. *The Interventionist*. Nashville: Abingdon Press, 1997.

_____. *The Very Large Church*. Nashville: Abingdon Press, 2000.

Schwarz, Christian. *Natural Church Development: A Guide to Eight Essential Qualities of Healthy Churches*. Carol Stream, IL: Church-Smart, 1996.

Scifres, Mary J. *Searching for Seekers: Ministry with a New Generation of the Unchurched*. Nashville: Abingdon Press, 1998.

Settle, Robert B., and Pamela L. Alreck. *Why They Buy: American Consumers Inside and Out*. New York: John Wiley & Sons, 1986.

Sharma, Poonam. *Guide to Starting Your Own Business: The Harvard Entrepreneurs Club*. New York: John Wiley and Sons, 1997.

Shawchuck, Norman. *Marketing for Congregations: Choosing to Serve People More Effectively*. Nashville: Abingdon Press, 1992.

Sheets, Dutch. *Intercessory Prayer*. Ventura, CA: Regal Books, 1996.

Shelly, Bruce, and Marshall Shelly. *The Consumer Church: Can Evangelicals Win the World without Losing Their Souls?* Downers Grove, IL: InterVarsity, 1992.

Shenk, David W., and Ervin R. Stutzman. *Creating Communities of the Kingdom*. Scottdale, PA: Herald Press, 1988.

Shenk, Wilbert R. *Write the Vision*. Harrisburg, PA: Trinity Press, 1995.

Simson, Wolfgang. *Houses That Change the World: The Return of the House Church*. Waynesboro, GA: OM Publishing, 2001.

Sjogren, Steve. *101 Ways to Reach Your Community*. Colorado Springs: NavPress, 2001.

_____. *Conspiracy of Kindness*. Ann Arbor, MI: Servant Publications, 1993.

Snyder, Howard. *Community of the King*. Downers Grove, IL: InterVarsity, 1977.

Snyder, Howard A., and Daniel V. Runyon. *Decoding the Church*. Grand Rapids: Baker, 2002.

Stanley, Paul D., and J. Robert Clinton. *Connecting: The Mentoring Relationships You Need to Succeed in Life*. Colorado Springs: NavPress, 1992.

Stark, Rodney. *The Rise of Christianity, How the Obscure, Marginal Jesus Movement Became the Dominant Religious Force in the Western World in a Few Centuries*. Princeton, NJ: Princeton University Press, 1997.

Stockstill, Larry. *The Cell Church.* Ventura, CA: Regal Books, 1998.

Stott, John. *Christian Mission.* Downers Grove, IL: InterVarsity, 1975.

Strobel, Lee. *Inside the Mind of Unchurched Harry & Mary: How to Reach Friends and Family Who Avoid God and the Church.* Grand Rapids: Zondervan, 1993.

Sullivan, Bill. *Ten Steps to Breaking the 200 Barrier: A Church Growth Strategy.* Kansas City, MO: Beacon Hill Press, 1988.

Sweet, Leonard. *AquaChurch.* Loveland, CO: Group Publishing, 1999.

Tichy, Noel. *The Leadership Engine: How Winning Companies Build Leaders at Every Level.* New York: Harper Business, 1997.

Tiffany, Paul, and Steven D. Peterson. *Business Plans for Dummies.* Foster City, CA: IDG Books Worldwide, 1997.

Tillapaugh, Frank. *Unleashing the Church.* Ventura, CA: Regal Books, 1982.

Van Yperen, Jim. "Conflict: The Refining Fire of Leadership." *Leaders on Leadership.* Ed. by George Barna. Ventura, CA: Regal Books, 1997.

Von Balthasar, Hans Urs. *Theo-Drama: Theological Dramatic Theory.* Vol. 1. Trans. by Graham Harrison. San Francisco: Ignatius Press, 1988.

Wagner, Peter. *Church Growth: State of the Art.* Wheaton, IL: Tyndale House, 1986.

_____. *Church Growth and the Whole Gospel: A Biblical Mandate.* San Francisco: Harper and Row, 1981.

_____. *Leading Your Church to Growth.* Ventura, CA: Regal Books, 1984.

_____. *The New Apostolic Churches.* Ventura, CA: Regal Books, 1998.

_____. *Our Kind of People: The Ethical Dimensions of Church Growth in America.* Atlanta, GA: John Knox, 1979.

_____. *Prayer Shield: How to Intercede for Pastors, Christian Leaders and Others on the Spiritual Frontlines.* Ventura, CA: Regal Books, 1992.

_____. *Strategies for Church Growth.* Ventura, CA: Regal Books, 1987.

_____. *Your Church Can Grow.* Ventura, CA: Regal Books, 1976.

Wardle, Terry. *Exalt Him! Designing Dynamic Worship Services.* Camp Hill, PA: Christian Publications, 1988.

Warren, Rick. *The Purpose-Driven Church.* Grand Rapids: Zondervan, 1995.

Weeden, Larry K. *The Magnetic Fellowship: Reaching and Keeping People*. Waco, TX: Word Books, 1988.

Weeks, John R. *Population: An Introduction to Concepts and Issues*. 7th ed. Belmont, CA: Wadsworth Publishing, 1999.

Weibe, Michael. *Small Groups: Getting Them Started, Keeping Them Going*. Downers Grove, IL: InterVarsity, 1976.

Weiss, Michael J. *The Clustering of America: A Vivid Portrait of the Nation's 40 Neighborhood Types and Their Values, Lifestyles and Eccentricities*. New York: Harper & Row, 1988.

Wheatley, Margaret. *Leadership and the New Science*. San Francisco: Berrett-Koehler Publishers, 1999.

White, James Emery. *Rethinking the Church: A Challenge to Creative Redesign in an Age of Transition*. Grand Rapids: Baker, 1997.

White, Randy. *Journey to the Center of the City: Making a Difference in an Urban Neighborhood*. Downers Grove, IL: InterVarsity, 1996.

Wiersbe, Warren W. *The Bible Exposition Commentary*. Vol. 1. Wheaton, IL: Victor Books, 1989.

Wills, Garry. *Certain Trumpets: The Call of Leaders*. New York: Simon and Schuster, 1994.

Witherington, Ben. *The Acts of the Apostles: A Socio-Rheotorical Commentary*. Grand Rapids: Eerdmans. 1998.

Wright, N.T. "How Can the Bible Be Authoritative?" *Vox Evangelica* 21(1991) 18-19.

Zigarelli, Michael A. *Management by Proverbs: Applying Timeless Wisdom in the Workplace*. Chicago: Moody Press, 1999.

MANUALS, WORKBOOKS, AND AUDIO AND VIDEO RESOURCES

George, Carl, and Robert Logan. *How to Lead and Manage the Local Church: Self-Study Kit*. Pasadena, CA: Charles E. Fuller Institute for Evangelism and Church Growth.

Hestenes, Roberta. *Building Christian Community through Small Groups*. Pasadena, CA: Fuller Theological Seminary.

Logan, Robert, and Jeff Rast. *Church Planter's Checklist*. Pasadena, CA: Charles E. Fuller Institute for Evangelism and Church Growth.

_____. *Church Planting Workbook*. Pasadena, CA: Charles E. Fuller Institute for Evangelism and Church Growth.

_____. *How to Daughter a Growing and Reproducing Church*. Pasadena, CA: Charles E. Fuller Institute for Evangelism and Church Growth.

_____. *A Supervisor's Manual for New Church Development*. Pasadena, CA: Charles E. Fuller Institute for Evangelism and Church Growth.

Logan, Robert, and Steve Ogne. *The Church Planter's Toolkit: A Self-Study Resource Kit for Church Planters and Supervisors*. Alta Loma, CA: CRM Publishing, 1991.

Ogne, Steven L., and Thomas P. Nebel. "Empowering Leaders through Coaching." Audiocassette. Carol Stream, IL: Church Smart Resources, 1995.

Ridley, Charles. *How to Select Church Planters*. Pasadena, CA: Charles E. Fuller Institute for Evangelism and Church Growth.

Wagner, C. Peter. *How to Plant a Church Self-Study Kit*. Pasadena, CA: Charles E. Fuller Institute for Evangelism and Church Growth.

RECOMMENDED WEB SITES THAT DEAL WITH CHURCH PLANTING

www.barna.org
www.castyourvision.net
www.census.gov
www.church-equipment.com
www.churchleader.net
www.church-marketing.com
www.church-planting.net
www.churchplanting4me.org
www.church-planting-solutions.com
www.churchplants.com
www.coachnet.org
www.namb.net
www.newchurches.com
www.NewChurchSpecialties.org
www.orchardgroup.org
www.percept1.com
www.Stadia.cc
www.zealforyourhouse.com

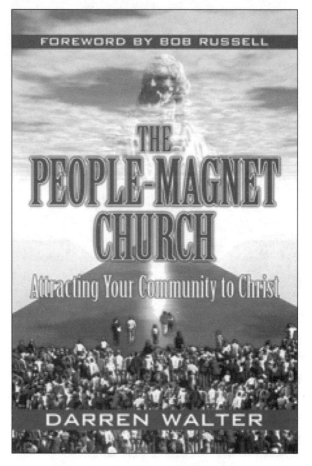